IFIP Advances in Information and Communication Technology 671

IFIP Advances in Information and Communication Technology

The IFIP AICT series publishes state-of-the-art results in the sciences and technologies of information and communication. The scope of the series includes: foundations of computer science; software theory and practice; education; computer applications in technology; communication systems; systems modeling and optimization; information systems; ICT and society; computer systems technology; security and protection in information processing systems; artificial intelligence; and human-computer interaction.

Edited volumes and proceedings of refereed international conferences in computer science and interdisciplinary fields are featured. These results often precede journal publication and represent the most current research.

The principal aim of the IFIP AICT series is to encourage education and the dissemination and exchange of information about all aspects of computing.

More information about this series at https://link.springer.com/bookseries/6102

Felix Bieker · Joachim Meyer ·
Sebastian Pape · Ina Schiering ·
Andreas Weich
Editors

Privacy and Identity Management

17th IFIP WG 9.2, 9.6/11.7, 11.6/SIG 9.2.2
International Summer School, Privacy and Identity 2022
Virtual Event, August 30 – September 2, 2022
Proceedings

 Springer

Editors
Felix Bieker
Office Data Protection Commissioner of
Schleswig-Holstein (ULD)
Kiel, Germany

Sebastian Pape ⓘD
Goethe University Frankfurt
Frankfurt, Germany

Andreas Weich ⓘD
Leibniz-Institut für Bildungsmedien|
Georg-Eckert-Institut
Braunschweig, Germany

Joachim Meyer ⓘD
Tel Aviv University
Tel Aviv, Israel

Ina Schiering ⓘD
Ostfalia Hochschule für Angewandte
Wissenschaften
Wolfenbüttel, Germany

ISSN 1868-4238   ISSN 1868-422X (electronic)
IFIP Advances in Information and Communication Technology
ISBN 978-3-031-31973-0   ISBN 978-3-031-31971-6 (eBook)
https://doi.org/10.1007/978-3-031-31971-6

Preface

In this volume, we present the proceedings of the 17th IFIP Summer School on Privacy and Identity Management, which took place from 30 August to 2 September 2022. While we initially planned to hold the summer school in Brunswick, Germany, we eventually had to move online, due to the ongoing COVID-19 pandemic and associated uncertainties.

The 17th IFIP Summer School was a joint effort among IFIP Working Groups 9.2, 9.6/11.7, 11.6, and Special Interest Group 9.2.2, in co-operation with Leibniz ScienceCampus Postdigital Participation Brunswick, CyberSec4Europe[1], and Forum Privatheit[2].

This IFIP Summer School brought together more than 40 junior and senior researchers and practitioners from different parts of the world and many disciplines, including many young entrants to the field. They met to share their ideas, build a network, gain experience in presenting their research, and have the opportunity to publish a paper through these proceedings.

As in previous years, one of the goals of the IFIP Summer School was to encourage the publication of thorough research papers by students and emerging scholars. To this end, it had a three-phase review process for submitted papers.

In the first phase, authors submitted short abstracts of their work. From 23 submitted abstracts, 20 abstracts within the scope of the call were selected for presentation at the school. Review was single blind with on average 2 reviews per paper. From those submissions, 14 were presented at the virtual conference.

After the school, authors submitted full papers of their work, which received two to three single-blind reviews by members of the Program Committee. Authors were then given time to revise and resubmit their papers for inclusion in these post-proceedings, and were offered in-depth shepherding where necessary. From those 12 submissions, 9 were finally accepted for publication.

The summer school was enhanced with 4 insightful and engaging keynotes:

- *Christian Buggedei:* "How to build organisations for privacy-friendly solutions",
- *Welde Tesfay:* "Empowering end users' privacy-related decision making with ML-enabled PETs",
- *Mary Shnayien:* "On privacy, (digital) media and reproductive rights in a post-Roe America", and
- *Os Keyes:* "Participation before Data: Historicising Trans Counterpower".

Furthermore, a total of five workshops and tutorials on topics related to privacy and identity management completed a diverse and educational program.

---

[1] https://cybersec4europe.eu/.
[2] https://www.forum-privatheit.de/.

The proceedings contain one keynote paper as well as a description for each of the workshops and tutorials.

We are grateful to all who contributed to the success of this summer school and especially to the Program Committee for reviewing the abstracts and papers as well as advising the authors on their revisions. We would also like to thank all supporting projects, the Steering Committee for their guidance and support, and all participants and presenters.

February 2023

Felix Bieker
Joachim Meyer
Sebastian Pape
Ina Schiering
Andreas Weich

Organization

General Chairs

Ina Schiering	Ostfalia University of Applied Sciences, Germany
Andreas Weich	Leibniz Institute for Educational Media and Georg Eckert Institute, Germany

Program Committee Chairs

Felix Bieker	ULD, Germany
Joachim Meyer	Tel Aviv University, Israel
Sebastian Pape	Goethe University Frankfurt, Germany

Steering Committee

Simone Fischer-Hübner	Karlstad University, Sweden
Michael Friedewald	Fraunhofer ISI, Germany
Marit Hansen	ULD, Germany
Eleni Kosta	Tilburg University, The Netherlands
Stephan Krenn	AIT Austrian Institute of Technology, Austria
Charles Raab	University of Edinburgh, UK
Kai Rannenberg	Goethe University Frankfurt, Germany
Stefan Schiffner	WWU Münster, Germany
Diane Whitehouse	EHTEL, Belgium

Program Committee

Florian Adamsky	Hof University of Applied Sciences, Germany
Vanessa Bracamonte	KDDI Research, Japan
Sébastien Canard	Orange Labs, France
Silvia De Conca	Vrije Universiteit Amsterdam, The Netherlands
Martin Degeling	Stiftung Neue Verantwortung, Germany
José M. Del Álamo	Universidad Politécnica de Madrid, Spain
Michael Friedewald	Fraunhofer ISI, Germany
Marit Hansen	ULD, Germany
David Harborth	Goethe University Frankfurt, Germany
Majid Hatamian	Google, Ireland
Tanja Heuer	Ostfalia University of Applied Sciences, Germany
Meiko Jensen	Karlstad University, Sweden
Stefan Katzenbeisser	University of Passau, Germany
Kai Kimppa	University of Turku, Finland
Agnieszka Kitkowska	Karlstad University, Sweden

Stephan Krenn	AIT Austrian Institute of Technology, Austria
Oliver Leistert	Leuphana Universität Lüneburg, Germany
Zoltan Mann	University of Duisburg-Essen, Germany
Silvia Masiero	University of Oslo, Norway
Lilian Mitrou	University of the Aegean, Greece
Frank Pallas	TU Berlin, Germany
Robin Pierce	University of Exeter, UK
Davy Preuveneers	KU Leuven, Belgium
Delphine Reinhardt	University of Göttingen, Germany
Kjetil Rommetveit	University of Bergen, Norway
Arnold Roosendaal	Privacy Company, The Netherlands
Stefan Schiffner	WWU Münster, Germany
Sandra Schmitz	Université du Luxembourg, Luxembourg
Yefim Shulman	Tel Aviv University, Israel
Stefan Strauss	Austrian Academy of Sciences, Austria
Niels van Dijk	Vrije Universiteit Brussel, Belgium
Mark Warner	Northumbria University, UK

Additional Reviewer

Mark Leiser

Sponsors

Contents

x   Contents

Keynote Paper

How to Build Organisations for Privacy-Friendly Solutions

Christian Buggedei[✉][iD]

Polypoly Enterprise GmbH, Hamburg, Germany
christian@buggedei.de
https://www.buggedei.de

Abstract. Personal data is a central corner stone of a broad variety of business models. But collecting and keeping this kind of data is risky and expensive for organisations, and potentially incorporates privacy risks for persons whose personal data is processed. This tension between risks and benefits is investigated with a focus on organisational aspects based on the perspective of the startup polypoly. The main focus is to split up the organisation to avoid conflicting interests.

This paper summarizes a keynote speech held on this topic at the 17 th IFIP Summer School on Privacy and Identity Management.

Keywords: data protection · organisational security · privacy risk mitigation

1 Introduction

Nearly every organisation has to deal with the processing of personal data these days. Especially recently founded organisations and startup companies with data-centric business models typically have the processing of personal data as a central element. Examples are delivery services that focus on managing routes and personal habits of their drivers, nonprofit organisations that try to address individual small-scale donor, or streaming services that focus on giving recommendations based on personal preferences.

Processing of personal data is thus one of the corner stones of modern organisations. To address privacy risks from the point of view of the organisation typically a broad range of technical and organisational measurements are employed. The present case study demonstrates how the startup company polypoly addresses privacy risks and derives short and long time mitigation measurements with a focus on organisational measurements.

2 Challenges for Organisations

The central assumption of organisations is that personal data, and processing it according to legal regulations for various commercial and non-commercial

---

The author worked as Senior Product Owner at polypoly.

© IFIP International Federation for Information Processing 2023
Published by Springer Nature Switzerland AG 2023
F. Bieker et al. (Eds.): Privacy and Identity 2022, IFIP AICT 671, pp. 3–7, 2023.
https://doi.org/10.1007/978-3-031-31971-6_1

purposes is in general positive. Of course, there are also a lot of use cases which are at least ethically questionable, but stopping the collection, processing and especially analysis of personal data altogether for that reason is cutting off our nose to spite our face.

If we want a media recommendation algorithm to work for us, it needs to know our preferences. Ensuring that a new prescription is compatible with our genetic preposition or has no contraindication with medication we already take needs access to our medical history.

Data is good, but there are inherent risks for it to be exploited for ethically questionable purposes. If an organisation works with data, it needs to prevent these exploits. To this end, we need to delve into a few topics:

2.1   Security as Baseline for Privacy

An important baseline to address privacy risks from the point of view of a company is an adequate level of security. Security and security practices in this context mean that the company is addressing security risks with adequate measurements such that no unauthorized or unintended entities can access the collected and processed personal data. This area is already widely covered by research and best practices. Standard practices include measurements as encryption, strong access control, network and operational security, audits, and so on.

It is important to keep in mind that good security needs to keep external attackers (malicious hackers for example) at bay as well as address internal weaknesses: Overwhelmed system administrators can make mistakes or authorized personnel could be targeted by phishing or advanced persistent threats.

Still, many organisations, especially recently founded ones, tend to underestimate the effort and scope of the task to secure data correctly.

2.2   Future Developments and Legal Regulations

Even if one has managed to create a good security infrastructure, there are ways that others can still exploit the data an organisation has collected. This could come in the form of a coercive government, a corporate buy-out, lawsuits - or even blackmail. Especially governments, law enforcement agencies and regulators could demand access to data based on legal regulations. Securing data is thus not only a technical challenge, but also a legal and organisational one.

In addition future developments need to be taken into account. There might be changes in the management and leadership of the organisation and organisations might face economic challenges. This might change business models and policies concerning the use of personal data. Also in the context of bankruptcy proceedings infrastructure of the organisation and thus also data might be sold to the highest bidder. In the context of policies for the processing and use of personal data, it is vital to consider such future scenarios.

2.3   Implications of Business Models

As Andrew Lewis wrote on Metafilter [1]: "If you are not paying for it, you're not the customer; you're the product being sold." An important question is how an organisation is funded. Funding usually comes with conditions attached, either explicitly or by the threat that it could be revoked at some future point in time.

Funding has a strong influence on the priorities concerning the use of data. A company that is financed through advertising for example will ultimately cave in to their advertisers demands. If one is funded by subscription fees of the users whose data is stored, they are the primary stakeholders. It is important to consider these potentially competing interests.

2.4   Cost of Data

Collecting and storing data is surprisingly expensive [2], even though the costs for computers and storage space have comparatively plummeted over the decades. But the amount of data we can easily collect has also increased significantly over time, and keeping it available for computations means that one cannot use the cheapest storage options.

Additionally, storing and processing data also means the cost of securing data, maintaining backups, factoring in possible fines for privacy violations, the costs for audits, mandatory data protection staff, and so on. When a huge amount of data from different sources is collected, organisations tend to lose track of what they have [3].

3   Tactics for Privacy-Friendly Organisations

In order to address the challenges described above, organisations should address the following tactics in their strategy. Since data is in general expensive, organisations should try to get rid of data and of conflicting interests. In addition, they should ensure that privacy is the cheapest option and the data subjects have the ultimate decision power over their data.

Pay the Piper, Order the Tune: Every organisation is ultimately beholden to those who finance them. Hence every organisation should strive to be financed by those whose interests they want to be most beholden to. When at any point an organisation realises to have competing interests, a valid option is to split up, to maintain integrity. In the following general considerations for organisations are summarized.

Plan for the Future: It cannot reliably foreseen what impact the future could have on personal data and the corresponding safeguards in the organisation. As a result, responsible data handling needs to take that into account and strive not to keep data for long periods of time. An even better option, considering the cost, is to avoid collecting data or delete data as soon as possible.

Make Privacy the Cheaper Option: If privacy depends on budgets, it is always in peril. But if privacy saves money, it is always the preferred option.

Empower Your Users: Once it is processed in a service of an organisation, end users have only legal recourse when it comes to data protection, but very little actual power over the data. Even the best practices rely mostly on informed consent. In many cases this consent choice is presented as all-or-nothing. Empowering the end users means that they need to have direct control over their data and have a true and meaningful choice when asked for consent.

4   Case Study Polypoly

The data privacy infrastructure startup polypoly strives to employ these tactics and to enable users to assert their right to privacy. Central elements are a service architecture ensuring that access to personal data cannot be gained without knowledge and consent of the data subjects. To prevent conflicts of interest, polypoly split up into different entities.

4.1   Organisational Structure - Splitting up in Different Entities

Despite the fact that this comes with overhead and organisational complexity, polypoly decided from the start that the organisation needs to be split up into three different entities, namely the cooperative, the foundation and the enterprise, each with its own area of responsibility and its own stakeholders.

None of these entities collects, stores or sells private data. The business relationship is between citizens and businesses. polypoly as a company only provides the platform, infrastructure and information for a user-centric data economy.

Cooperative: The Cooperative is financed and owned by its users which are European citizens. This entity builds and provides the Edge Data Ecosystem platform "the polyPod" enabling users to own, control and monetize their data themselves. The technical service polyPod is described in Sect. 4.2.

Enterprise: The Enterprise is financed and owned by business investors. Its task is to develop and operate software and services that enable companies to use and provide data-based services.

Foundation: The Foundation is created as a market neutral actor and funded by donations. It provides checks and balances for the ecosystem by making data flows transparent. Participants in the edge data ecosystem use this information to make self-determined decisions about the handling of data.

4.2   Service Architecture - The PolyPod

Since the compute resources available in smartphones are considerable, they can be used for data analysis. The central idea of the mobile and desktop app polyPod is to keep the data on the smartphone of the user and analyse it locally instead of transferring it to a central service. Hence personal data remains under the control of the data subject. This allows users control over their personal data and can be used as an important building block to realize privacy by default

5   Conclusion

Based on the tactics described above privacy of users can be ensured for the long term. This can be considered as important building blocks for a privacy by default strategy for data-driven services. Companies and organisations on the other hand can minimise the costs and efforts of data protection without actually compromising security. Cloud to Edge connectors allow for an integration into existing systems.

References

1. Andrew   Lewis,   Metafilter.   https://www.metafilter.com/95152/Userdriven-discontent#3256046. Last Accessed 06 Nov 2022
2. Statista,   AWS   costs.   https://www.statista.com/statistics/250520/forecast-of-amazon-web-services-revenue/. Accessed 06 Nov 2022
3. Facebook, Internal Facebook document written by Facebook privacy engineers about the company's challenges dealing with user data and privacy regulations. https://www.documentcloud.org/documents/21716382-facebook-data-lineage-internal-document/. Accessed 06 Nov 2022

Workshop and Tutorial Papers

Privacy-Enhancing Technologies and Anonymisation in Light of GDPR and Machine Learning

Simone Fischer-Hübner[1], Marit Hansen[2], Jaap-Henk Hoepman[1,3,4], and Meiko Jensen[1(✉)]

[1] Karlstad University, Karlstad, Sweden
{simone.fischer-huebner,meiko.jensen}@kau.se
[2] Unabhängiges Landeszentrum für Datenschutz Schleswig-Holstein, Kiel, Germany
marit.hansen@datenschutzzentrum.de
[3] Radboud University, Nijmegen, The Netherlands
jhh@cs.ru.nl
[4] University of Groningen, Groningen, The Netherlands
j.h.hoepman@rug.nl

Abstract. The use of Privacy-Enhancing Technologies in the field of data anonymisation and pseudonymisation raises a lot of questions with respect to legal compliance under GDPR and current international data protection legislation. Here, especially the use of innovative technologies based on machine learning may increase or decrease risks to data protection. A workshop held at the IFIP Summer School on Privacy and Identity Management showed the complexity of this field and the need for further interdisciplinary research on the basis of an improved joint understanding of legal and technical concepts.

1 Introduction

The European General Data Protection Regulation (GDPR) regulates the processing of personal data. Anonymised data does not fall under its legal regime (cf. Recital 26 of the GDPR, [1]). While the GDPR does not define the concept of "anonymisation", Recital 26 clarifies that "anonymous information"—e.g. as a result of the process of anonymisation—is information which does not relate to an identified or identifiable natural person. What does this mean? Recital 26 explains: "To determine whether a natural person is identifiable, account should be taken of all the means reasonably likely to be used, such as singling out, either by the controller or by another person to identify the natural person directly or indirectly. To ascertain whether means are reasonably likely to be used to identify the natural person, account should be taken of all objective factors, such as the costs of and the amount of time required for identification, taking into consideration the available technology at the time of the processing and technological developments."

The naive application of technical and organisational measures, specifically of so-called "anonymisation technologies", aiming at a successful anonymisation of

© IFIP International Federation for Information Processing 2023
Published by Springer Nature Switzerland AG 2023
F. Bieker et al. (Eds.): Privacy and Identity 2022, IFIP AICT 671, pp. 11–20, 2023.
https://doi.org/10.1007/978-3-031-31971-6_2

personal data does not guarantee that this aim is achieved: Several approaches reduce the identifiability of data subjects, but do not yield anonymous data (cf. [7]). Thus, there are multiple questions of interest concerning this theoretical state of anonymity, both from a legal and from a technical side. If data is not "sufficiently anonymised" (i.e. some kinds of anonymisation measures have been applied, but the identifiability of data subjects cannot be excluded to the necessary extent), it would still be considered personal data, hence the GDPR would apply in full—including obligations to protect the data and its processing with appropriate technical and organisational safeguards. Here, privacy-enhancing technologies play a major role, both as safeguards and as data minimisation tools. Concepts like differential privacy and privacy-preserving processing approaches based on e.g. homomorphic encryption or multi-party computation may provide strong guarantees of protection if applied correctly. Still, it is not an automatism that applying such techniques leads to anonymous data or to the level of data protection required by the GDPR. Hence, the major open question here is to determine when an anonymisation technique is "good enough" to reasonably consider its outcome as anonymous. Similarly, for pseudonymisation techniques it would have to be assessed whether the applied techniques result in pseudonymised data (as defined in Article 4(5) GDPR)[1].

Even if an anonymisation or pseudonymisation technique would not, or not always yield anonymised or, respectively, pseudonymised data, it could be valuable or even necessary for fulfilling the demands of the GDPR concerning appropriate technical and organisational measures due to its effects on reducing the risk for rights and freedoms of natural persons. In particular this encompasses technologies for reducing the identifiability of data subjects, e.g. by achieving pseudonymous data.

In this perspective, emerging technologies around machine learning and artificial intelligence play a special role. Machine-learning models need to be trained with input data to fulfil their respective purposes. This training data is often directly linkable to human individuals, therefore clearly not anonymous. Hence, the act of training a model itself may already constitute an act of processing of personal data—with all the legal consequences that arise from the GDPR for this. This poses multiple questions, e.g.: How can reasonable safeguards be set up here? How can they be validated? What level of protection is possible, and which learning approaches substantiate what level of protection of the training data?

Beyond that, also the model itself as outcome of the training phase may be classified as personal data if the linkability to human individuals from the training dataset is maintained by the learning approach. In particular, membership inference attacks [14] have demonstrated that machine-learning models may reveal which data subjects have contributed with their—potentially sensitive—personal data to the model training. For instance, if the model classi-

---

[1] Note that the GDPR defines the process of "pseudonymisation" with the outcome of "pseudonymised data" which is a subset of all kinds of "pseudonymous data" where the identity of the data subjects is hidden to some extent.

fies a medical disease, the fact that persons contributed data to the model may leak that these persons have this disease. This prompts further questions, e.g.: Under which conditions can a machine-learning model be classified as anonymous or pseudonymous? If the model may still be classified as personal data, under which conditions—potentially including additional technical and organisational measures—would it be lawful to forward the model to other legal entities under the GDPR? Can the linkability to the individuals from the training dataset be removed? Or at least aggregated or hidden to an extent that reasonably well reduces the risk of re-identification to substantiate anonymous data in light of the GDPR? If not, is it at least meeting the demand for strong safeguards with respect to processing?

In this context, recent research on usable privacy emphasises the need to explain privacy-enhancing technologies (PETs) with functional models detailing not only how a PET works but rather "why" it should be used [16], i.e. what are the benefits and implications for users or other types of stakeholders for using a PET. In particular, it has been pointed out that differential privacy should rather be explained as a reduction of the risk of re-identification and their practical implications for users (instead of emphasising other aspects such as privacy-utility trade-offs) [11,12].

Yet another twist in this game is the fact that much of this training of machine-learning models or the use of such models often happens in cloud systems hosted outside of Europe, mostly in the U.S., hence—according to the Schrems II decision of the Court of Justice of the European Union (CJEU)[2] — specific supplementary measures in addition to legal transfer instruments such as Standard Contractual Clauses (SCC) must be taken to legally transfer data to these third countries. Such supplementary measures could include the implementation of strong technical privacy-enhancing safeguards for the processing— which leads to exactly the same set of questions as before.

2   Workshop Summary

In order to address these questions and shed a light on the concept of anonymity in different application scenarios, we organised a one-hour workshop at the IFIP Summer School on Privacy and Identity Management in 2022, held online due to pandemic restrictions. The workshop participants consisted of a broad mix of different backgrounds, ranging from Ph.D. students to senior academics to representatives of industry.

The main task of the workshop consisted in two subsequent exercises around the concept of anonymity. In the first exercise, the participants were asked to align a set of different processing scenarios (with and without naming specific safeguard technologies like homomorphic encryption) along an axis ranging from *not anonymous* via *less anonymous, somewhat anonymous*, and *more anonymous* to *truly anonymous*, as is shown in the upper part of Fig. 1 (The lower part of

---

[2] https://curia.europa.eu/juris/liste.jsf?num=C-311/18.

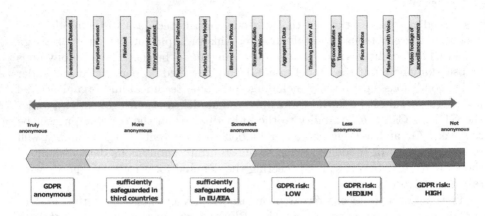

Fig. 1. The conceptboard presented to the workshop participants initially

the figure was hidden to the participants at this stage). This initial arrangement was set up intentionally, in order to foster discussion among the interdisciplinary audience. Obviously, these categories were—on purpose—not aligned with the terminology used in the GDPR or in other approaches for a more sophisticated terminology (cf. [3,13]. In particular, when regarding "anonymity" as a binary concept which directly determines whether the GDPR is applicable or not, there would be no space for "more anonymous" or "less anonymous" or for a notion of different "anonymity levels". A limitation to "truly anonymous" (i.e. "anonymous in the sense of the GDPR") would not have been helpful for fleshing out specific properties with respect to the degree of reducing the risk of re-identification.

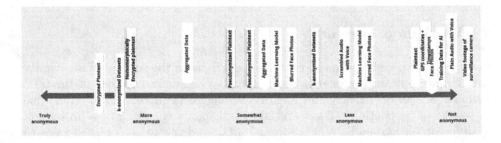

Fig. 2. The conceptboard result of Task 1

As one could expect, the task raised a lot of debates on its feasibility and validity, but led to a predominantly consensual result, where more advanced techniques were considered *more anonymous*, and unprotected data was considered *not anonymous*. No scenario or technique was considered *truly anonymous* (cf. Fig. 2). Along with this, a consensual agreement was that the information provided per scenario/technique was not sufficient and left a large room for debate and pitfalls, so the consensus was that "it depends". Beyond that, some interesting discussion findings were as follows:

- With the approach of k-anonymity, the participants agreed that the idea is: the higher the k, the *more anonymous* the data.
- With respect to machine-learning models, the more a model is considered explainable, the *less anonymous* the resulting model is,
- The participants agreed that data aggregation is a powerful mechanism, and a kind of slider, for decreasing the identifiability of individuals and thereby supporting anonymity.
- With regards to encrypted plaintext, it depends on who knows the secret key, and that it is only a matter of time until encryption could probably be broken.
- There was no one among the participants who said: something is *truly anonymous*. This was not challenged by anyone.
- There was an intense debate around the effort that is necessary to de-anonymise/re-identify data.
- With respect to "homomorphically encrypted plaintext", it was noted that additional information was kept in the ciphertext for analysis, and that this may leak information. In this line, it was highly debated whether homomorphic encryption was equivalent or weaker than standard symmetric encryption with respect to anonymity protection.
- On risk assessment, the participants stated that even if a risk is not likely, there may be a high damage.
- There was an intense discussion around the concept of emotion detection from video footage. It was stated, but also challenged, whether such a system, when utilising appropriate PETs, would be legal (especially in regard to compliance with the upcoming AI Act that forbids high-risk AI applications) and sufficient with respect to protecting anonymity.

In the second task, the lower part of the conceptboard was revealed, indicating a "mapping" of the given "anonymity levels" to relevant concepts from the data protection law domain. One aspect, taken from the risk assessment approach of data protection impact assessments (cf. Article 35 GDPR), mapped the "anonymity levels" to risk levels of *anonymous* (=no risk), *LOW* risk, *MEDIUM* risk, and *HIGH* risk. Additionally, two more categories shown were *sufficiently safeguarded in EU/EEA* and *sufficiently safeguarded in third countries*, implying that these "levels" were somewhat between *anonymous* and *LOW* risk level. Again, the participants were asked to adjust the position of the scenario/technology markers to this new scale, with results as shown in Fig. 3.

This time, the discussions were more critical concerning the task definitions, as large doubts were raised as to whether it is even possible to map the "anonymity levels" to these categories, and definitely not for the given scenario/technique markers given. The discussion clearly showed that it was not trivially possible to map these different concepts to a scale or to each other

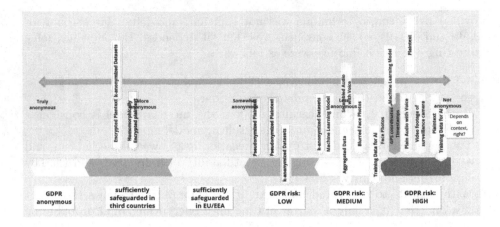

Fig. 3. The conceptboard result of Task 2

as was implied by the task descriptions given, and that more research would definitely be necessary to get to a better understanding of the interrelations of the different concepts interwoven here. Beyond that, some interesting discussion findings were as follows:

- It was suggested to phrase the task question differently: "Suppose I am in a high-impact environment, and the risk is depending on the data: how and how far can I reduce the risk?".
- We wondered on the actual delta of risk reduction, e.g. when data is encrypted compared to non-encrypted. What is the "amount of risk reduction"? Are there some techniques that always reduce the risk? Can we quantify the amount of risk reduction?
- The whole concept of anonymisation was challenged.
- It was discussed that the problem is much bigger: data protection is not the only leverage.
- An interesting find was a scenario in which applying a PET may be worse than not-applying a PET. If the use of PETs in machine learning reduces the accuracy of the trained model (by removing data that was relevant for the model computations), the application of PETs may lead to a situation where the use of the model is no longer "good enough" for the purpose, and should not be used at all.
- We identified a need for transparency, why a certain judgement is taken by a decision algorithm.

3   Open Challenges

In the workshop, we also raised the following questions that still constitute research challenges, as also touched upon above:

When using (data minimisation) PETs in a certain context, under which remaining (residual) risks:

- can data be considered as anonymous under the GDPR?
- may these PETs, potentially together with other measures, be assessed as appropriate technical and organisational measures for complying with the GDPR's principle for data protection by design and by default (Art. 25 GDPR)?
- can these PETs be considered as a supplementary measure for SCC for allowing non-EU Cloud usage (in compliance with the Schrems II CJEU decision and the European Data Protection Board's (EDPB) Recommendation 01/2020, [6])?
- can PETs render high-risk AI systems "acceptable" (in the meaning of compliance with the AI Act)?
- And finally: What other motivations or requirements, from legal, technical, organisational or economical backgrounds, may affect such implementations of PETs in real-world settings?

   The objective of posing these questions was to create awareness of challenges faced when approaching the questions (rather then answering them). In the following subsections, we discuss the second and third question further. For the discussion, we consider the use case of a company that plans to perform data analytics of sensitive data (about sick leaves taken by employees). As PETs, we consider data minimisation technologies for data analytics including (local or central) differential privacy.

3.1 Article 25 GDPR

Let us briefly consider Article 25 of the GDPR, entitled "Data protection by design and by default", in a bit more detail. It states in paragraph 1:

> Taking into account the state of the art, the cost of implementation and the nature, scope, context and purposes of processing as well as the risks of varying likelihood and severity for rights and freedoms of natural persons posed by the processing, the controller shall, both at the time of the determination of the means for processing and at the time of the processing itself, implement appropriate technical and organisational measures, such as pseudonymisation, which are designed to implement data-protection principles, such as data minimisation, in an effective manner and to integrate the necessary safeguards into the processing in order to meet the requirements of this Regulation and protect the rights of data subjects.

Although the title of this article appears to suggest that it constitutes an obligation to design systems with data protection as a core design requirement, Bygrave argues [4] the article is quite vague and generic, lacking clear guidelines and incentives to actually "hardwire" privacy-related interests into the design of systems and services. Others, like Jasmontaite et al. [10], do see elements of such an obligation and state that the data controller has to implement both technical and organisational measures in order to ensure that the requirements of the GDPR are effectively embedded in all stages of the processing activity.

Concrete guidelines to support the privacy-friendly design of systems and services from the very start do exist [8,9]. These are supported by additional privacy-enhancing technologies and design approaches further down the design process [5].

The situation is less clear for the specific case of machine learning. The European Data Protection Board, in its Guidelines on Data Protection by Design and by Default [2], note that for automated decision making and artificial intelligence based approaches, *accuracy* is a key concern. In particular because "inaccurate personal data could be a risk to the data subjects' rights and freedoms, for example when leading to a faulty diagnosis or wrongful treatment of a health protocol, or an incorrect image of a person can lead to decisions being made on the wrong basis".

The focus on accuracy is not by accident. The fundamental data protection principle of data minimisation is limited in its effect for machine learning that—by its very nature—requires a lot of detailed information both when being trained and when being used. And supposedly privacy-friendly approaches like federated learning that shift the processing to the end points or end user devices do prevent the *centralised* collection and processing of personal data, but not the processing of personal data per se.

3.2   Third Countries/Cloud Processing

In its judgment C-311/18 (Schrems II), the CJEU clearly pointed out that personal data protection must also be guaranteed if the data is transferred from the European Economic Area (EEA) to a third country. SCC mentioned in Article 46 GDPR were still declared as a valid contractual transfer instrument, but it was emphasised that at the same time SCC need to be complemented by supplementary measures to guarantee a levelof protection of the data transferred up to the EU standard. In Annex 2 of the EDPB's Recommendations 01/2020 [6] on measures that supplement transfer tools to ensure compliance with the EU level of protection of personal data, examples of supplementary measures including technical measures are given and discussed, including transfer of pseudonymised data.

While differential privacy or k-anonymity are not specifically listed as examples of technical measures, Stalla-Bourdillon et al. [15] argue that k-anonymity or differential privacy techniques could be considered as sufficiently secure pseudonymisation techniques if they are implemented as privacy-enhancing data transformation measures and sufficiently preclude a risk of re-identification. As pointed out in [14], differentially private models are, by construction, secure against membership inference attacks. Hence, differential privacy applied to machine-learning models (with a sufficient preclusion of the risk of re-identification), could in our use case be regarded as a suitable supplementary measure for outsourcing the model for data analytics e.g. to a non-European cloud service, or for using differential privacy combined with federated learning for creating a central model to be used in the cloud.

Still, given privacy-utility trade-offs that differential privacy implies, challenges remain for achieving a sufficiently low risk that can be accepted for the data processing in the responsibility of the respective controller without compromising on utility and thus on the privacy requirement for data accuracy.

4   Conclusion and Future Research Directions

While our short workshop could by no means solve all problems and answer all questions stemming from the complex situation of machine learning, PETs and the GDPR, the preparation process among the organisers and the interdisciplinary discussion with the participants provided an additional value

- in understanding legal demands from the GDPR and the Schrems II CJEU decision in the field of anonymisation, pseudonymisation and other measures for sufficiently reducing the risks for individuals,
- in comprehending properties, achievements and limitations of specific PETs,
- in grasping challenges concerning specific characteristics of machine learning with respect to personal data in different stages of processing,
- in conceiving the existing difficulties of applying and matching the identified legal demands in the respective field with respect to practical purposes of processing personal data, and
- in fostering a dialogue among researchers interested in privacy and identity management, PET developers, and organisations willing to employ PETs to promote compliance with Article 25 GDPR.

For achieving the objective of clarity on how to apply the GDPR, in particular concerning Article 25 GDPR, and of legal certainty concerning machine learning, manifold research questions have to be tackled in the near future, as described in the previous sections. This encompasses fundamental questions on identifiability as well as best practice solutions on specific cases to bridge the gap between data protection law and practice of development and usage of machine learning.

References

1. Agencia Española de Protección de Datos and European Data Protection Supervisor. 10 misunderstandings related to anonymization (2021). https://edps.europa.eu/system/files/2021-04/21-04-27_aepd-edps_anonymisation_en_5.pdf
2. European Data Protection Board. Guidelines 4/2019 on article 25. data protection by design and by default (2020). https://edpb.europa.eu/our-work-tools/our-documents/guidelines/guidelines-42019-article-25-data-protection-design-and_en
3. Bruegger, B.P.: Towards a better understanding of identification, pseudonymization, and anonymization (2021). https://uld-sh.de/PseudoAnon
4. Bygrave, L.: Data protection by design and by default: deciphering the EU's legislative requirements. Oslo Law Rev. 4(2), 105–120 (2017)
5. Danezis, G., et al.: Privacy and Data Protection by Design - from policy to engineering. Technical report, ENISA (2014). ISBN 978-92-9204-108-3. https://doi.org/10.2824/38623. https://www.enisa.europa.eu/activities/identity-and-trust/library/deliverables/privacy-and-data-protection-by-design

6. European Data Protection Board. Recommendations 01/2020 on measures that supplement transfer tools to ensure compliance with the EU level of protection of personal data (2020). https://edpb.europa.eu/system/files/2021-06/edpb_recommendations_202001vo.2.0_supplementarymeasurestransferstools_en.pdf

7. Finck, M., Pallas, F.: They who must not be identified-distinguishing personal from non-personal data under the GDPR. Int. Data Privacy Law **10**(1), 11–36 (2020). https://doi.org/10.1093/idpl/ipz026. ISSN 2044-3994

8. Hoepman, J.-H.: Privacy design strategies. In: Cuppens-Boulahia, N., Cuppens, F., Jajodia, S., Abou El Kalam, A., Sans, T. (eds.) SEC 2014. IAICT, vol. 428, pp. 446–459. Springer, Heidelberg (2014). https://doi.org/10.1007/978-3-642-55415-5_38

9. Hoepman, J.-H.: Privacy design strategies. The little blue book (2018). https://www.cs.ru.nl/jhh/publications/pds-booklet.pdf

10. Jasmontaite, L., Kamara, I., Zanfir-Fortuna, G., Leucci, S.: Data protection by design and by default: framing guiding principles into legal obligations in the GDPR. Eur. Data Prot. Law Rev. **4**(2), 168–189 (2018)

11. Karegar, F., Alaqra, A.S., Fischer-Hübner, S.: Exploring user-suitable metaphors for differentially private data analyses. In: Eighteenth Symposium on Usable Privacy and Security (SOUPS 2022), Boston, MA, pp. 175–193. USENIX Association (2022). https://www.usenix.org/conference/soups2022/presentation/karegar. ISBN 978-1-939133-30-4

12. Nanayakkara, P., Bater, J., He, X., Hullman, J., Rogers, J.: Visualizing privacy-utility trade-offs in differentially private data releases. arXiv preprint arXiv:2201.05964 (2022)

13. Pfitzmann, A., Hansen, M.: A terminology for talking about privacy by data minimization: anonymity, unlinkability, undetectability, unobservability, pseudonymity, and identity management, vol. 34 (2010). http://dud.inf.tu-dresden.de/literatur/Anon_Terminology_v0.34.pdf

14. Shokri, R., Stronati, M., Song, C., Shmatikov, V.: Membership inference attacks against machine learning models. In: 2017 IEEE Symposium on Security and Privacy (SP), pp. 3–18. IEEE (2017)

15. Stalla-Bourdillon, S., Rossi, A.: Why a good additional technical safeguard is hard to find–a response to the consultation on the EDPB draft recommendations 01/2020 on measures that supplement transfer tools to ensure compliance with the EU level of protection of personal data (2020). https://edpb.europa.eu/sites/default/files/webform/public_consultation_reply/response_sto_edpb_recommendations.pdf

16. Wu, J., Zappala, D.: When is a tree really a truck? Exploring mental models of encryption. In: Fourteenth Symposium on Usable Privacy and Security (SOUPS 2018), pp. 395–409 (2018)

From Research to Privacy-Preserving Industry Applications
Workshop Summary

Jesús García-Rodríguez[1], David Goodman[2], Stephan Krenn[3(✉)],
Vasia Liagkou[4], and Rafael Torres Moreno[1]

[1] University of Murcia, Murcia, Spain
{jesus.garcia15,rtorres}@um.es
[2] Trust in Digital Life, Waregem, Belgium
david@trustindigitallife.eu
[3] AIT Austrian Institute of Technology, Vienna, Austria
stephan.krenn@ait.ac.at
[4] Computer Technology Institute and Press "Diophantus", Patras, Greece
liagkou@cti.gr

Abstract. This paper summarizes the contents and presentations held at a workshop at the IFIP Summer School on Privacy and Identity Management 2022, focusing on privacy-preserving industry applications developed within the H2020 CyberSec4Europe project. In this document, we provide a short introduction to the project, and then explain three out of the seven vertical demonstrator cases considered within Cyber-Sec4Europe, focusing on fraud detection within the banking sector, job applications, and smart cities. For each of the selected demonstrators, we motivate the need for privacy and research in the domain, and then summarize the achievements made within the project.

Keywords: smart cities · privacy-preserving identity management · open banking

1 Introduction

CyberSec4Europe[1] is a European research project, designed as one of four pilot projects for the European Cybersecurity Competence Centre (ECCC), which was established in Bucharest, as an executive agency of the European Union in 2021. As such, the ambitions of CyberSec4Europe were multifold, with one of the main goals being to ensure that the European Union has all the capabilities required to secure and maintain a healthy democratic society, living according to European constitutional values, with regard to, for example, privacy and data sharing, and being a world-leading digital economy.

Authors are listed in alphabetical order, cf. https://www.ams.org/profession/leaders/CultureStatement04.pdf.

[1] https://cybersec4europe.eu/.

© IFIP International Federation for Information Processing 2023
Published by Springer Nature Switzerland AG 2023
F. Bieker et al. (Eds.): Privacy and Identity 2022, IFIP AICT 671, pp. 21–33, 2023.
https://doi.org/10.1007/978-3-031-31971-6_3

In order to identify common research directions, to scope a coherent research roadmap, and to prove the efficiency and added value of enhanced cybersecurity solutions, CyberSec4Europe selected seven vertical application domains in which multiple use cases and scenarios were researched, piloted, and evaluated:

- **Open banking** aims at identifying risks and vulnerabilities of various kinds of attacks, ranging from social engineering to malware. Furthermore, the demonstrator aims at preventing fraud and data loss in relation to monetary transactions by third parties in an open banking environment.
- **Supply chain security assurance** developed tools to make supply chain transactions traceable in all components, thereby increasing quality and integrity, and improving the detection of intentional or unintentional errors and manipulations – a key requirement for a quick response.
- **Privacy-preserving identity management** enables a distributed platform to manage identity and authenticated services. It is seeking to achieve strong, privacy-preserving authentication as well as providing consent for and controlling the data usage with privacy-preserving seamless ideals.
- **Incident reporting** was dedicated to the development of a secure and trustworthy sharing and reporting platform for security incidents, according to various procedures and methods.
- **Maritime transport** analyzed the entire maritime ecosystem, ranging from ports to ships, for cybersecurity challenges. The vertical supported stakeholders by detecting and modelling threats, developing responses, and assisting them with the related regulations and best practices.
- **Medical data exchange** was related to the sharing and protection of sensitive and/or personal medical data. The demonstrator realized a secure and trustworthy exchange of such information among actors with different objectives and requirements regarding security, data protection, and trust issues. Furthermore, the relevant legislation and policy frameworks were taken into consideration during the entire design.
- **Smart cities** connected cybersecurity challenges in an open smart city market environment based on the needs of three cities and their communities. It includes an ecosystem where new ideas, needs, best practices, lessons learned, and the information concerning are shared.

In the following sections, we will describe three demonstrator cases – open banking, privacy-preserving identity management, and smart cities – in more detail. The domains were selected in the light of the summer school's focus on privacy and identity management. For each of the verticals, we will provide a clear motivation and explain the added value of the developed solution.

2   Fraud Detection in Open Banking

Financial fraud is a global challenge today. As banking strategies focus on digitizing critical processes like opening a bank account or adding a recipient of funds to a bank account, it has become very easy for hackers to transact from their living room in a short period of time and without their physical identity being revealed. Moreover, they can attack multiple banks without having to change their way of working because banks today do not readily share information about fraud cases and related data. Finally, with new applications such as Instant Payment, which offer real-time money transfer services to bank users, it becomes even more difficult to combat fraud, since banks have no time for triggering counteractivities in the event of fraudulent transactions.

By facilitating information exchanges, banks can improve their ability to detect and respond to fraud in real time. For example, if a bank that detected a potential or real fraudulent IBAN (International Bank Account Number) could share that information with others, those other banks could then take this information into account and prevent the fraudster from using this IBAN for other fraudulent transactions.

In France, between 2017 and 2018, there was a significant increase in the number of fraudulent checks introduced across the entire banking network. The fraudster used the same mode of operation, involving opening an account with a specific bank, crediting the account with a fraudulent cheque from another bank, and transferring the credited funds to yet another bank account, in order to finally withdraw the money at an ATM before the fraud was discovered.

2.1   The OBSIDIAN Open Banking Network

In order to develop a solution that adheres to European values and legislation, CyberSec4Europe developed OBSIDIAN, the *Open Banking Sensitive Data Sharing Network for Europe*, which allows banks to pseudonymously share relevant information – specifically, IBANs – coming from fraudulent activities without violating either their customers' privacy or their own business confidentiality requirements.

At a high level, the message and information flow is as specified in the following and as also depicted in Fig. 1.

- Firstly, a fraud expert or a fraud detection system within a bank, say Bank A, detects a suspicious transaction and wants to use the OBSIDIAN network to check whether the beneficiary's IBAN has already been used in fraudulent transactions at other banks.
- Bank A thus pseudonymizes the suspicious IBAN (blue box) and sends it to the OBSIDIAN server, which serves as a pure proxy towards all other participating banks.
- Upon receiving the request, Bank B and Bank C compute pseudonyms on their known fraudulent IBANs (green and orange boxes, respectively). Furthermore, they add another layer of pseudonyms on the received request.
- All responses from Bank B and Bank C are again routed through the OBSIDIAN server, which forwards them to Bank A.
- Bank A now adds another layer of pseudonyms on the responses of Bank B and Bank C, and finally performs a simple comparison as to whether any of the results match the received re-randomized requests. This requires the commutative property of the deployed pseudonymization scheme.

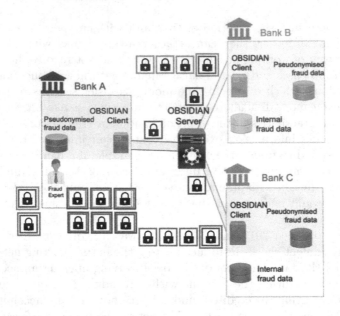

Fig. 1. OBSIDIAN overview

2.2   Evaluation

The key objectives of the demonstrator were the protection of banking secrecy, GDPR compliance, usability, and EU-wide availability.

At a high level, the achievement of these properties can be seen as follows. Regarding *banking secrecy*, it is important to note that no bank in the system is able to identify the sender of a request. That is, in the example flow above, Bank B is unable to decide whether the request came from Bank A or from Bank C, as the OBSIDIAN server acts as a proxy that hides the origin of a request. On the other hand, for the same reason, Bank A is unable to decide which banks reacted to the request, and where a potential match originated from. Furthermore, no party except for Bank A – including the OBSIDIAN server – learns anything about the result of the comparison.

With respect to *GDPR compliance*, it is important to note that the OBSIDIAN server does not store any data. Due to the pseudonymization mechanisms deployed, no party in the process can access IBANs in plaintext. Finally, to be compliant with the right for erasure, banks could take back their data whenever necessary.

Usability is achieved in two ways. Firstly, the technology does not involve complex cryptographic mechanisms or similar, and is thus easy to understand by non-IT experts. Secondly, integration of the solution into existing ecosystems is relatively easy, as it only requires connecting one host within a bank with a single server.

Finally, *EU-wide availability* is achieved by the scalability of the system, as processing a request does not cause relevant computational overhead for any party. Furthermore, by developing and testing the solution in Member States with the most restrictive secrecy laws, applicability to other countries follows. For instance, although the key information sources in the OBSIDIAN network are IBANs – belonging to potential fraudsters, terrorists or money launderers no less – in France an IBAN is considered to constitute personal data and as such the French national data protection authority CNIL stipulated that the exchange of IBANs would require the consent of the owners i.e., the potential fraudsters, terrorists or money launderers. However, after repeated interventions to overturn this ruling, the French authorities considered this added security a good practice that would help minimise the data protection risks.

Within CyberSec4Europe, other approaches for achieving the same functionality were analyzed and considered, e.g., based on MISP^2 (Malware Information Sharing Platform) or blockchain technologies. For a detailed comparison, we refer to the full evaluation report of our vertical [27].

3 Privacy-Preserving Identity Management

In an increasingly interconnected world, identity management systems offer a convenient and user-friendly way for authentication towards a broad range of application and systems. While in practice, such services are often offered by major cloud providers, privacy-preserving identity management has gained increasing attention in the academic world and beyond. The ambition of this demonstrator was to showcase the applicability of such privacy-enhancing technologies also beyond the usual application domains, and specifically with regards to job application portals.

On the one hand, there has been an increasing number of cases of faked university diplomas in many countries around the globe, e.g., [15,28]. What is therefore needed are efficient mechanisms to obtain strong guarantees about the authenticity of claimed qualifications already at early stages of a hiring process, in order to avoid unnecessary overhead, costs, and delays. On the other hand, it is well known that there exists a relevant bias in the hiring process; for instance, applicants are often discriminated against, because they belong to minorities [17]. Other discriminatory factors impacting the job market might include age [14] or gender [2]. What would thus be important are job application processes that do not reveal any sensitive information – like age, gender, or nationality – especially in a pre-selection stage, in order to guarantee fairness and to fight discrimination. The goal was therefore to develop an application portal that served the needs of both employers and employees.

3.1 Portal Design

The key technology used to resolve the tension between the different requirements were attribute-based credentials (or ABCs), first introduced by

---

^{2} https://misp-project.org/.

26   J. García-Rodríguez et al.

Chaum [10,11], and later refined and enhanced by various authors, leading, e.g., to prominent solutions like Microsoft's UProve [6,22] or IBM's Identity Mixer [7,9]. Further research in this area included, among others, [1,3,4,8,13,16]. In a nutshell, in an ABC system, users can receive digital certificates (so-called credentials) on personal attributes (e.g., name, date or place of birth) from an issuer. Later, they can selectively decide which attributes to reveal to a rely- ing party and which attributes to keep confidential, while the relying party still obtains formal end-to-end authenticity guarantees on the disclosed attributes.

In our demonstrator, ABCs are now used to give students formal digital certificates on obtained degrees, certifying their name, date of birth, type of degree, date of issuance, etc. When applying for a job, they can now selectively decide which information to reveal (e.g., type and name of degree) and which information to keep private (e.g., name or date of birth), while still convincing the relying party that an original credential was used for this computation. In order to ensure that users are aware of the information they reveal, we used drag- and-drop as an affirmative action according to Karegar et al. [18]. The specific library being used for ABCs is the OLYMPUS implementation by Torres Moreno et al. [21] (Fig. 2).

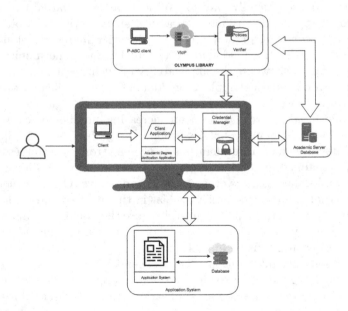

Fig. 2. High-level architecture of the job application demonstrator.

However, simply hiding certain attribute data from a diploma is by far not sufficient for a privacy-preserving job application process. As part of the develop- ment, an entire application portal was developed, guiding the applicant through all necessary steps, including the provisioning of standardized, anonymized tem- plate CVs asking only for the information relevant at pre-selection stage or similar. For instance, by only asking for relevant work experience in the last five years, metadata leaks allowing one to derive an applicant's age from the work experience can be reduced. Other aspects to be considered included, for example, the communication interface from the hiring team to the applicant: for instance, requesting an email address for follow-up questions may already leak sensitive information such as the applicant's name, which in turn may give indications regarding gender or country of origin. As part of the application process, therefore a simple anonymous mailbox was set up, through which any further communication could take place. Furthermore, to also achieve privacy on the network layer, the TOR[3] overlay network was used for all communication.

3.2 Evaluation

The main requirements for the demonstrator at hand can be clustered into the categories explained in the following.

Firstly, from an employer's point of view, it is important to ensure the *authenticity* of any received information in the application process. This directly follows from the soundness of the cryptographic primitives (i.e., attribute-based credential systems) being used.

On the other hand, to achieve *privacy* of applicants, several aspects need to be considered. From a technological point of view, ABC systems guarantee that undisclosed information is not leaked, by any means, to the relying party. Furthermore, different actions of the same user are fully unlinkable, i.e., if a user applies for different positions, this cannot be learned from the academic certificates being used. However, potential linkability through additional revealed information (e.g., contained in the CV) can only be avoided by strong education of applicants. Furthermore, it is worth noting that in the current implementation, the issuer of an academic degree is revealed due to the technology being used, which may not always be necessary in the first application round. This could be mitigated by using current techniques that allow hiding the issuer of credentials within a set of acceptable issuers [3,5,12].

Finally, regarding *usability*, we performed a study with more than 40 participants with different backgrounds. While most participants acknowledged the need for privacy-enhancing technologies in an online world, and despite having received detailed information material, guidelines, and briefings, many users still included sensitive information such as full names or nationality in documents uploaded to the application portal, thereby rendering parts of the privacy-guarantees of ABC systems meaningless. On the one hand, this shows a need for increasing user awareness, while on the other hand platforms need to give very clear guidelines and minimize the risk for accidental disclosure of information through the user.

For full details on the setup, requirements, and evaluation of the demonstrator, we refer the interested reader to [25–27].

---

[3] https://www.torproject.org/.

4 Smart Cities

Nowadays, most people worldwide live or work in cities, with the numbers tending to increase. So making cities comfortable and efficient environments in which people and businesses can thrive is a key issue in society. Following the trend towards digitisation and digitalisation, this is leading to many cities and metropolitan areas around the globe embracing the paradigm of "smart cities". With this, they aim at enabling innovation, economic growth, and well-being, ultimately increasing the living quality in these regions, and palliating issues like increasing pollution and resource usage.

One first step in this direction requires connecting data consumers and producers, allowing service providers to find and use data from the city as well as third-party data providers to achieve their goals. Such data-based services may address a large variety of domains, including, for example, mobility, energy efficiency, health, sustainable housing, or digital public services. What all these areas have in common are strong requirements regarding data sovereignty, quality, security, and privacy.

Indeed, smart platforms need to avoid privacy leaks at multiple levels, from data shared to platform interactions. Additionally, a security platform should protect the heterogeneous systems that compose the smart city environment, maintaining the required level of trust. A key security element for both topics is the platform's authentication and authorization framework.

4.1 City of Murcia

MiMurcia, Murcia's smart city project, consists of the FIWARE platform[4], which collects data from hundreds of sensors and other data sources such as parking service providers and public transport companies. The system includes, among others, information from agronomic sensors installed in parks and gardens, weather stations, noise sensors, traffic information, parking information, or public transport information.

Some of the potential applications of existing technologies and data range from reducing traffic congestion to improving the efficiency and sustainability of resource use (with particular interest in water resources) and the safety and overall well-being of citizens. In addition, promoting local commerce and improving interaction between city officials and citizens have also been identified as project objectives.

This demonstrator extended the security and privacy aspects of the existing platform by introducing a private identity management system that allows users to register and authenticate in the Smart-City ecosystem. Through this system, user privacy preferences are respected, and they can control how their personal information will be shared and used to identify them in the various services registered under the Smart-City project.

---

[4] https://www.fiware.org/.

Concretely, security tools based on XACML (eXtensible Access Control Markup Language) have been used to provide rule-based access control to the Smart City Platform data in conjunction with a self-sovereign privacy-preserving identity management solution based on OLYMPUS [21], to ensure that registered users (citizens, SMEs, and other services) have access to the Smart City Platform data. Smart-City data has been made available for search, discovery and access. Thus, the platform governs authorization through the XACML-based access control system, which is based on the DCapBAC model [23] and provides a distributed capability-based access control system. The integration of the identity management solution, and in particular its privacy-enhancing Attribute-Based Credentials (p-ABC), with this authorization framework enabled assurance of GDPR goals like minimal disclosure or non-traceability of user requests.

Additionally, a distributed ledger infrastructure (in particular, realized as Blockchain) was deployed to share, in a transparent and trustworthy manner, the public information necessary for the solution, from cryptographic material (e.g., public keys) to the services available and their approved access policies. This, along with the usage of the eIDAS framework as a source of a citizen's identity data, served to cement trust in the solution. Overall, the use of these technologies allowed us to provide privacy-friendly solutions that enable secure access to smart city data and services in the most efficient and flexible way, taking into account the diversity of devices and services in such a system.

A high-level view on the demonstrator architecture and main flow is given in Fig. 3.

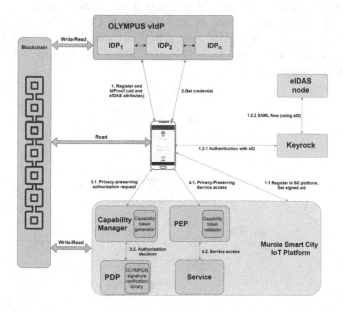

Fig. 3. High-level architecture of the smart cities demonstrator.

4.2   Evaluation

The test case executed in Murcia focused on the improvement of security and privacy aspects during interaction with the smart city platform, specifically for authentication and authorization. To validate the security, privacy and usability requirements, a two-fold validation strategy was followed: technical test cases and questionnaires with two target groups: developers and users. In the following, we give an overview on how they were addressed, and some insights coming from the evaluation process. For full details on the setup, requirements, and evaluation of the demonstrator, we refer the interested reader to [25–27].

From the platform's point of view, the *security* of the authorization process is key. The demonstrator has successfully developed a complete scenario, including integration with the traditional and widespread XACML. Specifically, the authorization framework is fully integrated with XACML access policies, with complex checks based on the Zero-Knowledge proofs of p-ABCs being possible. The security properties of p-ABCs ensure the authenticity of the presented data. What is more, the registration process improves trust in identity data through the use of eIDAS. However, this showed the limitations of current eIDAS, as its deployments failed to fulfil the necessities of most real-world applications, for example, with reduced availability of identity information, in some cases not even including the attributes deemed as mandatory, or lack of privacy mechanisms.

Users, on the other hand, want to be able to access the platform's services while their *privacy* is ensured. This has been achieved thanks to the properties of the p-ABC scheme used for authentication, which allow minimal disclosure and unlinkability. This work also showcased a remarkable issue in this field: the immaturity of standardization. W3C's Verifiable Credentials are the leading standardization element for p-ABC scenarios, but even in that case the structures for Zero-Knowledge-based authentication are sorely lacking, which implies further work is needed [24].

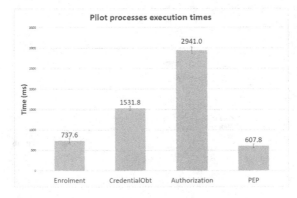

Fig. 4. Time taken for the various processes of authentication and authorization.

Lastly, for it to be applicable in practice, the system needs to have proper *usability*. Technical tests were used to achieve feasibility benchmarks for various processes (from enrolment to access through PEP), as shown in Fig. 4. Further, questionnaires have shown user insights on the feel of the solution, as well as the demonstrator and privacy topics in general. The results were positive, with approval criteria being met (e.g., percentage of people satisfied with the solution's approach for user consent), and came alongside interesting feedback for further improvements, such as "look-and-feel" of the system. Additionally, as one of the key findings, users overwhelmingly preferred technology enforced privacy solutions over relying on adhering to policies by service providers, which encourages further work on the topic.

5   Conclusions

In this workshop, we presented an overview of recent developments within the H2020 CyberSec4Europe project. Specifically, we presented three vertical demonstrators from different domains – open banking, privacy-preserving identity management, and smart cities. For each of the domains, we detailed the specific privacy requirements, and presented CyberSec4Europe's approach to address them. All demonstrators were evaluated in depth together with relevant stakeholders, and the resulting findings have been specified in detail in [27], from which also contributions to the project's research roadmaps and recommendations for further research have been derived [19,20].

Acknowledgements. The work leading to this workshop was funded by the European Union under the H2020 Programme Grant Agreement No. 830929 (CyberSec4Europe).

References

1. Belenkiy, M., Camenisch, J., Chase, M., Kohlweiss, M., Lysyanskaya, A., Shacham, H.: Randomizable proofs and delegatable anonymous credentials. In: Halevi, S. (ed.) CRYPTO 2009. LNCS, vol. 5677, pp. 108–125. Springer, Heidelberg (2009). https://doi.org/10.1007/978-3-642-03356-8_7
2. Birkelund, G.E., Lancee, B., Larsen, E.N., Polavieja, J.G., Radl, J., Yemane, R.: Gender discrimination in hiring: evidence from a cross-national harmonized field experiment. Eur. Sociol. Rev. **38**(3), 337–354 (2021)
3. Bobolz, J., Eidens, F., Krenn, S., Ramacher, S., Samelin, K.: Issuer-hiding attribute-based credentials. In: Conti, M., Stevens, M., Krenn, S. (eds.) CANS 2021. LNCS, vol. 13099, pp. 158–178. Springer, Cham (2021). https://doi.org/10.1007/978-3-030-92548-2_9
4. Bosk, D., Bouget, S., Buchegger, S.: Distance-bounding, privacy-preserving attribute-based credentials. In: Krenn, S., Shulman, H., Vaudenay, S. (eds.) CANS 2020. LNCS, vol. 12579, pp. 147–166. Springer, Cham (2020). https://doi.org/10.1007/978-3-030-65411-5_8
5. Bosk, D., Frey, D., Gestin, M., Piolle, G.: Hidden issuer anonymous credential. Proc. Priv. Enhancing Technol. **2022**(4), 571–607 (2022). https://doi.org/10.56553/popets-2022-0123

6. Brands, S.: Rethinking public key infrastructure and digital certificates - buildingin privacy. Ph.D. thesis, Eindhoven Institute of Technology (1999)
7. Camenisch, J., Herreweghen, E.V.: Design and implementation of the idemix anonymous credential system. In: Atluri, V. (ed.) ACM Conference on Computer and Communications Security - CCS 2002, pp. 21–30. ACM (2002). https://doi.org/10.1145/586110.586114
8. Camenisch, J., Krenn, S., Lehmann, A., Mikkelsen, G.L., Neven, G., Pedersen, M.Ø.: Formal treatment of privacy-enhancing credential systems. In: Dunkelman, O., Keliher, L. (eds.) SAC 2015. LNCS, vol. 9566, pp. 3–24. Springer, Cham (2016). https://doi.org/10.1007/978-3-319-31301-6_1
9. Camenisch, J., Lysyanskaya, A.: A signature scheme with efficient protocols. In: Cimato, S., Persiano, G., Galdi, C. (eds.) SCN 2002. LNCS, vol. 2576, pp. 268–289. Springer, Heidelberg (2003). https://doi.org/10.1007/3-540-36413-7_20
10. Chaum, D.: Untraceable electronic mail, return addresses, and digital pseudonyms. Commun. ACM **24**(2), 84–88 (1981). http://doi.acm.org/10.1145/358549.358563
11. Chaum, D.: Security without identification: transaction systems to make big brother obsolete. Commun. ACM **28**(10), 1030–1044 (1985). https://doi.org/10.1145/4372.4373
12. Connolly, A., Lafourcade, P., Perez-Kempner, O.: Improved constructions of anonymous credentials from structure-preserving signatures on equivalence classes. In: Hanaoka, G., Shikata, J., Watanabe, Y. (eds.) PKC 2022. LNCS, vol. 13177, pp. 409–438. Springer, Cham (2022). https://doi.org/10.1007/978-3-030-97121-2_15
13. Crites, E.C., Lysyanskaya, A.: Delegatable anonymous credentials from mercurial signatures. In: Matsui, M. (ed.) CT-RSA 2019. LNCS, vol. 11405, pp. 535–555. Springer, Cham (2019). https://doi.org/10.1007/978-3-030-12612-4_27
14. Dormidontova, Y., Castellani, M., Squazzoni, F.: Age Discrimination in Hiring: An Experimental Study in Italy. SocArXiv (2020)
15. ekathimerini.com: Minister admits number of civil servants with forged degrees was exaggerated (2013). https://www.ekathimerini.com/news/154846/minister-admits-number-of-civil-servants-with-forged-degrees-was-exaggerated/. Accessed 14 Dec 2022
16. Haböck, U., Krenn, S.: Breaking and fixing anonymous credentials for the cloud. In: Mu, Y., Deng, R.H., Huang, X. (eds.) CANS 2019. LNCS, vol. 11829, pp. 249–269. Springer, Cham (2019). https://doi.org/10.1007/978-3-030-31578-8_14
17. Kang, S.K., DeCelles, K.A., Tilcsik, A., Jun, S.: Whitened resumes: race and self-presentation in the labor market. Adm. Sci. Q. **61**(3), 469–502 (2016)
18. Karegar, F., Pettersson, J.S., Fischer-Hübner, S.: The dilemma of user engagement in privacy notices: effects of interaction modes and habituation on user attention. ACM Trans. Priv. Secur. **23**(1), 5:1–5:38 (2020). https://doi.org/10.1145/3372296
19. Markatos, E.: D4.5 - Research and Development Roadmap 3. CyberSec4Europe project deliverable (2022)
20. Markatos, E.: D4.7 - The Blue Book - A Future Horizon Roadmap in Cyber Security. CyberSec4Europe project deliverable (2022)
21. Moreno, R.T., et al.: The OLYMPUS architecture - oblivious identity management for private user-friendly services. Sensors **20**(3), 945 (2020). https://doi.org/10.3390/s20030945
22. Paquin, C., Zaverucha, G.: U-prove cryptographic specification v1.1 (revision2). Technical report, Microsoft Corporation (2013)
23. Ramos, J.L.H., Jara, A.J., Marín, L., Skarmeta, A.F.: Distributed capability-based access control for the internet of things. J. Internet Serv. Inf. Secur. **3**(3/4), 1–16 (2013). https://doi.org/10.22667/JISIS.2013.11.31.001

24. Rodríguez, J.G., Moreno, R.T., Bernabé, J.B., Skarmeta, A.F.: Towards a standardized model for privacy-preserving verifiable credentials. In: Reinhardt, D., Müller, T. (eds.) ARES 2021: The 16th International Conference on Availability, Reliability and Security, Vienna, Austria, 17–20 August 2021, pp. 126:1–126:6. ACM (2021). https://doi.org/10.1145/3465481.3469204
25. Sforzin, A.: D5.4 - Requirements Analysis of Demonstration Cases Phase 2. CyberSec4Europe project deliverable (2021)
26. Sforzin, A.: D5.5 - Specification And Set-Up Demonstration Case Phase 2. CyberSec4Europe project deliverable (2021)
27. Sforzin, A.: D5.6 - Validation of Demonstration Case Phase 2. CyberSec4Europe project deliverable (2022)
28. TimesKuwait: Investigations reveal millions spent on fake degrees (2019). https://timeskuwait.com/news/investigations-reveal-millions-spent-on-fake-degrees/. Accessed 14 Dec 2022

What is There to Criticize About Voice, Speech and Face Recognition and How to Structure the Critique?

Murat Karaboga$^{(\boxtimes)}$ ⓘ, Frank Ebbers ⓘ, Greta Runge, and Michael Friedewald ⓘ

Fraunhofer Institute for Systems and Innovation Research ISI, Karlsruhe, Germany
{murat.karaboga,frank.ebbers,greta.runge,
michael.friedewald}@isi.fraunhofer.de

Abstract. In view of a multitude of rapidly spreading applications based on voice, speech, and facial recognition technologies, there is a danger of criticism becoming fragmented and narrowed down to a few aspects. The workshop developed critiques of three application areas and collected initial suggestions on how these critiques could be categorized across multiple application areas.

Keywords: Facial Recognition · Speech Recognition · Voice Recognition · disease recognition · technology assessment

1 Introduction

Voice, speech and facial recognition technologies are becoming increasingly widespread in a broad range of applications. Voice and speech recognition, for example, are widely used in smart speakers and increasingly in call centers and for marketing. Facial recognition has become the subject of much public debate, mainly due to its use by law enforcement agencies, but it is also being used in many other areas – often in combination with voice and speech recognition: for example, to detect physical and mental illnesses, to recognize emotions, and (in China) to analyze the attention of schoolchildren. The corresponding media debate and NGO statements mostly focus on the use of facial recognition by police forces and place the danger of real-time mass surveillance at the center of criticism. However, other uses, such as disease and emotion recognition pose significant risks to individuals and society, too. Against the backdrop of the heated public and academic debate surrounding such recognition technologies, the workshop had two goals: on the one hand, to show the diversity of possible criticisms on the basis of the three fields of application. On the other hand, to try to develop criteria for categorizing these criticisms and to explore whether it would be possible to find categories that would allow for structuring the criticisms across all fields of application.

Methodologically, we built on our relevant findings from a comprehensive study on the technical, legal, and societal challenges posed by voice, speech, and facial recognition technologies, which we prepared on behalf of the Swiss Foundation for Technology

Assessment [1]. Thus, the initial part of the workshop served to introduce participants to the technological foundations and to provide entry points into the critique of voice, speech, and facial recognition technologies. Then, the participants were briefly introduced to the three application areas: 1) Smart speakers, 2) disease detection, and 3) police mass surveillance, each of which served as a starting point for discussion in the three breakout groups. These groups first collected what was critical about the respective application area and then developed a possible structuring of the points of criticism. Participants in the breakout sessions had different disciplinary backgrounds (law, economics and social science). At the end of the workshop, all groups reconvened and the results were consolidated. The following sections summarize the results from this process.

2   Technical Fundamentals of Voice, Speech, and Facial Recognition Technologies

Both face and voice recognition are biometric techniques, since they use attributes of the human body. They are typically used for either identification or verification of a person. In identification, an image or voice sample is compared with many others from a database (1:N), for example, to determine the name of a person. Verification, on the other hand, compares an image with a reference picture in a data base. Such a 1:1 comparison is typically used for authentication, i.e. to determine whether a person is actually who s/he claims to be. In principle, identification is the more difficult task because the comparison of one image or audio sample with a large number of other samples is a much more complicated computing process. With regard to performance, the decisive factor is whether the voice or face patterns found were recognized correctly and how well they match the voice or face patterns of other persons. Errors occur when parts of, for example, the face are recognized incorrectly due to poor camera resolution or the algorithms are unable to recognize the face [1]. The latter is also due to the input data quality with which the algorithms were trained. Such data bias has regularly led to the false recognition of people of colour [2].

It is also important to distinguish between speech recognition on the one hand and voice or speaker recognition on the other. The former involves the extraction of content and meaning from a statement, e.g., to enable the control of information systems by means of speech input. The latter refers to the aforementioned biometric procedure for recognizing persons, e.g., for authentication on a computer system [1].

In addition, there are also techniques to recognize patterns in images and audio samples other than a person's identity. Pattern recognition is used, for example, in the areas of disease or emotion recognition.[1] In both application areas, collected voice or facial expression patterns are compared with characteristics that are only assigned to emotions in one area and diseases in the other. By means of AI techniques, such as neural networks, anomalies in the speech pattern (spectrogram) or changes in facial

---

[1] Due to the workshop's focus on disease and emotion recognition, other application areas are not considered here. However, pattern recognition is the technical principle underlying many similar applications, such as the supposed recognition of sexual preferences based on facial recognition or the assessment of a person's dangerousness based on the analysis of their body movements.

expressions, e.g. in facial paralysis or anatomical changes due to genetic defects, can be detected and assigned. Similarly, facial movements can be interpreted as to what emotion they represent. In addition to the challenge of correctly recognizing voice, speech, or facial patterns already described above, disease and emotion recognition adds the fundamental challenge of matching these patterns to diseases and emotions. For example, a facial feature may be recognized correctly in itself, but whether something like the correct recognition of drooping corners of the mouth actually provides information about facial paralysis, represents the emotion "sad", or simply represents something else, such as an individual anatomical feature without any relation to disease or emotion, is scientifically disputed [3].

3   Criticism of Voice, Speech and Facial Recognition and Ways to Structure the Criticism

The discussions in the three breakout sessions all followed the same structure: first, group members were given a brief introduction to the respective application field. Then, possible points of criticism were collected. The workshop organizers had also prepared a collection of criticisms that would be used, if necessary, to trigger the discussion. The final step was a discussion to explore ways in which the points of criticism could be systematized supported by a virtual card sorting exercise.

3.1   Use Case: Smart Speaker

At the beginning of the session, the following written input was presented to the participants by the facilitator:

Smart speakers can be found in more and more households. Because they are intended to function as personal assistants, they are generally placed in living rooms and thus at the center of many people's private lives.

It turned out that out of the 5 participants, only one had set up a smart speaker in his home. The other attendees were reluctant, because of the privacy and security risks they attribute to the speakers and in particular its sensors. Due to this, a lively discussion started right away.

Points of Criticism Mentioned.   The overarching theme of criticism was *transparency*. Nearly all other criticisms boiled down to the fact that smart speaker manufacturers would not transparently document or communicate what the speakers record, what data is processed and what other information they derive from their users. It was mentioned that the manufacturers aimed for "black boxing" the technology with its data flows, algorithms and profiling mainly for reasons of ease of use. This was reinforced by potentially long data persistence, participants said. Furthermore, they criticized a lack of information about whether and which third parties are involved in data processing. Accordingly, misuse of data by providers but also by third-party providers and intelligence services was assumed. This misuse was seen by one participant as a "prerequisite for manipulation." This manipulation could be manifold and could be used to manipulate the results of an online search so that it leads to a phishing website, but could also be used for election manipulation or price discrimination, among other things.

Following this argument, it was argued that smart speakers would aim for a "data maximizing strategy" instead of data minimization. This means that smart speakers would collect as much data as possible by design, and only later it would be decided what kind of data was needed for the functionality of the device [4]. To counter this, participants suggested that manufacturers adopt a clear privacy by design strategy.

In addition, participants mentioned that most users may not be aware of the (potential) privacy and security risks they face from smart speaker use. The good usability (voice interaction with relatively good recognition performance) coupled with the anthropomorphism of the speakers were a "good and bad thing at the same time".

In addition to the technological criticism, the participants also saw room for improvement in the regulation of personal use. In their opinion, there were still very unclear rules about the data protection rights of third parties. For example, they said, one could legally install a smart speaker on one's balcony or near an open window and thus record the voices of one's neighbors.

Categorizing the Criticisms. While the discussion about the points of criticism was lively, it turned out that categorizing them is no easy task. Many privacy and security risks were seen as interrelated, which is why a clear separation would not be possible. After a few rounds of virtual card sorting, a grouping into "technical," "social," and "legal" proved to be the most promising and workable (see Fig. 1).

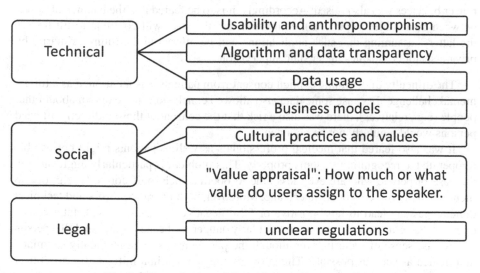

Fig. 1. Categorization of the criticism of smart speakers

3.2   Use Case: Detection of Medical Illnesses

The sessions started with an introduction to the application area with the following input:

Recognition of physical and mental illnesses from recordings of the voice or face is currently still largely experimental, but the first applications are already coming onto the market. They should enable the (early) detection of various diseases or impairments, such as Parkinson's, Alzheimer's, autism or depression. In addition, applications could be used to support therapy.

The moderator then pointed out the difference between applications used by medical professionals and applications that patients can use themselves for self-diagnosis, e.g., using their smartphones.

Discussion of the Criticism. In the course of the workshop, the participants raised a number of points of criticism. These included dangers arising from the fact that collected data is not processed on the devices of patients or medical staff, but on remote servers. In this context, there was also criticism that the collected data could also be processed for purposes other than the original ones. In addition, fears were expressed that processing could provide too far-reaching conclusions about health that patients would not have known with usual procedures and that they might not even want to know. If the proliferation of self-diagnosis and self-therapy apps shifted more responsibility to patients, it could overburden the patients and lead to psychological stress. In this context, it was also discussed that potential cost savings from such new technologies could be used to redistribute costs or increase profits instead of improving healthcare, by stagnating the level of healthcare despite the efficiency gains, for example, because cost savings are made in personnel. In the course of this discussion, the danger of an expansion of social power balances was also raised. Accordingly, it is to be feared that the balance of power between data subjects (patients), companies and the state will continue to tilt toward the latter – assuming that such applications will be offered in the future primarily by private-sector companies under state supervision.

The difficulty of obtaining explicit consent from patients was mentioned as a fundamental challenge. Because some data also allowed conclusions to be drawn about other people (e.g., relatives), there was also a risk that the consent of these indirectly affected persons would regularly not be obtained.

It was also feared that medical professionals as well as patients might not be able to operate the recognition systems properly. This problem is particularly aggravated in the case of people who are even less able to operate such tools correctly, e.g. due to mental health problems or advanced age. Moreover, both operating errors and technical deficiencies can lead to false-positive or false-negative detections – with fatal consequences. False-negative results are particularly dangerous because they can lull a person into a false sense of security, even though the person needs to be medically examined and treated as soon as possible. This problem may persist in a mitigated form even if patients forgo more invasive but accurate diagnostic methods for convenience, relying instead on voice-, speech-, and face recognition-based applications.

Categorizing the Criticism. With regard to the structuring of the critique, a three-way division into technology, law and ethics was also suggested for this use case. More precisely, data security was also subsumed under the term technical issues. Aspects of data protection law were sorted under the heading of law, and social issues were added to the ethical questions (see Fig. 2).

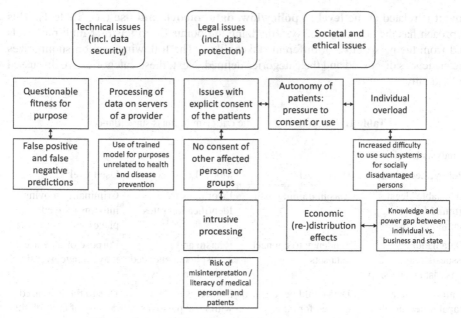

Fig. 2. Categorization of the criticism of disease detection

Issues of technical suitability were clearly assigned to the technical domain, but there were also issues that were considered to overlap with the legal domain. These include the use of training models for non-health purposes and processing on service provider servers. Challenges in the area of misinterpretation of analysis results were discussed as being at the intersection of technology, law, and ethics.

Issues of consent and intrusive processing, which is closely linked to the purposes of processing and transparent consent, were assigned to the legal area. Challenges regarding patient autonomy were assigned to the intersection between law and ethics.

Finally, the ethical aspects included individual overload, overburdening of disadvantaged persons, economic redistribution effects, and the widening imbalance of power between those affected and data processors and the state.

3.3   Use Case: Mass Surveillance

The following text was presented to the attendees at the beginning of the session as an introduction:

Facial recognition by police agencies can be used both in real-time to search for missing persons or fugitives in public places, train stations, etc., and ex-post to match crime scene footage with police databases during a police investigation. Real-time recognition in particular is the focus of criticism.

During the discussion, the participants decided to categorize the criticisms according to the structure inspired by a data model, since the basis of almost every surveillance technology is data, from which models are created and on the basis of which decisions are made. Data models indicate, among other things, what information is available and how it is related at the **level of policy/law, data, model, and use** (see Table 1). This approach has the advantage of systematizing the points of criticism at multiple levels and from the perspective of different stakeholders. The following section summarizes the criticisms discussed and the categories defined. Next, these categories are discussed individually.

Table 1. Categorization of the criticism of mass surveillance

Analysis Level			
Policy; Legal level	Data Level	Model Level	Use Level
"Unstable" legal ground for technology use	Bias in training data	Error rates vs. Identification rates	Criminality moving into unsurveyed places
Data handling issues/storage time/data ownership	Tendency to connect data sets	Racism and Transphobia encoded in the technology	Purpose of data use may change over time
Unlimited storage capabilities, no clear deletion periods	Data could be misused or used for other purposes	Strategies to deal with false positives	Due to the increased density of control, this can undermine trust in the state and the police
Function creep and sweeping interpretation of legal bases by law enforcement	Stigmatized or excluded on the basis of belonging to a particular social group		Fears could arise among the population regarding the misuse of data. Comprehensive data processing could undermine democratic values
Clandestine surveillance (no cooperation with citizens needed)			Permanent surveillance of everyday lives of large parts of the population
Securitization of society			General suspicion of the entire population
			Over-reliance on recognition results
			Unclear decision making (no transparency
Stakeholders			
Administration; Policy makers		Industry; Research; Academia	Security agencies (Police, Private security companies)

Policy; Legal Level. On the first level, the participants saw possible risks in the use of voice, speech and facial recognition technologies arising from an unclear legal situation regarding the use of technology. Further questions arose with regard to the legal handling of data, the storage period or access rights to (personal) data. In particular, the Group considered the expansion and far-reaching interpretation of the legal basis by law enforcement authorities to be a risk. For example, it was possible to use raw biometric data to draw further conclusions about personal characteristics and attributes beyond the actual purpose of use. This access to further information from raw data (function creep) and possible misuse would have to be prevented by means of suitable and holistic legal regulations. At the level of the society, the participants also discussed the concept of "securitization of society" [5]. This involves the gradual penetration of society by security technologies with the aim of controlling societal development in as many areas as possible. The workshop participants saw a special duty to act here for players from administration and politics.

Data Level. At the level of data, the participants discussed the risks of bias and distortion of data sets (data bias). Accordingly, the use of technologies based on biased training data could have discriminatory effects. The group discussed that these biases could promote stigmatization or exclusion based on belonging to a particular social group. Once individuals are treated differently based on surveillance and biased data sets, categorization per se is discriminatory and potentially impacts their opportunities and possibilities in various social settings, the group argued.

Model Level. At the model level, the participants first clarified that if the biometric data was collected by sensors, it was necessary to first prepare it for model-based analysis. The false acceptance rate (FAR) indicates the average number of false acceptances of a biometric security application and thus evaluates the precision of a biometric system. At the model level, the breakout session participants discussed the relationship of the FAR to the Equal Error Rate (EER) and the FAR. The EER is considered the most informative measure of the performance of a biometric system and is determined by the equality of correct and incorrect detections. However, these rates are not theoretical or derivable, but have to be determined on the basis of practical testing [6]. If multiple individuals have the same biometric characteristics and are therefore accepted as matching each other, this is also considered a mismatch - the uniqueness of the captured biometric characteristic therefore limits the smallest achievable FAR [7]. These technical characteristics are closely related to the risks posed by the nature of the database. Therefore, according to the participants, strategies need to be developed for dealing with false positives. Furthermore, stakeholders from industry, and academic research in particular should address the risks and develop solutions for "fair" data models. In addition, it was discussed that the model borders are fluid - and data models successively evolve. This could become a risk if purposes and goals other than those originally known and intended are pursued in the data collection process. According to the group, it is practically impossible for the data subjects to judge whether the collected data are evaluated for biometric characteristics or not.

Use Level. At the level of the use of voice, speech, and facial recognition technologies in the context of mass surveillance, participants discussed societal risks. Among them was the possibility that increased surveillance could lead to the relocation of criminal activities to less or non-surveillance locations. In addition, participants noted that the increased density of control by means of surveillance technologies can undermine trust in the state and the police (and democratic values). Mass surveillance via voice, speech and facial recognition technologies can give citizens the feeling that they are under general suspicion, which is an explicit vote of no confidence. Coupled with over-reliance on software results, it could also lead to non-transparent decisions. Finally, the group discussed how the permanent surveillance of everyday life of large parts of the population could lead to fear, self-censorship and conformist behavior among citizens (chilling effects).

4   Merging the Results

At the end of the workshop, the results of the breakout sessions were briefly summarized and a discussion on similarities regarding categorization began.

The discussion on smart speakers revealed a variety of criticisms of them.[2] Most of the raised points criticize the lack of transparency of the algorithms and data that are recorded and processed. According to the participants, the anthropomorphism of the speakers' voice and the character of the everyday interaction lead users not to perceive surveillance as such. Specifically, the criticisms can be found in production/sale of speakers, usage, social impact, fairness, user autonomy, transparency, security and trust. Similarly, discussions on the topics of disease detection and mass surveillance fostered a wide range of criticisms. In the case of disease detection, these included issues such as fitness for purpose, false positives, processing on uncontrollable servers, challenges in obtaining consent, risk of user misunderstanding, individual overload, and shifting power relations. In the case of mass surveillance, there were indeed overlaps, e.g. with regard to the points of misidentification and misuse. However, new points of criticism were also mentioned, including the erosion of societal trust and thus the erosion of democratic values or challenges posed by function creep.

Before a consolidation of the results regarding the categorization of the critiques was possible, the workshop ended though. Nevertheless, it should be mentioned at this point that, in addition to the rather classic division into the three pillars of technology, law and ethics, it is particularly the model-centered approach of the third breakout session that sounds promising. It allows the inclusion of several dimensions in the X-axis as well as in the Y-axis, e.g. by also allowing an assignment of the stakeholders.

5   Conclusion

Whereas just a few years ago discussions about recognition technologies were clearly focused on the area of facial recognition and the scope of government surveillance

---

[2] As this was a workshop with limited time capacities, it was of course not possible to provide an exhaustive survey of all conceivable points of criticism, so these points should rather be understood as an exemplary selection. For a more exhaustive discussion, see [1].

purposes, today we are already in a phase of massive proliferation of dozens of different applications into various areas of life.

Even though only a cursory summary of the results from the three breakout sessions was possible due to time constraints, the importance of this step for future work should nevertheless be emphasized here. The discussions in the workshop regarding the collection of criticisms of the three exemplary application areas of voice, speech, and face recognition technologies as well as the structuring attempts represent a valuable first step in keeping track of the critical aspects of these technologies in light of the increasingly confusing application landscape. In particular, the study of overlapping uses of data collected by voice, speech, and vision recognition technologies across different application domains and by different stakeholders is becoming increasingly important in light of this application diffusion. It would therefore be desirable if further research were carried out into developing evaluation matrices of such technologies, with which the various points of criticism can also be discussed and structured across different areas of application. Initial attempts are available, for example, in the form of the ethical matrix of Castelluccia and Métayer [8] or in the context of the publications around trustworthy AI [9].

References

1. Karaboga, M., Frei, N., Ebbers, F., Rovelli, S., Friedewald, M., Runge, G.: Automatisierte Erkennung von Stimme, Sprache und Gesicht: Technische, rechtliche und gesellschaftliche Herausforderungen. vdf Hochschulverlag AG an der ETH Zürich (2022). https://doi.org/10. 3218/4141-5
2. Lohr, S.: Facial Recognition Is Accurate, if You're a White Guy (2018). https://www.nytimes. com/2018/02/09/technology/facial-recognition-race-artificial-intelligence.html
3. Stark, L., Hoey, J.: The Ethics of Emotion in AI Systems (2020). https://osf.io/9ad4u/. https:// doi.org/10.31219/osf.io/9ad4u
4. Malkin, N., Deatrick, J., Tong, A., Wijesekera, P., Egelman, S., Wagner, D.: Privacy Attitudes of Smart Speaker Users. Proc. Priv. Enh. Technol. **2019** (2019). https://doi.org/10.2478/pop ets-2019-0068
5. Schuilenburg, M.: The Securitization of Society: Crime, Risk, and Social Order. New York University Press (2015). https://doi.org/10.18574/nyu/9781479854219.001.0001
6. Hornung, G.: Die digitale Identität: Rechtsprobleme von Chipkartenausweisen: digitaler Personalausweis, elektronische Gesundheitskarte, JobCard-Verfahren. Nomos (2005)
7. Strauss, S., Schaber, F., Peissl, W.: Biometrics: The body as universal ID? (ITA Dossier No.55en, April 2021) (2021). https://doi.org/10.1553/ita-doss-055en
8. Castelluccia, C., Métayer, D.L.: Analysing the Impacts of Facial Recognition Towards a Rigorous Methodology Position Paper. hal-02480647. 17 (2020)
9. Hallensleben, S., et al.: From principles to practice: an interdisciplinary framework to operationalise AI ethics (2020). https://doi.org/10.11586/2020013

Raising Awareness for Privacy Risks and Supporting Protection in the Light of Digital Inequalities

Yannic Meier[(✉)] [iD]

University of Duisburg-Essen, 47057 Duisburg, Germany
`yannic.meier@uni-due.de`

Abstract. Despite legal improvements in protecting privacy like the EU GDPR, most applied conceptions of privacy are individualistic, thus, still putting the responsibility for privacy management onto the users of digital technologies. A major problem with this approach is that it ignores obvious differences between user groups in being able to manage their privacy online. Recent studies show that factors like sociodemographic and -economic status create digital inequalities in people's digital behaviors, which is also true and particularly concerning for their privacy behaviors. Empirical works investigating means to assist users in their self-data management, however, are barely addressing these digital inequalities in their proposed solutions. Therefore, the present chapter will briefly summarize the empirical status quo of research focusing on privacy and digital inequalities and identify gaps in currently proposed solutions. In conclusion, it can be said that although initial research reveals digital inequalities in terms of people's privacy awareness, literacy, and behaviors, there appear to be neither empirical nor regulatory solutions to balance these inequities. Thus, I recommend that future research should more actively address and study the particular needs of vulnerable groups in finding ways of how to assist them to better manage their privacy on the internet.

Keywords: Privacy Protection · Digital Inequalities · Transparency · Privacy Literacy · Privacy Risk Awareness

1 Introduction

Using the Internet and digital technologies brings various advantages and facilitations for people's lives, but at the same time, people leave their footprints in these digital environments. Digital footprints – defined as "digitally traceable behavior and online presence associated with an individual" (Micheli et al., 2018, p. 243) – are being left behind because users are constantly required to actively provide personal information or to consent to an automated tracking of their data. However, not everyone leaves the same amount of tracks behind: some leave more detailed imprints than others while again others are more capable to conceal their traces by means of privacy protective strategies. Although individual privacy protection is viewed as a limited approach which

© IFIP International Federation for Information Processing 2023
Published by Springer Nature Switzerland AG 2023
F. Bieker et al. (Eds.): Privacy and Identity 2022, IFIP AICT 671, pp. 44–51, 2023.
https://doi.org/10.1007/978-3-031-31971-6_5

neglects privacy as a networked and collective social phenomenon and value (see Baruh & Popescu, 2017), current loopholes in legal approaches to privacy still necessitate individual self-protection. This approach, however, is specifically tragic since it creates and upholds inherent inequalities between different social classes and individual groups. This results in some user segments not being capable to adopt very easily applicable strategies like deleting cookies, withdrawing information, or not using websites and apps which can be counted to the most prominent protection strategies (Boerman et al., 2021; Matzner et al., 2016; Meier & Krämer, 2023). When it comes to more sophisticated and, thus, more effective strategies, the gap between user groups appears to be even larger. The more sophisticated privacy protective strategies get, the more awareness, knowledge, and skills are required to adopt them. Privacy risk awareness as well as protection knowledge and skills (also known as privacy literacy; Trepte et al., 2015) are main predictors of people's Internet privacy protection behaviors (Baruh et al., 2017; Büchi et al., 2017; Meier et al., 2020a). Recent studies with representative samples from the Switzerland and Germany revealed digital inequalities regarding people's internet privacy protection (skills) that can be traced back to sociodemographic differences. While Meier and Krämer (2023) found age and gender differences in people's privacy protective attempts with older persons and females using less protection online, Büchi et al. (2021) showed that especially internet skills (which are one of the main drivers of online protection) are unequally distributed among different user segments, and they depend on factors like age, education, and gender. While past research has primarily focused on exploring digital inequalities concerning people's privacy perceptions and behaviors, there appears to be a research gap aiming at balancing these inequalities. Although much research exists on how to inform users more transparently about potential privacy threats, for instance, by means of in situ measures such as privacy icons (Efroni et al., 2019), privacy warning messages (Ostendorf et al., 2022), or privacy scores (Meier & Krämer, 2022), these studies hardly consider that different user groups might require different kinds of information based on distinct needs or abilities. Moreover, there is no data about the consequences of unequally distributed privacy skills and knowledge, for instance, on the frequency of experienced privacy violations and how these in turn affect people's online behaviors (see Blank & Lutz, 2018; Lutz, 2019). In light of these research gaps, this chapter will outline the current state-of-the-art regarding privacy and digital inequalities and describe future directions how digital inequalities might be better addressed by privacy research.

2   Digital Inequalities

Scholars have identified multiple stages of digital divides that comprise differences in accessing information and communication technology (ICT), differences in ICT usage and skills, and differences in the outcomes of using ICTs (van Deursen & Helsper, 2015). Digital inequalities do not necessarily refer to people's access to ICT but describe how people with the same chances of access to ICTs differ in their usage patterns as well as in the experienced outcomes of using ICTs (Hargittai, 2021). Digital inequalities are basically social inequalities in terms of people's socio-economic status, for example, sex, age, education, employment status, or ethnicity that are transferred to the digital world (Robinson et al., 2015).

In the field of privacy research, multiple empirical studies found that sociodemographic factors can shape people's privacy perceptions, abilities, and behaviors. For instance, age seems to be negatively related to the frequency and quality of applying privacy protective measures (Büchi et al., 2021; Matzner et al., 2016; Meier & Krämer, 2023). At the same time, however, younger persons seem to find privacy risks less severe (Bol et al., 2018; Meier and Krämer, 2023). A similar pattern emerges when it comes to education: higher educated persons seem to protect themselves better (Büchi et al., 2021) but are less concerned for their privacy (Smit et al., 2014). Finally, gender differences have been found. Men seem to protect better and have higher protection skills than women (Büchi et al., 2021; Meier and Krämer, 2023). These inequalities seem to be exploited, for instance, by advertisers who target user groups with different (e.g., gender-stereotypic) content and might, thus, contribute to maintaining stereotypes or marginalization (Bol et al., 2020). Additionally, elderly, less educated, and persons with a lower income were found to be less confident in handling personal (health-related) information which deterred them from active usage (Park, 2021). These studies indicate that sociodemographic and -economic factors contribute to making some user groups more vulnerable in terms of less privacy protection and advertisement manipulation. Besides having a higher risk to experience privacy invasions, some user groups also seem to have lower advantages from using ICTs.

Apart from sociodemographic factors, other variables seem to contribute to privacy inequalities as well. For instance, Redmiles and Buntain (2021) found that a lack of trust in data processing and a high level of privacy concerns prevented people from certain online behaviors. Moreover, impulsive and intuitive decision-makers seem to share personal information more carelessly as they are rather reward-driven while ignoring possible negative consequences (Ostendorf et al., 2020, 2022). Lastly, privacy cynicism (i.e., feeling powerless, resigned, and mistrusting about the privacy practices of many internet corporations) seems to be related to less privacy protection, thus, constituting another vulnerable group (Lutz et al., 2020). Hence, vulnerable groups appear to exist not only within certain social classes but also among persons who share similar personality or attitudinal characteristics. However, digital inequalities are far from being fully understood as there are also studies that did not find empirical evidence for inequalities in people's privacy perceptions and behaviors based on sociodemographic variables (e.g., Boerman et al., 2021). Thus, more research is required that is based on large and nationally representative (but also cross-national) samples to better understand digital inequalities regarding privacy perceptions, skills, and behaviors of certain social classes and groups.

3 Current Approaches

In the EU, there are approaches to enhance transparency and to increase informational self-determination of users obligated by the GDPR. Websites must inform users about the handling of personal information in privacy policies and users must have the choice of whether to consent to the use of tracking mechanisms (e.g., cookies) that exceed what is technically required. Research data, however, illustrates the limitations of these approaches. Privacy policies are ignored by a great majority of users (European Commission, 2019) while cookie consent banners are largely evaluated as annoying and

problematic in several instances (Giese & Stabauer, 2022; Pastore, 2020). Privacy policies are written in ways that require the cognitive abilities and technical knowledge to
comprehend the textual information (Obar & Oeldorf-Hirsch, 2020), thus, excluding a
great majority of persons who either do not bring the skills or the motivation to read
privacy policies. Therefore, it can be argued that privacy policies in their current form are
contributing to inequalities in people's informedness about company privacy practices.
Not only would privacy policies need a revision in terms of general length and comprehension, so that an "average user" could extract important information from it. Privacy
policies should additionally be enhanced in a way to assist various user groups with
different needs, abilities, and levels of knowledge (e.g., children or elderly). Concerning
cookie banners, (i.e., pop-up windows informing about cookies and allowing users to
decide whether to accept or reject non-essential cookies) research points to shortcomings as well. Due to inconsistent presentation of these banners, users seem to behave
heterogeneously across different websites as mostly one-click options (i.e., "accept all"
and "reject all") are preferred to immediately close cookie banners (Giese & Stabauer,
2022; Pastore, 2020). These options, however, are not always present (especially the
reject option) and due to the usage of so-called dark patterns (e.g., highlighting or hiding
certain options) users are often manipulated to consent to extensive data tracking (Waldman, 2020). While these practices are certainly problematic to all users, there is a lack of
research investigating whether certain factors make some user groups especially resis-
tant or vulnerable to consent and dark patterns. Conceivably, due to a lack of awareness
or knowledge some users might be more prone to be tricked into consent which might
lead to unpleasant experiences or feelings of powerlessness. As a first step, it would be
in the interest of all users to make cookie banners uniform, with options to immediately
accept and reject all non-functional cookies, and without highlighting certain (invasive)
options. Also, privacy-by-default and privacy-by-design are very easily implementable
ways that might bridge the shortcomings of privacy policies and cookie banners and
could also address privacy issues caused by digital inequalities.

4   Current Research Gaps

Despite or because of the shortcomings in current implementations of legal obligations,
past research has developed and tested several ways of how to assist users in manag-
ing their privacy online. For instance, researchers suggest the usage of privacy nudges
(Acquisti et al., 2017), privacy icons (Efroni et al., 2019), privacy scores (Meier &
Krämer, 2022), warning messages (Ostendorf et al., 2022), or shortened privacy policies
(Meier et al., 2020b) to assist users in more informed and deliberate privacy behaviors.
While empirical findings point to the usefulness of some of these measures (Meier &
Krämer, 2022; Meier et al., 2020b; Ostendorf et al., 2022), there are still certain issues to
be considered. First and foremost, this strand of research tends to ignore interindividual
differences between users. This means that in most cases one intervention is tested for
its general functionality in one sample without considering that different user groups
might benefit from different interventions. So far, scholars have rather descriptively
investigated digital inequalities in the realm of privacy, but there appears to be a lack of
work designing and testing interventions to close gaps between user groups. Different

interventions, however, might be useful in distinct ways for different users. For instance, providing people with shortened privacy policies might still require a minimum level of knowledge to understand certain terms and the implication of privacy icons supposes training which might be more easily feasible for some user segments. Persons who make deliberate privacy decisions might benefit from more detailed information while impulsive and intuitive decision-makers might rather need short in situ interventions. A first indication for the latter claim can be seen in the study by Meier and Krämer (2022) who found that intuitive privacy decision-makers found the tested intervention (i.e., a Nutri-Score alike privacy risk indicator) more useful than rational decision-makers. Because of these subtle differences between various user segments that suppose distinct demands and needs, I argue that there is an urgent need to investigate which user groups (e.g., elderly or less educated persons) benefit from which type of interventions (e.g., providing detailed, step-by-step information) in order to assist and protect the most vulnerable user groups.

In addition, although empirical research studying privacy and digital inequalities is on the rise, very critical questions remain unaddressed so far. Especially research that examines the (negative) consequences of ICT usage is scarce. Previous research has primarily examined the third digital divide with respect to the positive outcomes (i.e., benefits) of ICT use, thus, neglecting the negative outcomes (e.g., privacy invasions) (Blank & Lutz, 2018; Lutz, 2019). However, not being able to adequately manage one's privacy online might lead to particularly sensitive negative experiences. Büchi and colleagues (2021) argue that especially marginalized groups run the risk of, for instance, increased privacy invasions which might negatively impact their psychological well-being and could reinforce existing social inequalities. Hence, there is an urgent need to better understand how sociodemographic and other factors not only deter people from experiencing positive outcomes of internet use but to simultaneously experience negative consequences, for instance, in the fashion of privacy invasions.

5   Next Steps

To conclude the chapter, I will provide an outlook on important possible next steps in privacy and digital inequalities research, considering the above-mentioned research gaps and demands. First, more work is needed to systematically *describe* digital inequalities regarding privacy. Previous works already indicate that sociodemographic factors play an important role in the ways of how people manage their privacy online (e.g., Büchi et al., 2021; Meier & Krämer, 2023; Park, 2021). Future studies should deepen the understanding of which variables (e.g., awareness, knowledge, skills, protection behaviors) are unequally distributed across social classes and focus on the causes of these inequalities. For instance, why do younger and more educated persons engage in better protection and why do women apparently manage their privacy less than men? Do they have an easier access to information or are these disparities due to differences in socialization? Future studies could shine light on these and further questions. Second, there is a need to study whether other social (e.g., having a migration background) and trait-like factors (e.g., impulsivity or privacy cynicism) *create* digital inequalities regarding privacy. It is conceivable that language barriers, cultural norms, or interindividual differences like being prone to immediate rewards complicate privacy protection and create particularly vulnerable groups. Also, it is unclear whether vulnerable groups are the same across different countries or cultures or whether these groups differ around the world. Third, more research is needed on how sociodemographic and other factors lead to inequities in people's *experiences* of privacy risks and invasions. The literature regarding digital inequalities has mainly focused on the experience of advantages (or lack thereof) of using ICTs. However, because not adequately managing and protecting one's personal data online can entail severe negative consequences for individuals, studying which factors make it more likely that people experience privacy invasions is of great importance (see also Blank & Lutz, 2018; Lutz, 2019). Fourth, previous works that focused on *transparency* remedies have largely neglected digital inequalities. This means that these works had the implicit assumption that certain transparency cues work similarly among different user groups. However, elderly persons might need different kinds of information than younger persons. Users who already have a high level of knowledge and skills are likely to still require in situ information about potential privacy threats, but perhaps not in such detail as less literate people. Therefore, future studies should compare different kinds of transparency cues and support measures to find out for which user group which kind of cue works best. Moreover, besides digital assistance, easily achievable and ubiquitous digital training possibilities and contact points for digital assistance might be further options to balance inequalities.

Ultimately, however, research and society should identify ways of how to balance and overcome digital inequalities because privacy is not an individual matter rather than a collective phenomenon (Baruh & Popescu, 2017). This means that it is hard if not impossible "for any one person to have privacy without all persons having a similar minimum level of privacy" (Regan, 2002, p. 399). Transparency measures such as personalized cues may be a fast and easy cure, but they do not heal the underlying misconception of privacy as an individual responsibility which neglects the networked and collective nature of privacy.

References

Acquisti, A., et al.: Nudges for privacy and security: understanding and assisting users' choices online. ACM Comput. Surv. (CSUR) **50**(3), 1–41 (2017). https://doi.org/10.1145/3054926

Baruh, L., Popescu, M.: Big data analytics and the limits of privacy self-management. New Media Soc. **19**(4), 579–596 (2017). https://doi.org/10.1177/1461444815614001

Baruh, L., Secinti, E., Cemalcilar, Z.: Online privacy concerns and privacy management: a meta-analytical review. J. Commun. **67**(1), 26–53 (2017). https://doi.org/10.1111/jcom.12276

Blank, G., Lutz, C.: Benefits and harms from Internet use: a differentiated analysis of Great Britain. New Media Soc. **20**(2), 618–640 (2018). https://doi.org/10.1177/1461444816667135

Boerman, S.C., Kruikemeier, S., Zuiderveen Borgesius, F.J.: Exploring motivations for online privacy protection behavior: insights from panel data. Commun. Res. **48**(7), 953–977 (2021). https://doi.org/10.1177/0093650218800915

Bol, N., et al.: Understanding the effects of personalization as a privacy calculus: analyzing self-disclosure across health, news, and commerce contexts. J. Comput.-Mediat. Commun. **23**(6), 370–388 (2018). https://doi.org/10.1093/jcmc/zmy020

Bol, N., Strycharz, J., Helberger, N., van de Velde, B., de Vreese, C.H.: Vulnerability in a tracked society: combining tracking and survey data to understand who gets targeted with what content. New Media Soc. **22**(11), 1996–2017 (2020). https://doi.org/10.1177/1461444820924631

Büchi, M., Festic, N., Just, N., Latzer, M.: Digital inequalities in online privacy protection: effects of age, education and gender. In: Hargittai, E. (ed.) Handbook of Digital Inequality, pp. 296–310. Edward Elgar Publishing (2021)

Büchi, M., Just, N., Latzer, M.: Caring is not enough: the importance of Internet skills for online privacy protection. Inf. Commun. Soc. **20**(8), 1261–1278 (2017). https://doi.org/10.1080/136 9118X.2016.1229001

Efroni, Z., Metzger, J., Mischau, L., Schirmbeck, M.: Privacy icons: a risk-based approach to visualisation of data processing. Eur. Data Prot. Law Rev. **5**(3), 352–366 (2019). https://doi.org/10.21552/edpl/2019/3/9

European Commission: Special Eurobarometer 487a: The general data protection regulation. European Commission (2019). https://cnpd.public.lu/content/dam/cnpd/fr/actualites/international/2019/ebs487a-GDPR-sum-en.pdf

Giese, J., Stabauer, M.: Factors that influence cookie acceptance. In: Fui-Hoon Nah, F., Siau, K. (eds.) HCI in Business, Government and Organizations, pp. 272–285. Springer, Cham (2022). https://doi.org/10.1007/978-3-031-05544-7_21

Hargittai, E.: Introduction to the handbook of digital inequality. In: Hargittai, E. (ed.) Handbook of Digital Inequality, pp. 1–7. Edward Elgar Publishing (2021)

Lutz, C.: Digital inequalities in the age of artificial intelligence and big data. Hum. Behav. Emerg. Technol. **1**(2), 141–148 (2019). https://doi.org/10.1002/hbe2.140

Lutz, C., Hoffmann, C.P., Ranzini, G.: Data capitalism and the user: an exploration of privacy cynicism in Germany. New Media Soc. **22**(7), 1168–1187 (2020). https://doi.org/10.1177/146 1444820912544

Matzner, T., Masur, P.K., Ochs, C., von Pape, T.: Do-it-yourself data protection—empowerment or burden? In: Gutwirth, S., Leenes, R., De Hert, P. (eds.) Data Protection on the Move. LGTS, vol. 24, pp. 277–305. Springer, Dordrecht (2016). https://doi.org/10.1007/978-94-017-7376-8_11

Meier, Y., Krämer, N.C.: The privacy calculus revisited: an empirical investigation of online privacy decisions on between- and within-person levels. Commun. Res. (2022). https://doi.org/10.1177/00936502221102101

Meier, Y., Krämer, N.C.: A longitudinal examination of internet users' privacy protection behaviors in relation to their perceived collective value of privacy and individual privacy concerns. New Media Soc. (2023). https://doi.org/10.1177/14614448221142799

Meier, Y., Schäwel, J., Krämer, N.C.: The shorter the better? Effects of privacy policy length on online privacy decision-making. Media Commun. **8**(2), 291–301 (2020b). https://doi.org/10.17645/mac.v8i2.2846

Meier, Y., Schäwel, J., Kyewski, E., Krämer, N.C.: Applying protection motivation theory to predict Facebook users' withdrawal and disclosure intentions. In: Gruzd, A., et al. (eds.) SMSociety 2020a: International Conference on Social Media and Society, pp. 21–29. Association for Computing Machinery (2020a). https://doi.org/10.1145/3400806.3400810

Micheli, M., Lutz, C., Büchi, M.: Digital footprints: an emerging dimension of digital inequality. J. Inf. Commun. Ethics Soc. **16**(3), 242–251 (2018). https://doi.org/10.1108/JICES-02-2018-0014

Obar, J.A., Oeldorf-Hirsch, A.: The biggest lie on the internet: ignoring the privacy policies and terms of service policies of social networking services. Inf. Commun. Soc. **23**(1), 128–147 (2020). https://doi.org/10.1080/1369118X.2018.1486870

Ostendorf, S., Meier, Y., Brand, M.: Self-disclosure on social networks - more than a rational decision-making process. Cyberpsychology: J. Psychosoc. Res. Cyberspace **16**(4), Article 2 (2022). https://doi.org/10.5817/CP2022-4-2

Ostendorf, S., Müller, S.M., Brand, M.: Neglecting long-term risks: self-disclosure on social media and its relation to individual decision-making tendencies and problematic social-networks-use. Front. Psychol. **11**, 543388 (2020). https://doi.org/10.3389/fpsyg.2020.543388

Park, Y.J.: Why privacy matters to digital inequality. In: Hargittai, E. (ed.) Handbook of Digital Inequality, pp. 284–295. Edward Elgar Publishing (2021)

Pastore, A.: Consent notices and cognitive cost after the GDPR: an experimental study [Doctoral dissertation, Catholic University of Portugal] (2020). http://hdl.handle.net/10400.14/31285

Redmiles, E.M., Buntain, C.L.: How feelings of trust, concern, and control of personal online data influence web use. In: Hargittai, E. (ed.) Handbook of Digital Inequality, pp. 311–325. Edward Elgar Publishing (2021)

Regan, P.M.: Privacy as a common good in the digital world. Inf. Commun. Soc. **5**(3), 382–405 (2002). https://doi.org/10.1080/13691180210159328

Robinson, L., et al.: Digital inequalities and why they matter. Inf. Commun. Soc. **18**(5), 569–582 (2015). https://doi.org/10.1080/1369118X.2015.1012532

Smit, E.G., Van Noort, G., Voorveld, H.A.: Understanding online behavioural advertising: user knowledge, privacy concerns and online coping behaviour in Europe. Comput. Hum. Behav. **32**, 15–22 (2014). https://doi.org/10.1016/j.chb.2013.11.008

Trepte, S., et al.: Do people know about privacy and data protection strategies? Towards the "online privacy literacy scale" (OPLIS). In: Gutwirth, S., Leenes, R., de Hert, P. (eds.) Reforming European Data Protection Law. LGTS, vol. 20, pp. 333–365. Springer, Dordrecht (2015). https://doi.org/10.1007/978-94-017-9385-8_14

Van Deursen, A.J., Helsper, E.J.: The third-level digital divide: who benefits most from being online? In: Communication and Information Technologies Annual. Emerald Group Publishing Limited (2015)

Waldman, A.E.: Cognitive biases, dark patterns, and the 'privacy paradox.' Curr. Opin. Psychol. **31**, 105–109 (2020). https://doi.org/10.1016/j.copsyc.2019.08.025

The Hitchhiker's Guide to the Social Media Data Research Galaxy - A Primer

Arianna Rossi[✉][iD]

SnT, University of Luxembourg, Esch-sur-Alzette, Luxembourg
arianna.rossi@uni.lu

Abstract. This short paper is a primer for early career researchers that collect and analyze social media data. It provides concise, practical instructions on how to address personal data protection concerns and implement research ethics principles.

Keywords: Privacy and Data Protection · Research Ethics · Social Media Data

1 Introduction

We often hear students and colleagues deplore that the legal and ethical principles concerning Information and Communication Technologies (ICT) research are too abstract to be easily applied and that hands-on guidelines would enable them to carry out their work more efficiently and more respectfully. When it comes to internet-mediated research, namely to the social media "data gold mine" [11], its richness and availability may lure researchers into drawing heavily from it. However, harvesting social media data for research purposes raises ethical concerns, as well as questions about its legitimacy and lawfulness: being able to easily access such data does not imply that everything is allowed.

This article provides essential pointers about data protection and research ethics to early career scientists when they mine social media data, i.e., when they use automated means to index, analyse, evaluate and interpret mass quantities of content and data [14]. They do not consist in a checklist that can be blindly and effortlessly followed, but they are rather meant to raise questions and reflections to which researchers should find thoughtful answers. Both (personal) data management and ethical practices are generally (i) reflective: scientists need to reflect on their own specific research practices and the associated risks; (ii) dialogical: scientists must continuously review their practices in light of new experiences and new knowledge [13].

We have described at length our own approach to social media data management and research ethics in [24]. This article simplifies what we have discovered about social media data mining and summarizes it in an accessible, jargon-free language directed to early career researchers without a background in law or

F. Bieker et al. (Eds.): Privacy and Identity 2022, IFIP AICT 671, pp. 52–65, 2023.
https://doi.org/10.1007/978-3-031-31971-6_6

ethics. We organize the topics in two main sections, i.e., Sect. 3 on personal data protection and Sect. 4 on research ethics, even though there is reciprocal influence on the decisions and measures that should be adopted, for instance because protecting the confidentiality of data is a fundamental ethical principle.

2   Social Media Data

2.1   What Kind of Data Do We Collect?

Our first concern should be about the type of data that we mine: data collected on the internet can consist of text, images, videos, audio, code, etc. They can be collected from websites or concern user's navigation data; from datasets in the public domain or that are protected by specific access and reuse conditions; they can be recorded by sensors, like the heartbeat or voice and video recording; and many more. This article focuses on a specific type of internet data: the tremendous quantity of information produced within social media platforms, consisting of text (e.g., opinions, comments, preferences, links, etc.), images (e.g., pictures, GIFs, etc.), videos, users' social networks, metadata like timestamps and location markers of publication, among the others.

2.2   From Which Social Media Do We Collect Data?

We may ask which platform is the most appropriate to study the phenomenon we intend to investigate. The major social networks provide API to allow developers to access their content, including Twitter, Reddit, YouTube, Discord, Instagram, Facebook, LinkedIn, TikTok, Tumblr.

Tip: We are usually required to register on the platform as developers, disclose our data mining intentions and obtain their approval. Outside such controlled settings, web scraping is generally prohibited by the terms and conditions of the platforms, even though Article 3 of the Directive (EU) 2019/790 (also known as the Directive on Copyright in the Digital Single Market) allows scientific institutions to perform text and data mining for non-commercial purposes [8].

3   The Protection of Personal Data

The General Data Protection Regulation (GDPR) is the main piece of legislation that protects personal information in the EU[1]. The GDPR is based on the principles of transparency, lawfulness and accountability. This section will also touch upon data minimisation, purpose limitation, accuracy, storage limitation and integrity and confidentiality.

---

[1] Text available at: https://gdpr-info.eu/.

3.1 Do We Collect Personal Data?

The GDPR defines personal data as "any information that relates to an identified or identifiable living individual" (Article 4). It is not always straightforward to determine whether certain pieces of information, when combined, can lead to the identification of a person: on social networks, personal data encompass usernames and pseudonyms, pictures and videos, location markers and timestamps, mentions of other users, shared user networks, etc.

Tip: We should not only consider individual data points, but their combinations. The support of the Data Protection Officer (DPO) of the university can help us determine whether we collect personal data and which ones.

3.2 Can We Fully Anonymize Personal Data?

It is very challenging to effectively anonymize data so that it becomes impossible to identify the person to whom they refer. For example, a simple search online of a social media post can retrieve its original version and its author [5,20]. Moreover, de-anonymization techniques can revert the process of anonymization [29]. Lastly, effective anonymization may lower the utility of the data [3,19].

Tip: There are dedicated applications available online for anonymizing certain types of data[2]. However, merely masking identifiers (e.g., by replacing a personal name with a code) is not an anonymization technique, but rather a pseudonymization technique. In such cases, the data are still considered personal data that can be stored, if security measures and other data protection mechanisms are in place.

3.3 What Data Do We Need and Why?

A good research data management plan is based on a prior reflection on what data are actually needed, adequate and relevant to the purpose, how to collect them, as well as when and how to dispose of them, with the overall goal of minimizing data collection and retention (data minimization principle (Article 5(1)(c))). The purpose must be specified and the (further) processing or re-use of data must be compatible with such purpose [7] (e.g., data that were initially collected for scientific research cannot be repurposed for marketing).

Tip: Although it is sometimes difficult to strictly determine the types of data that will be necessary for the analysis before it starts, defining the purpose as specifically as possible and limiting data collection and storage to the strictly necessary has the benefit of lowering the risks that we need to mitigate. As a consequence, it we can simplify the data management measures we need to put in place.

---

[2] E.g., https://arx.deidentifier.org/ and https://bitbucket.org/ukda/ukds.tools. textanonhelper/wiki/browse/.

3.4   On Which Ground Do We Collect Data?

Personal data processing needs to be justified by a legal basis. For research purposes, the legal basis may be consent, public interest or legitimate interest (Article 6) [7], and may be additionally regulated by national law.

   Tip: It is recommended to seek guidance from the DPO to determine the most appropriate legal basis. If this is consent, only under specific conditions it is lawful: it must be freely given, specific, informed and unambiguous (Article 4(11) and Article 7); additionally, it must be explicit if the data are of sensitive nature (e.g., health data, religious beliefs, etc. see Article 9 GDPR). Note that no matter the legal basis, a different ("ethical") consent to participation to scientific research must be obtained (see Sec. 4.2).

3.5   How Risky and What Kind of Impact Has Our Research on the Concerned Individuals?

When our activities are likely to result in high risks for the rights and freedoms of the individuals to whom the personal data refer (Article 35(1)), a Data Protection Impact Assessment (DPIA) becomes necessary [1]. The DPIA offers a structured way to assess and mitigate the risks entailed in data processing [15], when for example this implicates a systematic, extensive and automated evaluation (e.g., profiling) and when sensitive data are processed on a large scale.

   Tip: Consulting with the DPO will clarify the need for a DPIA and the procedures. The project "Privacy in Research: Asking the Right Questions"[3] offers a dedicated online course, a roleplay game and a booklet [15], while official EU guidelines provide practical guidance questions [9].

3.6   How Do We Ensure the Confidentiality of the Data?

We can protect the confidentiality of personal data against unauthorized access via various (organizational and technical) security measures, for example encryption that irreversibly converts the data into an unreadable form, unless for those having the decryption key [27]; storage on the institutional GitLab and internally hosted servers (versus external clouds); strong authentication procedures; access control measures [27] that authorize or prohibit certain actions depending on the user role (e.g., students vs senior researchers); reversible pseudonymization that removes certain identifiers (multiple approaches exist, see [10]) and allows for the re-identification of users and for their consent gathering and withdrawal (see also Sec. 4.2).

   Tip: The university often provides applications for anonymizing, pseudonymizing, encrypting and securely storing, transferring and sharing the data. Check the institutional IT catalogue or ask the DPO and the technical service of your institution. For a non-exhaustive list of open source tools for pseudonymization, refer to [25].

---

[3] https://sites.google.com/rug.nl/privacy-in-research/home?authuser=0.

3.7   How Do We Limit the Storage of the Data?

We can keep personal data only as long as necessary [21], then they should be deleted or anonymized. However, institutional and funding policies often impose to keep the data for longer periods of time out of data integrity and transparency reasons. This is why an exception applies to scientific research [7], provided that it is justified and security mechanisms are implemented [17].

Tip: Check institutional and funding policies to find out the required storage period and dispose mechanisms for the subsequent data deletion.

3.8   How Do We Ensure the Transparency of Our Data Practices?

Before the data collection starts, we need to inform the concerned people about what we do with their personal data, why we are authorized to gather them, how we are going to use them, and about their rights (Articles 13–14). When we indirectly collect personal data from a social media platform, rather than directly from the concerned individuals, and when informing thousands would constitute a disproportionate effort [7,17], it is admissible to draft a public notice addressed to the people that may be impacted by the research study. The notice must be easily accessible and easy to understand (Article 12).

Tip: The DPO or the Institutional Review Board (IRB) usually provide standard privacy notices that must be tailored to the specific case and can be published on the website of the research project. To be sure everybody understands, we should use plain language and a conversational style, and clarify technical jargon; to allow for skim reading, we should highlight the main words and structure the document in sections with informative headings [2,23]. Moreover, we can devise a short notice [26] that is periodically published on the social media (e.g., a tweet) to warn users of the (imperceptible) data collection and of the opt-out option detailed in Sect. 4.2, with a link to the full public notice on the website.

3.9   How Do We Enable the Exercise of Rights?

Data protection envisages several rights for the individuals to whom data refer: the right to access (Art. 15), rectify (Art. 16), erase (Art. 17) and transfer (Art. 17) their data, as well as to ask to limit (Art. 18) and object to processing (Art. 21), which would prevent us from using the data. If the legal basis is consent, we need to provide an easy way to withdraw consent (Art. 7(3)). Individuals can also submit complaints to the relevant data protection authority (Art. 77), but this should be the last resort: it is advisable to seek to solve all controversies beforehand.

Tip: We need to establish appropriate measures for people to act upon their rights. For example, describe how exactly we enable them to access their data and put in place user-friendly mechanisms to do so.

3.10 Useful Resources on Data Protection Compliance

Additional guidance with examples is provided in [21] and the other sources cited throughout this section. Institutions and national research bodies usually provide resources as well. In the Appendix A, we provide a diagram that guides researchers through the process.

4 Research Ethics in Practice

Similarly to data protection approaches, research ethics decisions are based on judgement calls [13]: what constitutes ethical behaviour depends on the context where the study occurs [30] and is guided by the researchers asking the right questions. Thus, ambiguity, uncertainty and disagreement are inevitable [13], especially to solve ethical dilemmas on internet-mediated data where best practices may not be established. Valuing interdisciplinary knowledge and collective problem-solving is a helpful way to answer such dilemmas, as well as resorting to the organizational and sectorial code of conduct. Further, in many universities, the ethical authorization of the Institutional Review Board should be sought before starting a study.

4.1 Research on Social Media Data Equals Research with Human Subjects

In Europe, the collection and analysis of social media data is considered research with human subjects and must therefore abide by the same ethical safeguards [16]. The difference, however, is that the authors of online contents are largely unaware that their input may be collected and reused elsewhere for scientific purposes [12,22], unless they are directly told so. Thus, their participation to our research study cannot be considered voluntary nor informed, which raises novel challenges.

4.2 How May We Respect the Autonomy, Privacy, and Dignity of Individuals and Communities?

Public Vs. Private Information. People disclose information on social media platforms even on sensitive, intimate topic to feel like they belong to a community and share their experiences. Despite its availability and seemingly public nature, we should not lightheartedly scrape, analyze, or report such information in other context. We may infer what constitutes acceptable behaviour from contextual elements. For instance, content disclosed on a password-protected group is likely more private [16] than content published with a visible and retrievable hashtag that contributes to a public debate. Moreover, when the information is sensitive (e.g., sexual orientation, health-related issues, etc.) or concerns minors, it may cause harm if it is divulged outside of its intended context.

Tip: We should ask whether the scientific benefits of the disclosure to a different audience in a different context outweigh the possible harms [16]. The answer may also be negative. Depending on the cases, the permission of the authors, of the group moderator or of the legal guardian should be sought [12,31].

Anonymity and Confidentiality. By implementing confidentiality measures, we mitigate the risk of increased vulnerability, embarrassment, reputation damage, or prosecution of the subjects of the study [28]. Since public social media posts are retrievable via a simple online search, when we republish e.g., verbatim quotes in articles, it is difficult to conceal the authors' identities.

Tip: We should not quote verbatim contents without a good reason [12] or ask for the authors' permission (this is where pseudonymization can be handy). Paraphrasing the content can constitute a viable solution [16] in this respect, however it may impact data accuracy and integrity (Sec. 4.3).

Informed Consent and Withdrawal. Based on the disclosure of the practices and risks involved in the study, informed consent allows individuals to freely express their willingness to join or abstain as research participants, under the condition that they should be able to withdraw their consent whenever they desire. In large-scale data mining, seeking consent from each potential participant may be impracticable [13], though. In such cases and when the collection concerns non-sensitive, visibly public data (see Sect. 4.2) [16], providing transparency about the research study [12] (see also Sec. 3.8) and the possibility to withdraw (i.e., retrospective withdrawal [16] or opt-out) may be considered sufficient.

Tip: The consent to research participation ("ethical consent") is always required and differs from the ("legal") consent that may or may not constitute the legal basis for personal data processing (see Sect. 3.4). Whenever possible, ethical consent for data scraping from research participants should be sought. Otherwise, we can aggregate data and ask consent for republication of individual quotes or images. If the information is sensitive and not visibly public, it is advisable to ask the permission to use it to the group moderator, at least. We should also set up procedures to allow impacted users to contact us to opt-out from the study and delete or exclude their data from any further processing.

4.3   Scientific Integrity

This principle concerns the quality, integrity and contribution of a piece of research [16].

Data Quality. Data should not be tampered nor transformed in an unreasonable manner to ensure the validity of the research findings and conclusions [16]. Moreover, data coming from social networks may be produced by bots and exclude those voices and experiences that are absent from the platform. Further, we do not know whether the data made available via the platform's APIs is representative and complete. Lastly, inaccurate and even misleading inferences [16] may be generated through data analysis.

Tip: We should be aware of and mitigate such risks, starting with a transparent account of such shortcomings. We should also resort to an anticipatory assessment of the entailed risks and balance them against the envisaged benefits deriving from the research study. When the risks outweigh the benefits and mitigation measures do not suffice, we need to find alternative ways to get to the scientific answers we seek.

Minors. As the minimal age requirement to register on many social media is 13, we may unwittingly involve minors and their data in our study without the necessary authorization of their legal guardian [16].

Tip: At present, there seems to be no reliable manner to exclude minors' data from data collection. Thus we should report the results only in an aggregate form and paraphrase quoted if we intend to republish them.

4.4   Social Responsibility

This principle enshrines that researchers should act in the public interest by respecting social structures of (online) communities, avoiding their disruption, and thoughtfully balancing the positive and negative consequences of a piece of research [16].

Invasive Research and Dual Use. Building on the tension between public and private domain (Sec. 4.2), there may be certain communities that do not welcome being under the spotlight nor analyses of their disclosures in a trustworthy online environment. Stretching the meaning of dual use, it is paramount to reflect in an anticipatory manner on whether the data, code or knowledge that we produce can be used to harm the society (e.g., job loss, discrimination), the environment (e.g., pollution, global warming), living beings' health and safety (e.g., military applications), and the rights and freedoms (e.g., privacy) [4]. We should also propose measures to mitigate such risks or even avoid certain research activities if deemed too risky.

Tip: We should apply the proportionality principle which requires that ethical checks and procedures should be proportional to the assessed risks and potential harms [16] and weight the benefits of the findings against the harms in each research context, as part of a research impact assessment.

Risks for Researchers. Using social media can expose researchers to cyber-risks (e.g., cyberbulling, stalking and media pillories) as well as physical threats, which can lead to professional and personal consequences like loss of scientific reputation and anxiety.

Tip: Such risks must be mitigated, especially when they concern early stage researchers, mainly through institutional preparedness [18].

Compensation. It is common practice to reward research participants for their time and efforts, but doing so with data that was collected indirectly is cumbersome or even impossible.

Tip: We may reciprocate with enhanced knowledge based on the publication of the study results [12].

4.5   Maximise Benefits and Minimise Harm

Confidentiality and security measures, precautions against using minors' data, processes for consent collection and withdrawal, as well as oversight over the ethicality of the process and the validity of the research, are meant to minimize the risks for participants and researchers, while maximizing the research benefits [16].

4.6   Useful Resources on Research Ethics

Additional guidance with examples is provided in [6,13,16] as well as in professional code of conducts, like the ACM code[4].

5   Limitations

The content of this article is meant to be a primer and must be taken critically as each research study has its own features and what applies to one case may not apply to seemingly similar ones. Since it oversimplifies many topics, we invite the readers to explore the proposed bibliography resources and beyond. Moreover, this short guide has not been tested in use and is not complete: for example, sustainability as an ICT ethical principle is not mentioned. Moreover, researchers should get acquainted with FAIR principles (i.e., findable, accessible,

---

[4] https://www.acm.org/code-of-ethics.

interoperable, reusable)[5] for data management and be able to choose the appropriate licenses for software[6] and data[7]. To get a broader understanding of such issues, DCC provides how-to guides and checklists on their website[8], whereas CESSDA has published a complete guide to data management online[9] that can be learnt through a serious game[10].

6 Conclusions

In a nutshell, the main points to retain are:

1. Start planning the data management process and contact the DPO and the IRB well before you start the data collection as it may take time to receive an authorization;
2. Ask for support from more experienced researchers and to those with complementary experiences;
3. Check the institutional resources (e.g., code of ethics; consent templates; security-enhancing tools; data protection training; etc.) available to you;
4. It is safer to assume that social media data and metadata are personal data, rather than the contrary;
5. Analysing information published online counts as research on human subjects, thus the same ethical safeguards should be upheld;
6. Thus, ethical consent to research participation should be sought; under certain conditions, transparency and opt-out may suffice;
7. Actual anonymization is hard to achieve, while pseudonymization allows for re-identification (i.e., to contact the users, enable them to opt-out, uphold data integrity) but other technical and organizational measures are needed.

Acknowledgements. This work has been partially supported by the Luxembourg National Research Fund (FNR) - IS/14717072 "Deceptive Patterns Online (Decepticon)" and the H2020-EU grant agreement ID 956562 "Legally-Attentive Data Scientists (LeADS)". The main content of this work was published in extend form in [24] and re-elaborated thanks to the comments of colleagues, students and data management experts.

---

[5] https://www.go-fair.org/fair-principles/.
[6] https://choosealicense.com/.
[7] https://ufal.github.io/public-license-selector/.
[8] https://www.dcc.ac.uk/guidance/how-guides.
[9] https://dmeg.cessda.eu/Data-Management-Expert-Guide.
[10] https://lod.sshopencloud.eu/.

A   Appendix A

See the Fig. 1.

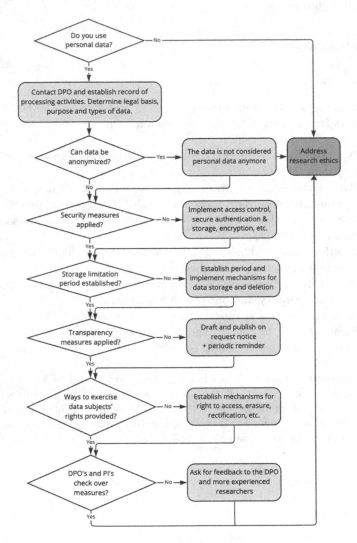

Fig. 1. Decision diagram for data protection measures

References

1. Article 29 Data Protection Working Party: Guidelines on data protection impact assessment (DPIA) and determining whether processing is "likely to result in a high risk" for the purposes of regulation 2016/679 (2017). https://ec.europa.eu/newsroom/just/document.cfm?doc_id=47711

2. Article 29 Data Protection Working Party: Guidelines on transparency under regulation 2016/679, 17/EN WP260 rev.01 (2018–04). https://ec.europa.eu/newsroom/article29/redirection/document/51025
3. Article 29 Working Party: Opinion 05/2014 on anonymisation techniques (2014). https://ec.europa.eu/justice/article-29/documentation/opinion-recommendation/files/2014/wp216_en.pdf
4. Benčin, R., Strle, G.: Social responsibility in science and engineering (2015–06). https://satoriproject.eu/media/1.c-Social-responsibility.pdf
5. Beninger, K., Fry, A., Jago, N., Lepps, H., Nass, L., Silvester, H.: Research using social media; users' views (2014). https://www.natcen.ac.uk/media/282288/p0639-research-using-social-media-report-final-190214.pdf
6. Commission, E.: Horizon 2020 guidance - how to complete your ethics self-assessment (2018). https://eneri.eu/wp-content/uploads/2018/10/H2020-Guidance-How-to-complete-your-ethics-self-assessment.pdf
7. Ducato, R.: Data protection, scientific research, and the role of information. Comput. Law Secur. Rev. **37**, 105412 (2020). https://doi.org/10.1016/j.clsr.2020.105412, https://www.sciencedirect.com/science/article/pii/S0267364920300170
8. Ducato, R., Strowel, A.M.: Ensuring text and data mining: remaining issues with the EU copyright exceptions and possible ways out. Eur. Intell. Prop. Rev. **43**(5), 322–337 (2021). https://papers.ssrn.com/abstract=3829858
9. European Data Protection Supervisor: Accountability on the ground part II: Data protection impact assessments & prior consultation (2018). https://edps.europa.eu/sites/edp/files/publication/18-02-06_accountability_on_the_ground_part_2_en.pdf
10. European Network and Information Security Agency: Pseudonymisation techniques and best practices: recommendations on shaping technology according to data protection and privacy provisions. Publications Office (2019). https://data.europa.eu/doi/10.2824/247711
11. Fiesler, C., Beard, N., Keegan, B.C.: No robots, spiders, or scrapers: Legal and ethical regulation of data collection methods in social media terms of service. In: Proceedings of the International AAAI Conference on Web and Social Media, vol. 14, pp. 187–196 (2020). https://ojs.aaai.org/index.php/ICWSM/article/view/7290
12. Fiesler, C., Proferes, N.: "participant" perceptions of twitter research ethics. Soc. Media + Soc. **4**(1), 2056305118763366 (2018). https://doi.org/10.1177/2056305118763366
13. Franzke, A.S., Bechmann, Anja, Zimmer, M., Ess, Charles M.: Internet research: Ethical guidelines 3.0: Association of internet researchers (2019). https://aoir.org/reports/ethics3.pdf
14. Future TDM: D3.3+ baseline report of policies and barriers of TDM in europe (2016). https://project.futuretdm.eu/wp-content/uploads/2017/05/FutureTDM_D3.3-Baseline-Report-of-Policies-and-Barriers-of-TDM-in-Europe.pdf
15. Hoorn, E., Montagner, C.: Starting with a DPIA methodology for human subject research (2018). https://www.rug.nl/research/research-data-management/downloads/c2-dataprotection-dl/dpia_guidance_doc_v1_pub.pdf
16. Kaye, L.K., et al.: Ethics guidelines for internet-mediated research (2021). https://www.bps.org.uk/sites/www.bps.org.uk/files/Policy/Policy%20-%20Files/Ethics%20Guidelines%20for%20Internet-mediated%20Research.pdf. ISBN: 978-1-85433-796-2

17. Kuyumdzhieva, A.: General data protection regulation and horizon 2020 ethics review process: ethics compliance under GDPR. Bioethica. **5**(1), 6–12 (2019). https://doi.org/10.12681/bioeth.20832, https://ejournals.epublishing.ekt. gr/index.php/bioethica/article/view/20832

18. Marwick, A.E., Blackwell, L., Lo, K.: Best practices for conducting risky research and protecting yourself from online harassment. In: Data & Society Guide, p. 10. Data & Society Research Institute (2016). https://datasociety.net/wp-content/ uploads/2016/10/Best_Practices_for_Conducting_Risky_Research-Oct-2016.pdf

19. Mészáros, J., Ho, C.h.: Big data and scientific research: the secondary use of personal data under the research exemption in the GDPR. Hungarian J. Legal Stud. **59**(4), 403–419 (2018). https://doi.org/10.1556/2052.2018.59.4.5, https:// akjournals.com/doi/10.1556/2052.2018.59.4.5

20. Narayanan, A., Shmatikov, V.: De-anonymizing social networks. In: 2009 30th IEEE Symposium on Security and Privacy, pp. 173–187 (2009). https://doi.org/ 10.1109/SP.2009.22, ISSN: 2375-1207

21. Officer, I.C.: Guide to the UK general data protection regulation (UK GDPR). https://ico.org.uk/for-organisations/guide-to-data-protection/guide-to-the-general-data-protection-regulation-gdpr/

22. Proferes, N.: Information flow solipsism in an exploratory study of beliefs about twitter. Soc. Media + Soc. **3**(1), 2056305117698493 (2017). https://doi.org/10. 1177/2056305117698493

23. Rossi, A., Ducato, R., Haapio, H., Passera, S.: When design met law: design patterns for information transparency. Droit de la Consommation = Consumenterecht : DCCR. **122**, 79–121 (2019). https://orbilu.uni.lu/bitstream/10993/40116/1/A. %20Rossi,%20R.%20Ducato,%20H.%20Haapio%20et%20S.%20Passera.pdf

24. Rossi, A., Kumari, A., Lenzini, G.: Unwinding a legal and ethical ariadne's thread out of the twitter's scraping maze. In: Privacy Symposium 2022 - Data Protection Law International Convergence and Compliance with Innovative Technologies (DPLICIT). Springer Nature (2022). https://doi.org/10.1007/978-3-031-09901-4_10

25. Rossi, A., Arena, M.P., Kocyijit, E., Hani, M.: Challenges of protecting confidentiality in social media data and their ethical import. In: 1st International Workshop on Ethics in Computer Security (EthiCS 2022) Co-located with the 7th IEEE European Symposium on Security and Privacy, pp. 554–561. IEEE (2022). https://doi. org/10.1109/EuroSPW55150.2022.00066

26. Schaub, F., Balebako, R., Durity, A.L., Cranor, L.F.: A design space for effective privacy notices. In: Proceedings of Eleventh Symposium On Usable Privacy and Security (SOUPS 2015), pp. 1–17 (2015). https://doi.org/10.5555/3235866. 3235868

27. Stallings, W.: Operating system security (chapter 24). In: Computer Security Handbook, pp. 24.1–24.21. Wiley, 6 edn. (2014). https://doi.org/10.1002/ 9781118851678.ch24

28. Townsend, L., Wallace, C.: The ethics of using social media data in research: a new framework. In: Woodfield, K. (ed.) The Ethics of Online Research, Advances in Research Ethics and Integrity, vol. 2, pp. 189–207. Emerald Publishing Limited (2017). https://doi.org/10.1108/S2398-601820180000002008

29. Tripathy, B.K.: De-anonymization techniques for social networks. In: Dey, N., Borah, S., Babo, R., Ashour, A.S. (eds.) Social Network Analytics, pp. 71–85. Academic Press (2019). https://doi.org/10.1016/B978-0-12-815458-8.00004-9, https://www.sciencedirect.com/science/article/pii/B9780128154588000049

30. Vitak, J., Shilton, K., Ashktorab, Z.: Beyond the Belmont principles: Ethical challenges, practices, and beliefs in the online data research community. In: Proceedings of the 19th ACM Conference on Computer-Supported Cooperative Work & Social Computing, pp. 941–953. ACM (2016). https://doi.org/10.1145/2818048.2820078
31. Williams, M.L., Burnap, P., Sloan, L.: Towards an ethical framework for publishing twitter data in social research: Taking into account users' views, online context and algorithmic estimation. Sociology **51**(6), 1149–1168 (2017). https://doi.org/10.1177/0038038517708140

Selected Student Papers

Valuation of Differential Privacy Budget in Data Trade: A Conjoint Analysis

Michael Khavkin$^{(\boxtimes)}$ and Eran Toch

Department of Industrial Engineering, Tel Aviv University, Tel Aviv 6997801, Israel
khavkin1@mail.tau.ac.il, erant@tauex.tau.ac.il

Abstract. Differential privacy has been proposed as a rigorous privacy guarantee for computation mechanisms. However, it is still unclear how data collectors can correctly and intuitively configure the value of the privacy budget parameter ε for differential privacy, such that the privacy of involved individuals is protected. In this work, we seek to investigate the trade-offs between differential privacy valuation, scenario properties, and preferred differential privacy level of individuals in a data trade. Using a choice-based conjoint analysis ($N = 139$), we mimic the decision-making process of individuals under different data-sharing scenarios. We found that, as hypothesized, individuals required lower payments from a data collector for sharing their data, as more substantial perturbation was applied as part of a differentially private data analysis. Furthermore, respondents selected scenarios with lower ε values (requiring more privacy) for indefinitely-retained data for profit generation than for temporarily-retained data with a non-commercial purpose. Our findings may help data processors better tune the differential privacy budget for their data analysis based on individual privacy valuation and contextual properties.

Keywords: Differential Privacy · Privacy Budget · User Preferences · Willingness-to-Accept · Conjoint Analysis

1 Introduction

Anonymization has become the fundamental step in privacy protection and data minimization, acting as one of the critical principles in compliance with privacy-related laws. Privacy-related laws and regulations, such as the European General Data Protection Regulation (GDPR) [20] and its American equivalents California Consumer Privacy Act (CCPA) and the Health Insurance Portability and Accountability Act (HIPAA), have raised data collectors' awareness to privacy and contributed to the empowerment of individuals through increased transparency of data handling processes. Anonymization is often used as a Privacy-Enhancing Technique (PET) to deal with the risk of releasing Personally Identifiable Information (PII), i.e., any information that is linkable to an individual's identity or to her personal attributes, by either direct or indirect means. This has made privacy-preserving data analysis more relevant, especially in providing business insights in many real-world applications, such as census surveys

© IFIP International Federation for Information Processing 2023
Published by Springer Nature Switzerland AG 2023
F. Bieker et al. (Eds.): Privacy and Identity 2022, IFIP AICT 671, pp. 69–84, 2023.
https://doi.org/10.1007/978-3-031-31971-6_7

[7], healthcare [12], and so forth. However, as previously demonstrated [23], anonymization does not always act as a silver bullet, primarily when statistical analyses are performed.

Rigorous privacy constraints, such as differential privacy [13], have been proposed to prevent adversarial re-identification of sensitive information from data analysis outcomes. Under differential privacy, individual-level values cannot be inferred from aggregate data, even in the presence of an adversary with background knowledge. A privacy parameter typically controls the level of differential privacy, denoted by the parameter ε and referred to as privacy budget [15]. The privacy budget limits the privacy loss incurred by an individual when her personal data is used in an analysis. In the context of differentially private mechanisms for data analysis, the privacy budget is translated to the amount of noise that is added to the analysis output to guarantee privacy. In general, setting an appropriate value of ϵ is an unsolved problem open to interpretations and heuristics, as there is no upper bound on the value of ε, and no gold standard for its selection exists [14,19]. For example, reported privacy budget values in previous works range from 0.1 to $\ln(3)$ [15] and as high as 14 in Apple's implementation [29]. Moreover, the relativeness of ε to the data domain and analysis type adds another dimension of complexity to its selection process since it may require a high degree of domain expertise from the data processor.

User-Centered-Design (UCD) principles have been developed to extend the initiative of *Privacy-by-Design* development [6], which encourages involving end-users in the design process of privacy in information systems. Although these principles help increase the cooperation of individuals in contributing their data for an analysis [17], they posed an additional challenge due to a possibly significant deviation in privacy preferences and varying privacy valuations among individuals. This has raised the need for personalized differential privacy [17], according to which personal privacy levels are set individually at a user-level and then aggregated to a general privacy budget. However, we cannot expect individuals to provide the data processor with their preferred value of ε directly, as this task is non-trivial, even for domain experts.

The challenge of privacy budget selection has been intensified in data markets [27], where individuals trade their personal data by selling it to data collectors (e.g., organizations), who in turn present them with monetary compensation for their privacy loss (also referred to as Transactional Privacy [26,27]). User interaction with privacy, particularly Transactional Privacy, is strongly connected to human behavior and personal valuation. The decision-making process of users (also referred to as *privacy-calculus* [10]) involves weighting the privacy risks of disclosing personal information, on the one hand, and the personal benefits from this act, on the other hand. Accordingly, if the benefits outweigh the privacy risks, users are expected to disclose sensitive information. Hence, the decision-making process of individuals in data trade is represented, often unconsciously, by the evaluation of multiple trade-offs between multiple factors. Previous evaluation of privacy-utility trade-offs in the health recommender systems [30] and e-commerce [31] domains has emphasized the importance of studying human-related factors to increase acceptance of privacy mechanisms and understand their impact on individuals' willingness to share personal data. Nevertheless, most previous works investigated the impact of privacy valuation on decision-making processes without establishing specific research questions that relate to differential privacy, in particular.

Extending the existing literature on decision-making processes under differential privacy, we investigated the influence of behavioral and contextual factors on the willingness to share data in data trade under differential privacy. These factors reflect the privacy preferences of individuals participating in a data-sharing scenario. In particular, we examined these trade-offs' influence on the value of ε, which the data processor can later use to apply a differential privacy mechanism to data analysis. To that end, we performed a choice-based conjoint analysis, where we asked 139 participants to select their most preferred scenario, described by a set of attributes, in the context of three data-sharing use cases involving medical, financial, and behavioral data.

Contribution. In this paper, we considered the human-related aspects of selecting ε for differential privacy. We compared the potential impact of varying privacy preferences and scenario properties on the selected privacy budget ε. In addition, we investigated whether individuals' differential privacy valuation is aligned with the expected theoretical payment scheme for data trade under differential privacy.

The remainder of this paper is structured as follows. In Sect. 2, we review related work concerning privacy valuation and provide a brief overview of differential privacy. In Sect. 3, we describe our experimental design and present our findings in Sects. 4 and 5. Finally, we conclude this paper in Sect. 6.

2 Background and Related Work

2.1 Anonymization and Differential Privacy

Statistical Disclosure Limitation techniques [3] have been proposed as a type of anonymization that generates an anonymized dataset with a specific format designed to reduce disclosure risk. Such methods implemented the idea of *"hiding in a crowd"*, reducing the uniqueness of a record among all other records in a dataset. Such protection methods achieved anonymization by performing generalization, suppression, or both. However, these methods have been found [23] to be vulnerable to cases where the adversary has broader background knowledge about individuals in a dataset than one would anticipate.

Differential privacy (DP) [13] has been proposed as a mathematically rigorous privacy guarantee that provides plausible deniability. According to differential privacy, the maximal change in a randomized algorithm's output on two neighboring datasets is bounded by the privacy budget parameter ε. This parameter controls the maximum amount of information that can be learned about any individual's data through the analysis of a dataset. In other words, the outcome of any analysis is equally likely, up to a multiplicative factor, independent of whether any individual's data is present in the analyzed dataset. Formally, a randomized mechanism $\mathcal{A}$ satisfies ε-differential privacy concerning two neighboring datasets D and D', differing in precisely one record, and for every subset of possible outputs $\mathcal{S}$, if and only if

$$Pr[\mathcal{A}[D] \in \mathcal{S}] \leq \exp(\varepsilon)Pr[\mathcal{A}[D'] \in \mathcal{S}] \tag{1}$$

Differential privacy is commonly achieved through noise-addition mechanisms, such as Laplace mechanism [15], Gaussian mechanism [15], or exponential mechanism [24]. For example, for an analysis function and Laplace mechanism, noise is sampled randomly from the Laplace distribution and added to the function's output. The amount of added noise is directly and inversely controlled by the privacy budget ε, i.e., the lower ε, the noisier the output is (but more private), and vice versa. In the context of personalized differential privacy [17] for computations between a data collector and multiple individuals, each individual selects a personal privacy specification, which is then aggregated to a single general privacy budget.

Previous works argued that although the privacy budget parameter ε of differential privacy is theoretically well-defined, there is a challenge in configuring it in practice [14,16,19]. Reported privacy budget values in previous works ranged from 0.1 to $\ln(3)$ [15] and as high as 14 in Apple's implementation [29], but these may serve as a rough estimation and may not be suitable for any use case. Moreover, the change in the risk of learning anything about a non-participating individual, as opposed to a participating individual whose data is used for a data analysis, is bounded by a multiplicative exponential factor of e^{ε}. Hence, even small changes in ε are translated to large deviations in that risk.

From a practical point of view, the selection of ε in real-world applications [14] was also accompanied by the challenge of relativeness to the data domain and analysis type. This has presented organizations with the requirement of hiring a dedicated domain expert with knowledge of differential privacy to circumvent the challenges in the selection process, which ultimately can hinder the deployment of differential privacy into information systems. Furthermore, the difficulty in comprehending differential privacy and its implications among laypeople has been extensively studied [11,31] to improve the general acceptance of differentially private methods. Other criticized challenges relate to increased computational resources and the need for suitable computing environments [4].

2.2 Privacy Valuation Under Differentially Private Data Trade

Personal privacy valuation and segmentation of privacy attitudes [21] have been used to explain the rationality behind privacy calculus [10]. Acquisti et al. [2] stated that the value of privacy depends on how private the data is, i.e., the less private the information is, the lower it is valued, and vice versa. Privacy valuation is commonly measured in monetary units by the individual Willingness-to-Accept (WTA) [2], i.e., the lowest price that individuals are willing to accept for sharing their personal information. Alternatively, valuation has been considered as the Willingness-to-Pay (WTP) for the protection of personal sensitive information [2]. However, deeper examination using common experience and surveys [1] showed a paradox between privacy attitudes and user behavior, which has later been referred to as the privacy paradox [5]. Namely, the privacy preferences that individuals declare are not always the ones they reveal (i.e., *"users do share data but value not sharing data"* [30]). Several cognitive and behavioral factors have been researched to explain the rational behind the privacy paradox and extend it, including privacy attitudes and sharing attitudes [9]. These have been found to be almost decoupled in the context of data sharing experiences with positive sentiment (i.e., people forget about privacy when they perceive sharing data as beneficial or pleasurable).

In the context of differentially private data trade, this observation was used for devising a payment scheme that is both fair for the individual who shares personal data and profitable enough for the data processor. For example, Jung et al. [18] proposed a fair negotiation technique which leverages the concept of social welfare, i.e., the participant's benefit from a transaction in a negotiation. Following that negotiation, the connection between ε and the price individuals were willing to sell their personal data for was controlled by an exchange rate (dollar value per ε value).

However, since differentially private data analysis is more accurate with large datasets, including data from many individuals can be expensive for the data collector. To reduce query costs for the data collector, Nget et al. [25] proposed a balanced query-based pricing mechanism that finds a sample of data owners to be included in a differentially private data analysis, using a price menu, derived from individuals' privacy preferences. Alternatively, in cases where data owners struggle to valuate their privacy, several pre-calculated payment schemes have been generated for data owners to choose from [2,22].

Although several user studies [2,28] have been conducted to understand attitudes towards data trade in general, and data protection within a data trade environment in particular, no extensive empirical investigation with users has been conducted to investigate the alignment of theoretical pricing mechanisms with real-world behavior under differentially private data trade. Furthermore, in spite of the comprehensive literature on privacy valuation, it still lacks sufficient research on how to help individuals correctly valuate their differential privacy, based not only on their subjective assessment, but also on data and setting properties (e.g., data type, collection purpose and etc.).

3   Research Method

Inspired by the methodology of Valdez et al. [30], a conjoint analysis was performed to investigate the decision-making process of individuals under a differentially private data sharing scenario. A conjoint analysis [8] is a common research method typically employed for product and pricing research and frequently used across different industries. We consider hereafter a use case of a two-sided data market where individuals trade their personal data with a data collector, who in turn aggregates the data to perform a statistical data analysis that satisfies differential privacy. This use case corresponds to an "interactive use" of differential privacy, where aggregate data is used to calculate statistics, rather than masking the individual data records themselves in an offline manner. The total cost of the data analysis for the data collector is the sum of compensations to all participating individuals for their incurred privacy loss.

For simplicity, in our case we defined analysis of personal data as a histogram query, computed on the collected data of individuals who had agreed to share their data. This selection was based on reviewing recent real-world use cases, where differential privacy has been successfully implemented [7]. Furthermore, such analysis type allows us to analyze differential privacy in terms of added noise scale, with a global sensitivity [15] of 1. This property leads to an inverse relationship between the privacy budget ε and the added noise scale, namely the scale of the noise is $1/\varepsilon$, and its value is sampled from Laplace distribution with parameters $(0, 1/\varepsilon)$ (i.e., Laplace mechanism [15]).

3.1 Experimental Design

For the experimental design, a standard setting of conjoint analysis was used. In our experiments, participants were asked to perform several choice-based tasks, where they select their most preferred scenario, described by a set of attributes, in the context of data sharing scenarios across three domains: (1) medical sensitive data (e.g., relating to the existence of diabetes); (2) financial data (.e.g., income); and (3) behavioral data (e.g., Internet browsing history). To that end, we collected the responses of 139 participants to choice-based tasks, each answering 10 rounds of random decision tasks of three choices, representing three settings of sharing scenarios.

Three data-related and two user-related categorical attributes were used in the conjoint choice tasks. For the data-related attributes, we included the disclosed information type, its retention period and sharing purpose, to define the scenario for a single choice in the task.

As a proxy to the differential privacy budget, we included a noise scale attribute, representing the minimum perturbation that an individual would prefer to be added to the output of an underlying data analysis, to protect her shared personal data. Accordingly, the privacy budget was logarithmically split to five ranges between 0.05 and 2 (maximal assumed privacy budget), corresponding to noise scales, i.e., lower noise scales correspond to higher range of ε values (and vice versa). The noise scale was used instead of directly presenting a privacy budget, since it is inversely tied to the value of ε [15], and it would be difficult for people to interpret a continuously distributed value.

A monetary privacy valuation factor was presented as a value in the range of 1\$ − 100\$ (split to five sub-ranges), representing different WTA valuations. In total, the decision tasks have been randomly sampled from a set of 450 (3 × 2 × 3 × 5 × 5) factor value combinations. Table 1 summarizes the considered attributes in the study.

Table 1. Considered attributes in the choice-based conjoint analysis. Each combination of attribute levels (i.e., values) describes a setting of a data sharing scenario under differential privacy.

Attribute	Description	Attribute levels
Sensitive disclosed data	Type of collected data	(Medical) Existence of Diabetes; (Financial) Income; (Behavioral) Browsing History
Retention period	Retention period of data	Indefinite; Temporary
Sharing purpose	The purpose for which the personal data is collected	Research; Revenue generation; Improvement of services
Data sharing compensation price (*Willingness-to-Accept*)	Lowest price that individuals are willing to accept for sharing their personal information	1\$ – 100\$
Differential Privacy Level (*prop. to noise scale, lower noise scales correspond to higher ε ranges*)	Expected differential privacy level to be satisfied by the data processor	1 ($1.0 \leq \varepsilon \leq 2.0$); 2 ($0.5 \leq \varepsilon \leq 1.0$); 3 ($0.2 \leq \varepsilon \leq 0.5$); 4 ($0.1 \leq \varepsilon \leq 0.2$); 5 ($0.05 \leq \varepsilon \leq 0.1$)

As an introductory explanation to the questionnaire, all participants were provided with a short description of the study and differential privacy. We adapted the general description of differential privacy from Xiong et al. [31], which has been studied to best enhance comprehension among laypeople and increase their willingness to share information. In total, 1390 choice selections were considered, ignoring incomplete responses and click-through completions (1% of responses)[1]. Figure 1 illustrates a screenshot of a single decision task presented to a participant.

Participant Statistics. The participants were recruited via MTurk platform, with restriction to people from the U.S. with at least 90% approval rate and at least $1,000$ approved assignments. Each respondent was paid 0.6\$ for an estimated 7 min work. The participants consisted of $N = 77$ (55%) male and $N = 62$ (45%) female participants. Participants varied in age, spanning across all age groups: $N = 48$ (34%) in $18 - 34$, $N = 67$ (48%) in $35 - 54$, and $N = 24$ (18%) were 55 and above. Reported highest level of education has also spanned across all categories: $N = 19$ (14%) indicated a high-school education or less, $N = 100$ (73%) indicated high education degree, and $N = 20$ (13%) reported other non-degree education.

---

[1] Full survey protocol and evaluation code are available at https://github.com/iWitLab/valuating_differential_privacy_budget.

Question 1

Please carefully review the choice options detailed below, then choose your most preferred scenario.
Which of these choices do you prefer?

	Choice 1	Choice 2	Choice 3
Retention period (Retention period of collected personal data by the data processor)	Indefinitely	Temporary	Temporary
Differential privacy level: 1 (lowest) - 5 (highest) (Expected differential privacy level to be satisfied by the data processor)	1	3	4
Data sharing compensation price (Lowest price that individuals are willing to accept for sharing their personal information)	1$	50$	10$
Sharing purpose (The purpose for which personal data is collected)	Research	Research	Research
Sensitive disclosed data (Type of collected data)	(Medical) Existence of Diabetes	(Financial) Income	(Behavioral) Browsing History

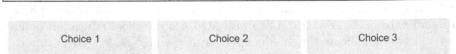

Fig. 1. Screenshot of one decision choice task in the distributed questionnaire. Each column refers to a different setting of a differentially private data sharing scenario. Participants were asked to choose their preferable scenario setting out of the presented options. Order of attributes was randomized for each participant to prevent any biased selection according to the appearance order.

3.2   Comparison to Theoretical Behavior

Prior to carrying out the study, we examined the theoretical relationship between the amount of added noise for satisfying differential privacy and the value of WTA, to compare it with that induced from the survey's collected answers. Following our methodology (in Sect. 3.1 above), we considered the scale of the added noise and not the privacy budget ε explicitly, to be consistent with the attributes in the conjoint analysis survey.

As has been demonstrated in previous differential privacy studies dealing with balanced data trade pricing [22], increasing the noise scale of perturbation can lower the data processor's price. Hence, we would expect to see a logarithmic decrease in the payment that individuals will receive from a data collector, when the amount of added noise increases. This can be explained by the low utility of a perturbed analysis output when a large amount of noise is added to it, up to an extent where it might become useless for the purposes of the data collector. Thus, we can overall assume a similar pricing scheme for contributing individuals, according to which a noisier analysis output leads to a lower disclosure risk for contributing individuals, allowing them to compromise on a lower payment.

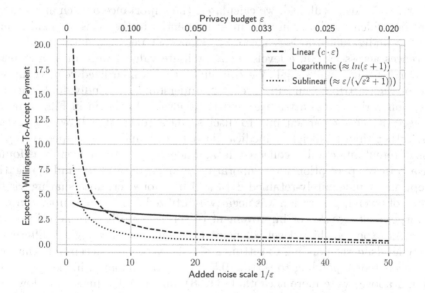

Fig. 2. Theoretical expected WTA (Willingness-to-Accept) payment as a function of added noise scale. Noise scale is derived from the privacy budget ε for a differentially private analysis, with Laplace noise scale of $(1/\varepsilon)$. Payment distribution is shown for three schemes - linear, sub-linear and logarithmic.

We adopted the definitions of Nget et al. [25] for a theoretical payment scheme in a data market setting. Figure 2 shows the expected relationship between added noise scale and the WTA values for three types of payment schemes. For a linear payment function $(c \cdot \varepsilon)$, the data subject can set any value for some linear constant c to increase his profit, resulting in highly untruthful privacy valuation. Alternatively, for logarithmic and sub-linear schemes, the decay in the WTA payment is slower but is different between the two functions. Logarithmic payment schemes represent conservative risk-averse individuals, whose ε is small, whereas sub-linear schemes are more suitable for liberal risk-seeking individuals, whose ε is large (i.e., tend to compromise on privacy for reward).

4   Results

The analysis of the trade-offs in the selection of a differentially private data sharing scenario was performed twofold. First, we computed the relative importance of each included attribute in the conjoint analysis, with respect to its levels. Then, we compared the distributions of WTA and ε values for varying scenario properties.

4.1   Trade-Offs in Individual Decision-Making

Similarly to Valdez et al. [30], we calculated the importance of each attribute to determine which attributes are the most influential in the decision-making process of an individual who is requested to share her personal data. In addition, preferences across attribute levels (i.e., attribute values) were measured using part-worth utility analysis [8]. We computed the standardized relative importance of each attribute and its levels, to understand how individuals' privacy perception varies across attributes and their levels. As shown in Fig. 3, it was more acceptable for participants to disclose data concerning browsing history (1.2), rather than financial or medical data (−1.25 and 0.05, respectively). In terms of retention period of collected data, a neutral preference trend was found, with a positive perception for temporarily-retained data (1.0), and a negative perception for indefinitely-retained data (−1.0). Moreover, data sharing for the purpose of revenue generation was negatively utilized (−1.4), in comparison with the purposes of research or improvement of service, which were perceived positively. As expected, high levels of noise (i.e., guaranteeing higher differential privacy levels, corresponding to setting $\varepsilon \leq 0.2$), were more acceptable than low noise levels (corresponding to setting $0.5 \leq \varepsilon \leq 2$). Similarly, higher payments (50\$ and above) were more acceptable (1.38) among individuals than low payments (−1.33), which may cause individuals to decline sharing their data, even when shared for a benevolent purpose.

The relative importance of attributes (at a granularity of an attribute) for a preference decision is shown in Fig. 3 by color and descending order of importance (top to bottom). Overall, the most dominant factor among participants when choosing a preferred sharing scenario was their Willingness-to-Accept, i.e., the amount of money they are willing to receive for sharing their personal data. This was an expected outcome of a trade market, where both sides wish to maximize their profits. The second most relevant factor was the differential privacy level

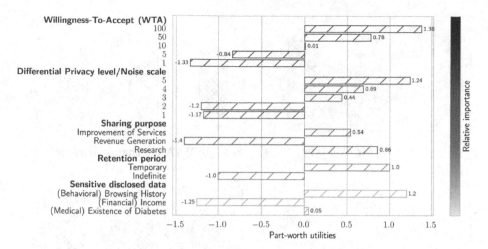

Fig. 3. Relative importance of attribute levels (standardized part-worth utilities)

(offered by the privacy budget ε and its corresponding incurred noise). The purpose for which the data is requested was considered more relevant than its retention period. Relatively to other attributes, the data type (i.e., sensitive disclosed attribute) received the lowest weight in the decision making process of participants.

We computed the mean WTA values for the combination of two attributes: the sensitive disclosed data type and its sharing purpose. The mean WTA values were normalized to a $[0, 1]$ scale for easier comparison. We conducted a statistical Kruskal-Wallis test, with a significance level of $\alpha = .05$, to find differences in the values of WTA and ε with respect to different sharing properties, with additional pairwise Dunn's post-hoc testing (with Bonferroni correction).

Overall, as seen in Fig. 4, the mean WTA value is statistically significantly higher in scenarios where the data is retained indefinitely, in comparison with a temporary retention ($\chi^2(1) = 241.156, p < .001$). Similarly, we found statistically significant differences with respect to the shared sensitive attribute ($\chi^2(2) = 7.634, p = .02$). Disclosure of medical sensitive data (e.g., the existence of diabetes) was considered more "expensive" for data owners to disclose, than financial income data ($p = .02$), and when data is retained indefinitely rather than temporarily by the data recipient (Fig. 4a). However, there were no significant differences in WTA between scenarios involving financial and behavioral browsing data, or between medical and behavioral browsing data ($p = .64$ and $p = .39$, respectively).

Furthermore, statistically significant differences in WTA values were observed with respect to different sharing purposes, depicted in Fig. 4b ($\chi^2(2) = 272.478, p < .001$). The mean WTA value was statistically significantly higher when data is shared for the purpose of revenue generation than when it is used for research or improvement purposes ($p < .001$), but no significant differences were found between the two non-revenue-related purposes ($p = .90$). This implies

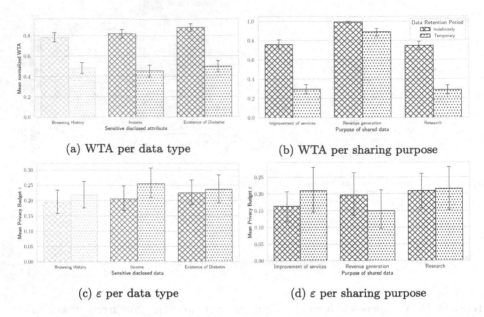

(a) WTA per data type   (b) WTA per sharing purpose

(c) ε per data type   (d) ε per sharing purpose

Fig. 4. Effect of scenario properties on mean normalized Willingness-to-Accept (WTA) and mean ε values

that individuals may be more concerned about scenarios involving sensitive data, which may be used by the data collector for unknown periods of time and ultimately for commercial purposes. In turn, the raised concerns may be translated to higher compensation demands, which are expressed by higher WTA values.

The same analysis was performed with respect to the mean ε value that corresponds to the desired differential privacy level of individuals (Fig. 4c). As previously noted, due to the inverse relationship between ε and the differential privacy level, we expected to see lower ε values for more privacy-demanding data types. The mean ε value in selected scenario choices was not found to be lower for scenarios involving medical data (e.g., existence of diabetes) than for scenarios analyzing financial data ($\chi^2(2) = 1.019, p = .6$). This can be explained by the low relative importance that respondents assigned to the sensitive disclosed data attribute (Fig. 3).

Moreover, the ε values were higher for scenarios where data is retained temporarily than indefinitely, implying that participants considered such retention periods less risky, in comparison with indefinite retention, which was associated with more demanding privacy guarantees (translated to lower ε values). In addition, differences in mean ε values were found between scenarios where data is shared for the purpose of revenue generation and research ($p = .04$), with higher ε values for the latter (Fig. 4d).

4.2   Distribution of WTA Payments Under Differential Privacy

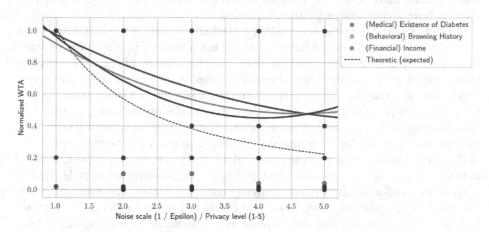

Fig. 5. Normalized mean Willingness-to-Accept (WTA) payment value as a function of differential privacy level (determined by the value of ε).

In Fig. 5, for each type of sensitive disclosed data, we plotted the relationship between the normalized mean WTA values and the selected privacy budget, translated to the amount of added noise. A polynomial regression line was fitted for each type of sensitive disclosed data, based on the combinations of analyzed attributes from the conjoint analysis. Comparing the shown fitted curves with the theoretical relationship of Nget et al. [25] in Sect. 3.2, we can see a similarity. To confirm our hypothesis about this similarity, we conducted a Mann-Whitney non-parametric statistical test with a significance level of $\alpha = .05$, according to a null hypothesis that both the theoretical and the surveyed WTA values correspond to the same distribution. We found that the distributions were similar for the scenario of sharing browsing data ($U = 4204.0, p = .052$) and medical sensitive data ($U = 5001.0, p = .051$), confirming our null hypothesis, but not for financial income data ($U = 8867.0, p < .001$). Furthermore, overall, the mean WTA values for the medical scenario were higher than those for other data types across all differential privacy noise scales.

5   Discussion

In terms of differential privacy valuation, we saw that individuals presented a pragmatic view of the trade setting, focusing on their personal *profit* and the *way* their data is processed. Moreover, this pragmatic attitude was also reflected in the selection of the differential privacy levels, considering temporary retention periods less risky than indefinite retention. This was associated with less demanding privacy guarantees, translated to the setting of higher ε values.

Furthermore, differences in mean ε values across scenarios with different sharing purposes can imply that participants considered research-purposed analysis as safer than an analysis for the purpose of revenue generation, and thus assigned lower privacy expectations for such scenarios.

In fact, we can use the above results for the benefit of both the individuals and the data collector, who often have contradicting interests, i.e., individuals wish to maximize their payment, while the data collector aims at minimizing compensation expenses. It implies that when data collectors have a limited monetary budget for the collection of data, they can offer individuals a lower payment, by injecting more noise to the outputs of the differentially private computation. On the other hand, if individuals wish to increase profit, they may want to compromise on their privacy, by allowing data processors to use a less perturbed version of their information (closer to their original data). Hence, we can expect individuals to demand higher compensation for either more sensitive data, or less noisy outputs of a differentially private analysis (and vice versa). However, although this observation partially supports the theoretical pricing model of Nget et al. [25], it varies across different data types and can be accurate for only some data types, such as medical data.

A large-scale conjoint analysis with higher coverage of data types and scenarios is required to make conclusive conclusions for broader audiences of data processors. In addition, closer examination of correlations between demographics, such as age of data owners, and privacy valuation with respect to sensitive data types is also of interest, and is left as future work. Nevertheless, our findings can be taken into account by data processors when designing and applying differential privacy mechanisms on individual-related data, and in particular, when selecting a privacy budget for a data analysis.

6 Conclusions

Through a choice-based conjoint analysis ($N = 139$) of a data trade scenario under differential privacy, we investigated the trade-offs between differential privacy valuation, scenario properties and the preferred differential privacy level, which can later be used by a data processor to set a privacy budget ε. We concluded that the differential privacy valuation, measured by individual Willingness-to-Accept (WTA), is similar to the theoretical payment schemes for differential privacy in a data trade environment. Furthermore, we found that respondents preferred scenarios with a lower privacy budget ε (requiring a higher degree of privacy) for data that is retained indefinitely for the purpose of profit generation, than temporarily for a non-commercial purpose. From the data collectors' perspective, our conclusions can be employed to better tune the differential privacy budget for an individual-related data analysis, in a way that will optimize the expenses of data collectors, on one hand, and protect the privacy of individuals, on the other hand.

Acknowledgments. This work was partially supported by a grant from the Tel Aviv University Center for AI and Data Science (TAD).

References

1. Acquisti, A.: The economics of personal data and the economics of privacy (2010)
2. Acquisti, A., John, L.K., Loewenstein, G.: What is privacy worth? J. Leg. Stud. **42**(2), 249–274 (2013). https://doi.org/10.1086/671754
3. Adam, N.R., Worthmann, J.C.: Security-control methods for statistical databases: a comparative study. ACM Comput. Surv. (CSUR) **21**(4), 515–556 (1989). https://doi.org/10.1145/76894.76895
4. Agrawal, N., Binns, R., Van Kleek, M., Laine, K., Shadbolt, N.: Exploring design and governance challenges in the development of privacy-preserving computation. In: Proceedings of the 2021 CHI Conference on Human Factors in Computing Systems, pp. 1–13 (2021). https://doi.org/10.1145/3411764.3445677
5. Barth, S., De Jong, M.D.: The privacy paradox-investigating discrepancies between expressed privacy concerns and actual online behavior-a systematic literature review. Telematics Inform. **34**(7), 1038–1058 (2017). https://doi.org/10.1016/j.tele.2017.04.013
6. Birnhack, M., Toch, E., Hadar, I.: Privacy mindset, technological mindset. Jurimetrics **55**, 55 (2014). https://doi.org/10.2139/ssrn.2471415
7. Bureau, U.C.: The modernization of statistical disclosure limitation at the U.S. census bureau (2021). https://www2.census.gov/cac/sac/meetings/2017-09/statistical-disclosure-limitation.pdf
8. Cattin, P., Wittink, D.R.: Commercial use of conjoint analysis: a survey. J. Mark. **46**(3), 44–53 (1982). https://doi.org/10.1177/002224298204600308
9. Coopamootoo, K.P., Groß, T.: Why privacy is all but forgotten. Proc. Priv. Enhancing Technol. **2017**(4), 97–118 (2017). https://doi.org/10.1515/popets-2017-0040
10. Culnan, M.J., Armstrong, P.K.: Information privacy concerns, procedural fairness, and impersonal trust: an empirical investigation. Organ. Sci. **10**(1), 104–115 (1999). https://doi.org/10.1287/orsc.10.1.104
11. Cummings, R., Kaptchuk, G., Redmiles, E.M.: I need a better description: an investigation into user expectations for differential privacy. In: Proceedings of the 2021 ACM SIGSAC Conference on Computer and Communications Security, pp. 3037–3052 (2021). https://doi.org/10.1145/3460120.3485252
12. Dankar, F.K., El Emam, K.: Practicing differential privacy in health care: a review. Trans. Data Priv. **6**(1), 35–67 (2013)
13. Dwork, Cynthia: Differential privacy. In: Bugliesi, Michele, Preneel, Bart, Sassone, Vladimiro, Wegener, Ingo (eds.) ICALP 2006. LNCS, vol. 4052, pp. 1–12. Springer, Heidelberg (2006). https://doi.org/10.1007/11787006_1
14. Dwork, C., Kohli, N., Mulligan, D.: Differential privacy in practice: expose your epsilons! J. Priv. Confident. **9**(2), 689 (2019). https://doi.org/10.29012/jpc.689
15. Dwork, C., Roth, A., et al.: The algorithmic foundations of differential privacy. Found. Trends Theor. Comput. Sci. **9**(3–4), 211–407 (2014). https://doi.org/10.1561/9781601988195
16. Garfinkel, S.L., Abowd, J.M., Powazek, S.: Issues encountered deploying differential privacy. In: Proceedings of the 2018 Workshop on Privacy in the Electronic Society, pp. 133–137 (2018). https://doi.org/10.1145/3267323.3268949
17. Jorgensen, Z., Yu, T., Cormode, G.: Conservative or liberal? personalized differential privacy. In: 2015 IEEE 31St International Conference on Data Engineering, pp. 1023–1034. IEEE (2015). https://doi.org/10.1109/ICDE.2015.7113353

18. Jung, K., Park, S.: Privacy bargaining with fairness: privacy-price negotiation system for applying differential privacy in data market environments. In: 2019 IEEE International Conference on Big Data (Big Data), pp. 1389–1394. IEEE (2019). https://doi.org/10.1109/BigData47090.2019.9006101
19. Kohli, N., Laskowski, P.: Epsilon voting: Mechanism design for parameter selection in differential privacy. In: 2018 IEEE Symposium on Privacy-Aware Computing (PAC), pp. 19–30. IEEE (2018). https://doi.org/10.1109/PAC.2018.00009
20. Koops, B.: Directive 95/46/EC general data protection regulation. Tech. rep., European parliament and council (2016). https://ec.europa.eu/info/law/law-topic/data-protection_en
21. Kumaraguru, P., Cranor, L.F.: Privacy indexes: a survey of Westin's studies. Carnegie Mellon University, School of Computer Science, Institute for Software Research International (2005)
22. Li, C., Li, D.Y., Miklau, G., Suciu, D.: A theory of pricing private data. ACM Trans. Database Syst. (TODS) 39(4), 1–28 (2014). https://doi.org/10.1145/2691190.2691191
23. Machanavajjhala, A., Kifer, D., Gehrke, J., Venkitasubramaniam, M.: l-diversity: Privacy beyond k-anonymity. ACM Trans. Knowl. Discov. Data (TKDD) 1(1), 3 (2007). https://doi.org/10.1145/1217299.1217302
24. McSherry, F., Talwar, K.: Mechanism design via differential privacy. In: 48th Annual IEEE Symposium on Foundations of Computer Science (FOCS2007), pp. 94–103. IEEE (2007). https://doi.org/10.1109/FOCS.2007.66
25. Nget, R., Cao, Y., Yoshikawa, M.: How to balance privacy and money through pricing mechanism in personal data market. arXiv preprint arXiv:1705.02982. https://arxiv.org/abs/1705.02982
26. Poikela, M., Toch, E.: Understanding the valuation of location privacy: a crowdsourcing-based approach. In: Proceedings of the 50th Hawaii International Conference on System Sciences (2017). https://doi.org/10.24251/hicss.2017.241
27. Riederer, C., Erramilli, V., Chaintreau, A., Krishnamurthy, B., Rodriguez, P.: For sale: your data: by: you. In: Proceedings of the 10th ACM Workshop on Hot Topics in Networks, pp. 1–6 (2011). https://doi.org/10.1145/2070562.2070575
28. Staiano, J., Oliver, N., Lepri, B., de Oliveira, R., Caraviello, M., Sebe, N.: Money walks: a human-centric study on the economics of personal mobile data. In: Proceedings of the 2014 ACM International Joint Conference on Pervasive and Ubiquitous Computing, pp. 583–594 (2014). https://doi.org/10.1145/2632048.2632074
29. Tang, J., Korolova, A., Bai, X., Wang, X., Wang, X.: Privacy loss in apple's implementation of differential privacy on MacOS 10.12. arXiv preprint arXiv:1709.02753 (2017). https://arxiv.org/abs/1709.02753
30. Valdez, A.C., Ziefle, M.: The users' perspective on the privacy-utility trade-offs in health recommender systems. Int. J. Hum Comput. Stud. 121, 108–121 (2019). https://doi.org/10.1016/j.ijhcs.2018.04.003
31. Xiong, A., Wang, T., Li, N., Jha, S.: Towards effective differential privacy communication for users' data sharing decision and comprehension. In: 2020 IEEE Symposium on Security and Privacy (SP), pp. 392–410. IEEE (2020). https://doi.org/10.1109/SP40000.2020.00088

Promises and Problems in the Adoption of Self-Sovereign Identity Management from a Consumer Perspective

Marco Hünseler[1] and Eva Pöll[2(✉)]

[1] Bonn-Rhein-Sieg University of Applied Sciences, Sankt Augustin, Germany
marco.huenseler@h-brs.de
[2] University of Münster, Münster, Germany
eva.poell@uni-muenster.de

Abstract. Online identification is a common problem but so far resolved unsatisfactorily, as consumers cannot fully control how much data they share and with whom. Self-Sovereign Identity (SSI) technology promises to help by making use of decentralized data repositories as well as advanced cryptographic algorithms and protocols. This paper examines the effects of SSIs on responsible, confident, and vulnerable consumers in order to develop the missing understanding of consumer needs in SSI adoption and define preconditions and necessary considerations for the development of SSI-based platforms and applications.

Keywords: blockchain · self-sovereign identity · SSI · criticism · consumers · triad model · vulnerable consumer · confident consumer · responsible consumer

1 Introduction

Digitalisation found its way into all parts of everyday life [27], from studying and applying to a new job to entertainment and using online platforms to keep in touch with friends. A common entry requirement is to register and authenticate one's identity during which personal information is requested. All means of commonly used digital identification today have in common that consumers cannot fully control how much data they disclose and to whom. A current technology promises a solution: the concept of Self-Sovereign Identity (SSI) aims to give back full control to the consumer, while allowing a broad applicability [2]. But albeit these promises, consumers still barely adopted it [16]. The research done in the section of SSIs so far does not focus on the consumer as a central part, but rather highlights technical aspects [3,16,27]. We find that a consumer-focused perspective is underrepresented in the research of SSI so far. This paper looks into the promises of SSI and how consumers can access them. Precisely, we seek to answer the following questions:

1. Can SSI solve the problem of easy and user-centric identification online?
2. Is this solution available and advantageous for all consumers, or does it differ, depending on the consumer type?

© IFIP International Federation for Information Processing 2023
Published by Springer Nature Switzerland AG 2023
F. Bieker et al. (Eds.): Privacy and Identity 2022, IFIP AICT 671, pp. 85–100, 2023.
https://doi.org/10.1007/978-3-031-31971-6_8

To supply an answer we will first set the context, stating the problem of digital identity management systems and pointing out shortcomings in current solutions. Also we present Micklitz's triad model of the responsible, the confident, and the vulnerable consumer, to fathom the characteristics of consumers in the following. Thirdly, the technical basics of SSI are introduced and then the promises it holds are presented. The fourth section moves on to the problems that consumers face. Finally, we sum up our findings, that most consumers can benefit from the use of SSIs, given that a widely-adopted ecosystem of related software, hardware and services exists.

2 How to Manage One's Digital Identity?

Even though the identification and authentication of consumers are fundamental for digital participation, it is still considered as "one of the major present challenges in the World Wide Web" [3]. A digital identity is the partial representation of a real-world entity. Usually the entity is a person, but digital identities can also represent legal persons, i. e. a company or institution, or physical objects [27]. A digital identity holds a number of attributes, i. e. information about the entity that can be used to identify it (e. g. name, date of birth) [17]. Attributes can also be used to claim something about the entity, such as associated bank credentials or which groups it associates with [2].

2.1 The Current State of Digital Identities

One of the most common models for establishing an online identity today is the *isolated model*. In the isolated model, consumers register accounts and identify themselves and share their data separately with each service provider [14]. From a consumer perspective, this model shows some flaws: Every service provider is in full control over the data shared with them and it is complicated to keep an overview over all service providers one has ever shared any information with. The lack of overview makes it difficult to exercise rights related to data privacy such as updating personal data or revoking consent to use it [27]. In order to help with the management burden, consumers often reuse passwords for several accounts [27]. These can subsequently be stolen if any one of the service providers fails employ proper security measures, oftentimes leading to a compromised online identity [17]. Solutions like password managing software need digital literacy, as in being aware of the risk and the knowledge how to mitigate it.

One solution to ease the burden and centralise an identity scattered across several accounts are *Single Sign-On (SSO)* providers. They offer to create a central digital identity on their platform and communicate this identity towards other platforms. Still, the data governance remains with the providers, which have an economic rather than protective interest in the data [12]. Thus the consumer gives up control over their digital identity, granting access and insight, practically transferring the authority to these providers [27]. Furthermore, it

allows the authentication providers to gather even more data (e. g. by tracking user behaviour) [17] which they might use without the consumer's actual
consent [12].

Another alternative are state-issued digital identities (*National ID Cards*):
These are useful in cases where an unambiguous mapping between a specific natural or legal person and their online identity is needed (e. g. regulated industries
such as banking) [24]. In order to provide their citizens with a strong way to
prove their identity online multiple states around the world provide their citizens with ID cards that are electronically readable, digitally verifiable [19] and,
for example in the European Union (EU), operable across the union [5]. However, the EU Commission finds that adoption of this service remains low and
subsequently tries to establish a successor to the current scheme, based on SSI
principles [6].

2.2 Consumer Models

At the core of EU regulations is the model of an ideal consumer who is genuinely willing and able to search, understand and use necessary information on
a topic sufficiently well [1]. This model is widely criticised to bypass reality, in
posing idealistic rather than realistic expectations of competences and capacities
on consumers. It also overestimates that relevant information is available and
accessible for all consumers [28]. An alternative to this idealistic model is brought
forward by Micklitz who proposes a dynamic consumer model, made up of three
overlapping consumer types (the *triad model*), consisting of *responsible, confident*
and *vulnerable consumers* [18]. Each type represents a set of behavioural patterns
that characterise strengths and weaknesses and allows an internal differentiation,
aiming for tailored support for each type, protecting the weaker, without patro-
nising the stronger consumers [18,28]. The *responsible consumer* is close to the
ideal consumer also applied in EU law, but acknowledging that consumers only
have limited cognitive capacities. Thus, they are best supported with accessible,
thorough, and ideally also processed, additional information. They can and want
to take full responsibility in their decision process [1]. The *confident consumer*
is de facto the most common role [15]. These consumers aim for fast and easy
consumption decisions and therefore rely on the judgement of others. In lifting
some responsibility from them, e. g. by offering certified products and services,
these consumers are supported in their decision-making. To offer them further
information is only partially helpful, as they do not wish to spend much time
on getting informed before making a decision [18]. *Vulnerable consumers* are
barely capable to fathom the complexity of the respective consumption context
and are hardly able to decide intentionally in their best interests. This might
be due to cognitive limits (age, disability, ...), or a language barrier. They need
profound protection, for example by laws and institutions, regulating markets
and business practices [18].

As the triad model is still novel, the boundaries between consumer types
remain vague and are in need of further research [1]. To illustrate the differentiation, habits of agreeing to general standard terms and conditions (GTC)

of software products can be used: Responsible consumers are genuinely interested in the topic at hand and will consequentially invest time and effort to gather background information and make a well-informed decision. Thus, they would read the GTC thoroughly and – if they disagree with the terms – try to find a different solution. Confident consumers, however, will agree to the terms, without reading or even skimming through the text. They trust jurisdictional standards to protect their interests. Vulnerable consumers might agree to the GTC, without having the ability to understand what they agreed to and what the terms and conditions imply.

2.3   Introduction to SSI

While established identification systems offer a central place to store data, but without sufficient control over the data for the consumer, Self-Sovereign Identity (SSI) promises to establish consumers as "the rulers of their own identity" [2]. The term SSI surfaced in 2011 [20] and gained momentum with Allen's manifesto on ten fundamental principles for SSI in 2016.

The basic building blocks for SSI systems are Decentralised Identifiers (DIDs), Verifiable Credentials (VCs), and Verifiable Presentations (VPs) [3]. DIDs are an address (similar to an URL) that can be resolved to a DID document which can in turn contain information such as cryptographic keys or information about a subject [26]. Using DIDs, it is possible to issue and receive VCs [25]. VCs consist of information about a particular identity such as the address, or banking information, but can also represent certificates (like university degrees) or state-issued identities [31]. Consumers can use these credentials attached to their identifiers to create VPs – a set of consumer-chosen claims originating from the VCs issued to them – in order to prove aspects of their choice regarding their identity to third parties [25]. VCs are used to selectively reveal personal information to a service provider [3], e. g. to register on a streaming platform or to apply for a job. In this process the data remains under control of the consumer, as the data is stored with them. They can use their issued credentials without the permission or any further participation of either the service provider or issuer [12,31].

Additionally to these basic building blocks, more components are necessary to operate a service which can be used by consumers: On the technical side, protocols, algorithms and data formats for exchanging or revoking credentials, network communication, cryptographic key management or the management of credential-related data (such as DIDs, VCs or revocation information) inside a central data registry (e. g. blockchain) are needed. Organizational arrangements concern the operation of the managing organization itself, public relations, the software provided, the central data registry and related policies such as entities allowed to read, write and verify the registry, associated costs, and terms for using the provided services [7].

To guide the ongoing development of SSI Allen proposed ten conceptual principles for identity management systems in his manifesto, demanding transparency, fairness, and protection for consumers [2]: (i) *Existence:* an individual exists beyond their online identity, they cannot solely exist digitally; (ii) *Control:*

the individual has control of the central aspects of their identity and is supported in this by trustworthy and secure algorithms; (iii) *Access:* the individual must have access to all information that is known about them; (iv) *Transparency:* the system and its algorithms must be transparent in how they work and how they are managed; (v) *Persistence:* the individual is able to use their digital identity as long as they choose to; (vi) *Portability:* the online identity should be portable across systems and jurisdictions; (vii) *Interoperability:* the digital identity is interoperable, i. e. individuals can use their identity where they want to (i. e. as widely as possible); (viii) *Consent:* no parts of an individual's identity are used without their consent; (ix) *Minimalization:* an individual should be able to minimise disclosed data, i. e. they only have to share as much personal information as strictly necessary; and (x) *Protection:* the individual's rights and freedom are protected, including cases where the needs of consumers and identity networks may conflict [2].

2.4   Criteria to Evaluate SSI from a Consumer Perspective

To assess which consumer types could benefit from SSIs to which extent, we examine various aspects related to the technology. In this we conceptually combine the consumer model by Micklitz with the insights of current SSI literature. The results are summarised in Table 1. First, we consider if for the ten principles put up by Allen [2] the potentials of SSI can outweigh the risks and difficulties for each consumer type (Sect. 3.1, Sect. 4.1). In the second part (Sect. 3.2, Sect. 4.2), we examine typical aspects related to implementation decisions, such as usability and market factors. The third part presents two illustrative use cases that are commonly referred to as examples where SSI can benefit consumers (Sect. 3.3, Sect. 4.3).

3   Promises: The Concept of Self-Sovereign Identity as a Solution

SSI claims to be the "vision for how we can enhance the ability of digital identity to enable trust while preserving individual privacy" [2]. In the following these promises are analysed and differentiated for the three consumer types. In a second step (Sect. 4) they will be contrasted to the cases in which consumers cannot access the promise.

3.1   Promises in Allen's Manifesto

Existence. Allen highlights in his manifesto the relevance of the individual holding the identity. However, even with multiple overlapping digital identities, the individual exists beyond these descriptions and must be respected as an autonomous entity [2]. An ecosystem that respects the whole existence and sovereignty of a person is advantageous to all consumer types (Table 1: Existence).

Table 1. Potential of correctly implemented SSI properties for consumers, weighted against possible risks

	Vulnerable	Confident	Responsible
Existence	▲	▲	▲
Control	○	▲	▲
Access	▲	▲	▲
Transparency	○	▲	▲
Persistence	ϟ	○	○
Portability	○	○	○
Interoperability	○	○	○
Consent	ϟ	○	▲
Minimalization	ϟ	○	▲
Protection	○	○	▲
Key Management	ϟ	ϟ	▲
Trust Management	ϟ	ϟ	▲
Wallet/Agent Availability	ϟ	○	▲
Costs	ϟ	ϟ	○
Healthcare	○	○	▲
Professional Certification	○	○	▲

Legend: ▲: high potential to access benefits; ○: benefits are accessible, given certain preconditions, mitigating risks or difficulties; ϟ: risks outweigh the benefits or the ability to use this aspect is not given

Control, Consent. Using SSI, consumers can gain exclusive control over their digital identities and exercise sole authority over whom they share related data with. For confident and responsible consumers, this is a significant advantage over established isolated identity systems or SSO providers (Table 1: Control). Setting the consumer at the centre of control over their data also satisfies the need for informational self-determination, which is also proclaimed by the EU[1] and which could be realized by SSI if it is consistently implemented [30]. Consumers also benefit from being able to grant or revoke consent to use their identity at all times. In centralised systems this would only be possible when assuming identity providers are fully trustworthy. In order to give consent, consumers need to understand what exactly they consent to, including what consequences this decision entails. Especially responsible consumers are assumed to be able to give informed consent decisions and thus able to profit from extensive control over their data sharing practices (Table 1: Consent).

Access. The access property promises users to always be able to retrieve all data that is related to their identity while at the same time this data is only accessible for others with their permission [2]. This is an universal advantage for every consumer type in comparison to traditional systems, where identity

---

[1] The Court of the EU deduces the right to information self-determination from article 8.1 of the Charter of Fundamental Rights of the EU: "Everyone has the right to the protection of personal data concerning him or her" [10].

providers are able to store and share data at their own discretion and possibly without asking for consent of the consumer.

Transparency. The transparency property states that operational matters (i. e. governance, algorithms, software) should be freely accessible and publicly visible by everyone [2]. Responsible consumers are likely to profit the most from this property because they are the most likely to actually check that the system works in their own interest while confident consumers can choose to rely on assessments by institutions they trust or the public hand as with open-source software in general.

Persistence, Portability, Interoperability. Providing a digital identity that is self-managed with the possibility of using it across different user agents and across services (portability), widely accepted (interoperability) and guaranteed to be usable for an extended period of time (persistence) is a promise no other identity system architecture has delivered on to date [2,6]. In principle (given an established infrastructure), all types of consumers could benefit from a central place to manage *all* of their registrations, certificates, permissions and further data about them. It enables them to see with whom they share their data and offers a central place to manage granted permissions. It also offers them a uniform experience, i. e. they only need to learn how to manage their identity using the provided tools once. Especially responsible consumers could freely choose which software they trust and move between alternatives, if they find one that better fits their needs. Consumers could rely on being able to use their established identities how they see fit and even dispose of it, provided they are still able to control it (i. e. hold the relevant cryptographic keys).

Minimalization, Protection. The selective disclosure of a subset of attributes related to the consumer's identities brings high potential to increase privacy, especially for responsible consumers who are expected to understand the implications of sharing their data. Correctly implemented and used, it is a property that could lead to significant reduction of data sharing and thus possibility for misuse, for example by only providing a proof of possession of information, instead of sharing the information itself (through zero-knowledge-proof algorithms) [12] (Table 1: Minimalization). Similarly, the protection requirement, stating that the employed algorithms should be censorship-resistant and decentralized, protects the rights of the individual and can benefit all consumers in upholding their sovereignty and integrity.

3.2 Promises of Related Technology and Concepts

Key and Trust Management. Both key and trust management enable users to take full control over the use of their digital identity and an autonomous assessment of relationships to other people, organizations and things inside the SSI ecosystem. Cryptographic keys are used to prove aspects about the consumer's identity and restrict access to use this identity to the key holders. Using advanced key management techniques [21], consumers can take appropriate measures to counter the risk of losing their keys or make stolen keys unusable.

The measures include distributing parts of the key material to commercial providers, people they trust, or creating analogue backups on paper. However, they must set up these measures preventively, which primarily responsible consumers can be expected to do (Table 1: Key Management).

Additionally, consumers need to know to whom exactly they reveal their data. They consequently need a way to correlate cryptographic keys (of relying parties such as online services) to real-world identities. Centralized solutions solve this by regulating who is able to guarantee a specific identity, which potentially limits the freedom of consumers [16]. Using SSIs however, consumers are able to manage trust relationships by themselves, i. e. they choose which issuers they trust to make claims about themselves and others. This includes checking that corresponding cryptographic key material is legitimately owned by these issuers. Using these techniques, especially responsible consumers could implement a fully sovereign Web-of-Trust that does not rely on institutional credential issuers [4] (Table 1: Trust Management). Furthermore, this could lead to the development of new use cases that are difficult to implement using established technology (e. g. to transitively grant friends' trusted friends access to one's flat).

Wallet and Agent Availability. A diverse ecosystem of wallets and agents, i. e. applications consumers use to participate in the SSI ecosystem, can lead to healthy competition and the availability of functionally rich software that is easy to use and able to help consumers fulfilling their needs. Assuming wide adoption, there is a high probability that a suitable solution for every type of consumer exists. Confident consumers could benefit from software products that align with their interests and support them in making safe decisions (i. e. have sensible defaults that protect them, are easy to use and provide them with support options in case problems arise).

3.3   Promises for the Real World

Healthcare. Today's healthcare systems often rely on different types of proof and certificates consumers need to handle in order to access medical services. For example, they need a proof of insurance in order to be treated and then obtain prescriptions, medical reports or other certificates regarding their health. The methods in use are often not interoperable (e. g. prescriptions in digital form obtained in one EU country can usually not be redeemed in another [9]) and often not internationally accepted (e. g. Switzerland does not accept prescriptions from EU countries at all [9]). SSI offers the potential to provide interoperable solutions that are privacy-friendly and offer consumers control over the processing and sharing of their health-related data [23,33]. All consumer types would generally benefit from such a solution.

Professional Certification. A common use case is the need to present educational credentials to interested parties, for example when applying for a job, changing the school or university. Oftentimes, only specific information like whether a degree was awarded or claims about the distribution of certain grades are required. SSI is able to simplify the proof of having obtained a certain degree and thus processes needing this information [11, 24]. Because credential issuance can be frictionless and offered by various institutions, even online or short term courses could issue them. All consumer types could highly benefit from this possibility to quickly demonstrate all facets of their specific skillset and help them to compete on the job market [11].

4   Problems: Limits of Usability of the Concept of Self-Sovereign Identity

SSI seems to answer the call for user-centric identity management with sparkling promises. However, in light of practice, not all promises can be kept, especially for vulnerable and confident consumers. This section examines where risks occur among the promises made and what additional difficulties SSI brings about.

4.1   Broken Promises in Allen's Manifesto

Persistence, Portability, Interoperability. To be able to use the same digital identity across several platforms is said to be a main reason for the adoption of SSI [22]. So far, this remains a promise. No standard has evolved yet, which would lay the foundation for this [27]. On the contrary, currently there are more than 130 methods to implement DIDs [29]. While projects like Sovrin [24] or European Self-Sovereign Identity Framework (ESSIF) [8] aim to provide a technical and organizational foundation for a widely-used SSI ecosystem, their solutions are not readily usable for consumers, yet. While Sovrin is generally usable, standards, e. g. for advanced key management techniques, that facilitate complex aspects of using SSI are not implemented by now [21]. ESSIF and the related European Identity Wallet [6] are not yet available either. This makes it risky for consumers as well as for the industry to settle on one implementation, as it might not be supported long-term or will not be adopted broadly [27]. But specifically wide adoption, and thus also broad applicability, are among the main factors for consumers to use a technology [16, 22]. Thus, the settled implementation that is assumed by Allen [2] and that would benefit all three consumer types, is not yet available. Consumer must invest effort to maintain an overview of all options on the market and understand their advantages and in case switch to a new application. Confident consumers, however, seek quick and easy decisions and would rather stick with a solution they chose once than adopting a new one [15]. The need for a settled ecosystem is even more evident for vulnerable consumers who do not have the capacities to make an informed decision on an implementation in the first place. Therefore, currently the ability to use the same identity across different platforms and in several environments is obstructed, restraining portability and interoperability to be only conditionally advantageous for all consumers (Table 1: Portability, Interoperability). Due to the missing standard and the ongoing development also the promise of persistence is only conditionally applicable for consumers until a standard is settled. For vulnerable consumers persistence might also bear the further risk of credentials persisting past their intended use. Both, knowing about the criminal use of a credential and the process of revoking it are assumed to be complex [16] and thus above the abilities of vulnerable (and confident) consumers (Table 1: Persistence).

Control, Consent. By definition SSI allows the user to have central control over their identity [2]. However, this might be difficult to utilise for vulnerable consumers, who have a very low digital literacy, obstructing their ability to actually understand and intentionally use SSI applications (Table 1: Control). Technical research highlights the advantage of enhanced privacy and security through SSI (i. e. consent in [2]) as well as minimization of the data that needs to be shared [12]. But despite these findings consumer oriented studies show "that privacy concerns are of little importance" for consumers [22]. They would value convenience higher than privacy [16,30] and experience sharing personal data as "a part of modern life" [22]. This corresponds to the result of Kenning and Wobker stating that confident consumers are the most common type [15], and also corresponds to our understanding that confident consumers aim for convenient rather than more secure solutions. SSI cannot solve the problem that the consumer remains responsible for sharing their data [27]. Especially vulnerable and confident consumers are often not literate or willing enough to consent to what parts of their identity is used and how. These types need to be supported by presenting data sharing requests in a way that nudges consumers to question their action and reflect over whether it is in line with their own interests. Responsible consumers should be trusted to have sufficient digital literacy to manage their data responsibly. Vulnerable consumers, however, are under higher risks in the aspect of consent and need more support: Here it would be advisable to set up certified intermediaries or mechanisms that restrict which data is reasonable to share in the consumer's interest [18,22] (Table 1: Control, Consent). Note that restricting consumers in such a way contradicts control and consent requirements put up by SSI.

Minimalization. The protection of personal data is made even more difficult by the industry's greed for data, which SSI might even aggravate: Although SSI enables the minimization of disclosed private data [2], this does not yet mean that the industry will also submit to this option. Still, they can ask for whatever data they please as a condition of entry – very much like what is common practice now [13]. The interests might rise further as it can be assumed that information extracted from externally verified credentials could be more valuable than, potentially false, data entered directly by consumers. Also aligning to current practice, platforms might continue to ask for additional information as a proof of authorisation (e. g. asking for credit card credentials to prove one's age) [27]. Confident and vulnerable consumers will be open to disclose this data, when they should actually be reluctant to do so. Furthermore, SSI might open new contexts of data collection where current solutions for digital identification are too elaborate, e. g. when entering a building [27]. Once the information is disclosed, it is stored with the service providers and under their control, making it hard for consumers to enforce the rights on their personal data [3]. Thus, consumers carry a high responsibility with regard to their data. While responsible consumers can be expected to handle the risk, vulnerable and confident consumers are incapable to do so and should be supported by juridical frameworks and employing nudges.

Protection. While responsible consumers can be expected to inform themselves sufficiently to claim their own position in the trade-off between transparency and anonymity as well as choosing applications with secure data storage, vulnerable and confident consumers are missing the literacy or interest to do so. They can only benefit from the property of protection under the condition that standards and regulations in which they trust are in place to protect them.

4.2 Broken Promises of Related Technology and Concepts

Wallet and Agent Availability. SSI demands additional effort to learn to use the new mechanisms that it introduces and that consumers are barely used to, e. g. agents, wallets and cryptographic keys. This poses a hurdle on less literate consumers [16,27]. While it is desirable to have different options for SSI-related software, especially wallets, it also makes it harder to choose a safe solution. To support confident consumers public clues should be offered (e. g. certifications) to protect them from malware or products that do not sufficiently secure the sensible information that is stored with them. Vulnerable consumers should not be left alone with the choice of software and key management, but be supported by intermediaries, software regulations or strong public clues. Still, security risks in using wallets remain for vulnerable as well as confident consumers.

Key Management. Connected to the risks in using wallets are the risks of managing cryptographic keys. The complex mechanisms of cryptography with private and public keys are hard to understand [27], thus it might be hard for confident, but especially for vulnerable consumers to keep the private key secret and yet memorised [3,20]. A lost private key is impossible to restore (very much in contrast to resetting a forgotten password), blocking the consumer permanently from accessing their data. Furthermore, if a private key is disclosed to a criminal, the consumers privacy is diminished and their identity might be stolen. Vulnerable and confident consumers are barely expected to be able to manage their keys on their own without putting their assets at high risk. A mitigation of the additional responsibility is to introduce an intermediary who manages the keys in place of the consumer. This hybrid approach would still enable responsible consumers to manage their keys themselves, while supporting confident and vulnerable consumers at the same time [32].

Trust Management. To be able to share their data responsibly, consumers need to know, whom they disclose information to, i. e. if the entity actually is, who it claims to be and if it is authorised to grant the claimed credentials. Following a self-sovereign approach, consumers should be able to choose who to trust by themselves. However, the problem to transfer trust relationships to the digital world by cryptographic means remains [3]. One mitigation might be the use of a Web-of-Trust (see above), which offers a decentralized approach on trust

that fits well to SSI [4]. Alternatively, classical hierarchical models like a Public
Key Infrastructure, involving institutions that are considered trustworthy, can
be used to delegate the decisions who to trust. Although these entities might
help to anchor trust in a network, they are also valuable targets for attackers.
Depending on the implemented process on how consumers decide whom to trust,
central trust anchors are prone to be forged [13]. While responsible and confident
consumers should be able to identify fake identities when they are supported
by public clues (similar to the verified badge on social networks), vulnerable
consumer will be at risk to fall for scams with forged identities Table 1: Trust
Management.

Costs. The operation of a SSI platform requires financial investments, providing
the infrastructure and gaining a profit margin [27]. Thus it is to be expected
that consumers have to pay fees at least for certain operations [16,27]. However,
because this is a serious hindrance to adoption, costs should be as low as possible
[22]. Consumers appear to prefer free solutions over paid options with higher
privacy or security [22]. This can be assumed to apply especially to vulnerable
and confident consumers. Responsible consumers, however, can be expected to
act according to those study participants who value privacy and were willing to
pay for more secure systems [22]. Thus, responsible consumers would still prefer
a good, free solution, but if that is not available, they would choose to pay a fee.

4.3 Broken Promises in the Real World

The healthcare sector is in high demand of digitalization, which SSI could push
forward. As described above, all three consumer types could benefit from an
SSI ecosystem in terms of healthcare. In this use case especially the aspects
of interoperability and control come into effect, which are both (conditionally)
advantageous for all consumer types. Most of all, consumers will be hindered
by having to adjust to a new procedure and system. If this learning effort is
supported by intermediaries and good software, also confident and vulnerable
consumers will be able to benefit (Table 1: Healthcare). The same argument
applies in case of professional certification. If the weaker consumer types can be
enabled to use the SSI system, they would be able to benefit from it (Table 1:
Professional Certification).

4.4 Further Issues

Aside from the promises that cannot be delivered on so far, some aspects of
usability are also impeding widespread consumer adoption of SSI. Current solutions of identity management are usually based on registering with username
and password, which is quick, well-known to all consumers and thus highly
convenient. This convenience is hard to outweigh with the advantages of SSI,
especially as it is based on complex mechanisms that are hard to understand
[27] and benefits like increased privacy and data security are of little interest
to most consumers [22]. The on-boarding is already too complicated for broad

adoption [16]. Particularly if a second device is need for logging in consumers are disturbed in their convenience and thus hesitant to adopt [27]. Also indirect network effects hamper the adoption: as soon as a significant amount of users join a SSI system, others will follow. Vice-versa, consumers will perceive the low adoption as a signal that it is not lucrative to join, yet [16].

Even if a certain SSI system is eventually generally accepted, this might cause further problems: If it is easily possible to ask for verified credentials, it might become normal to prove (verifiably) various qualities that are currently accepted without proof (e. g. language skills or soft skills in a job application). But it seems questionable if every quality can indeed be standardized to be able to prove it. This endeavour, of general standardization of one's identity, seems normatively outdated and also appears to contradict Kenning and Wobker's idea that a digital identity is never able to wholly cover a person's existence.

5 Answer: SSI is a Promising Solution for Most Consumers

In a digitalised world, there is a strong need for reliable digital identities. In reality, however, consumers' digital identities are scattered throughout many different services or are controlled by few commercial providers. SSI claims to be the "vision for how we can enhance the ability of digital identity to enable trust while preserving individual privacy" [2]. We find, however, that in practice, depending on the particular consumer, conceptual risks associated with the concepts of SSI itself remain, in addition to the risks of current implementations. Still, most consumers could benefit from a widely available SSI ecosystem.

Especially responsible consumers benefit from SSIs, because it enables them to both, taking unprecedented control over their digital identity and additional convenience in completing day-to-day tasks. Due to their higher digital literacy and interest to understand the technology, they are able to effectively use SSIs and prevent the entailed risks. As shown in Table 1, this consumer type benefits in most categories and is only hampered by the practical limitations of currently available implementations. Confident consumers, the biggest group, seek for convenience and will choose an easy, accessible solution over a more secure one. Thus, they are less likely to adopt SSI in the first place, but if they do, confident consumers are prone to struggle in the contexts of security and privacy. These struggles are similar to difficulties in current identity management solutions, and could be mitigated by a widely available and trustworthy software and hardware ecosystem that is able to support them with decisions related to consent and technical challenges. Especially when SSI is broadly adopted, they can benefit from an easier control of their digital identity. Vulnerable consumers however can barely benefit from using SSIs because they are likely struggling to use the technology and are incapable to asses and handle the implied risks. Still, with support of a reliable software and hardware ecosystem and further with intermediaries that can protect them in more sensitive aspects, they might become enabled to use SSIs.

We diagnose that currently available solutions fall short of the promises made and cannot provide them to all consumer types. By today, wallet software and agent services are not widely available and barely used. A single SSI ecosystem that is widely in use and that could deliver on the stated requirements has not been established. Even if adoption rises, issues related to providing a safe, yet useful environment to all consumers are hard to solve, especially while maintaining full control and decentralization properties demanded by proponents. However, assuming a widely-used SSI ecosystem emerges (especially enabled by a settled standard for SSI), most of the stated advantages could be realized for most consumers, making SSI a promising solution for managing and conveniently using digital identities online.

Acknowledgements. The BlockTechDiVer project is supported by funds of the German Federal Ministry for the Environment, Nature Conservation, Nuclear Safety and Consumer Protection (BMUV) based on a decision of the Parliament of the Federal Republic of Germany via the Federal Office for Agriculture and Food (BLE) under the innovation support programme.

References

1. Achilles, N.: Vom Homo Oeconomicus zum Differenzierten Verbraucher: Ana-lyse von Begriff. Entwicklung und neuen Herausforderungen des verbrauchervertragsrechtlichen Leitbildes auf EU-Ebene. Nomos (2020)
2. Allen, C.: The Path to Self-Sovereign Identity (2016). http://www.lifewithalacrity.com/2016/04/the-path-to-self-sovereign-identity.html
3. Brunner, C., Gallersdörfer, U., Knirsch, F., Engel, D., Matthes, F.: DID and VC: untangling decentralized identifiers and verifiable credentials for the web of trust. In: ICBTA 2020. Association for Computing Machinery (2020). https://doi.org/10.1145/3446983.3446992
4. Caronni, G.: Walking the web of trust. In: IEEE 9th International Workshops on Enabling Technologies (2000). https://doi.org/10.1109/ENABL.2000.883720
5. European Parliament and Council. Regulation (EU) No 910/2014 of the European Parliament and of the Council of 23 July 2014 on electronic identification and trust services for electronic transactions in the internal market and repealing Directive 1999/93/EC (2014). http://data.europa.eu/eli/reg/2014/910/oj/eng
6. European Parliament and Council. Proposal for a Reglation of the European Parliament and of the Council amending Regulation (EU) No 910/2014 as regards establishing a framework for a European Digital Identity (2021). https://eur-lex.europa.eu/legal-content/EN/TXT/?uri=CELEX:52021PC0281
7. Davie, M., Gisolfi, D., Hardman, D., Jordan, J., O'Donnell, D., Reed, D.: The trust over IP stack. IEEE Commun. Stand. Mag. **3**(4), 46–51 (2019). https://doi.org/10.1109/MCOMSTD.001.1900029
8. European Commission. High-level scope (ESSIF). https://ec.europa.eu/digital-building-blocks/wikis/pages/viewpage.action?pageId=555222265
9. European Commission. FAQS - presenting a prescription abroad. https://europa.eu/youreurope/citizens/health/prescriptionmedicine-abroad/prescriptions/faq/index_en.htm

10. European Union: Charter of fundamental rights of the European union. Off. J. Eur. Union **C83**, 53 (2010)
11. Grech, A., Sood, I., Ariño, L.: Blockchain, self-sovereign identity and digital credentials: promise versus praxis in education. Front. Blockchain **4**, 616779 (2021). https://doi.org/10.3389/fbloc.2021.616779
12. Ishmaev, G.: Sovereignty, privacy, and ethics in blockchain-based identity management systems. Ethics Inf. Technol. **23**(3), 239–252 (2020). https://doi.org/10.1007/s10676-020-09563-x
13. Ishmaev, G., Stokkink, Q.: Identity management systems: singular identities and multiple moral issues. Front. Blockchain **3**, 15 (2020). https://doi.org/10.3389/fbloc.2020.00015
14. Jøsang, A., Pope, S.: User centric identity management. In: AusCERT Asia Pacific Information Technology Security Conference (2005). https://www.mn.uio.no/ifi/english/people/aca/josang/publications/jp2005-auscert.pdf
15. Kenning, P., Wobker, I.: Ist der, "mündige Verbraucher" eine Fiktion? Zeitschrift für Wirtschafts- und Unternehmensethik **14**(2), 282–300 (2013). https://doi.org/10.5771/1439-880X-2013-2-282
16. Kubach, M., Schunck, C.H., Sellung, R., Roßnagel, H.: Self-sovereign and Decentralized identity as the future of identity management? In: Open Identity Summit 2020. Gesellschaft für Informatik e.V. (2020). https://doi.org/10.18420/ois2020_03
17. Lyons, T., Courcelas, L., Timsit, K.: Blockchain and Digital Identity. White paper, EU Blockchain Observatory and Forum (2019). https://www.eublockchainforum.eu/sites/default/files/report_identity_v0.9.4.pdf
18. Micklitz, H.-W.: The future of consumer law - plea for a movable system. Zeitschrift für Europäisches Unternehmens- und Verbraucherrecht **2**(1) (2013)
19. Pöhn, D., Grabatin, M., Hommel, W.: eID and self-sovereign identity usage: an overview. Electronics **10**(22), 2811 (2021). https://doi.org/10.3390/electronics10222811
20. Piekarska, M., Lodder, M., Larson, Z., Young, K.: When GDPR Becomes Real. White paper, Rebooting the Web of Trust (2018). https://github.com/WebOfTrustInfo/rwot5-boston/blob/master/final-documents/gdpr.pdf
21. Reed, D., Law, J., Hardman, D., Lodder, M.: DKMS (Decentralized Key Management System) Design and Architecture v4. https://github.com/hyperledger/aries-rfcs/blob/0323c5ae/concepts/0051-dkms/dkms-v4.md
22. Roßnagel, H., Zibuschka, J., Hinz, O., Muntermann, J.: Users' willingness to pay for web identity management systems. Eur. J. Inf. Syst. **23**(1), 36–50 (2014). https://doi.org/10.1057/ejis.2013.33
23. Shuaib, M., Alam, S., Alam, M.S., Nasir, M.S.: Self-sovereign identity for healthcare using blockchain. In: Materials Today: Proceedings (2021). https://doi.org/10.1016/j.matpr.2021.03.083
24. Foundation, S.: Sovrin: A Protocol and Token for Self-Sovereign Identity and Decentralized Trust. White paper (2018). https://sovrin.org/library/sovrin-protocol-and-token-white-paper/
25. Sporny, M., Longley, D., Chadwick, D.: Verifiable Credentials Data Model v1.1. W3c recommendation, World Wide Web Consortium (W3C) (2022). https://www.w3.org/TR/vc-data-model
26. Sporny, M., Longley, D., Sabadello, M., Reed, D., Steele, O., Allen, C.: Decentralized Identifiers (DIDs) v1.0. W3c recommendation, World Wide Web Consortium (W3C) (2022). https://www.w3.org/TR/did-core

27. Strüker, J., et al.: Self-Sovereign Identity - Grundlagen, Anwendungen und Potenziale portabler digitaler Identitäten. White paper, Projektgruppe Wirtschaftsinformatik des Fraunhofer-Instituts für Angewandte Informationstechnik FIT (2021). https://www.fim-rc.de/wp-content/uploads/2021/06/Fraunhofer-FIT_SSI_Whitepaper.pdf
28. Strünck, C., et al.: Ist der "mündige Verbraucher" ein Mythos? Statement at the BMELV, Scientific Advisory Board on Consumer and Nutrition Policy (2012)
29. Swick, R.: Director's decision on did 1.0 proposed recommendation formal objections. https://www.w3.org/2022/06/DIDRecommendationDecision.html
30. Uhlmann, M., Pittroff, F., Lamla, J.: Vertrauensinfrastrukturen der digitalen Gesellschaft. In Der vertrauende Verbraucher. Zwischen Regulation und Information. Verbraucherzentrale NRW (2020). https://doi.org/10.15501/978-3-86336-922-4_2
31. Urbach, N.: Selbstbestimmte Identitäten zur Stärkung der digitalen Souveränität. (Vortrag 8) (2022). https://www.verbraucherforschung.nrw/sites/default/files/2022-02/zth-8-urbach-selbstbestimmte-identitaeten-zur-staerkung-der-digitalen-souveranitaet.pdf
32. Wang, F., De Filippi, P.: Self-sovereign identity in a globalized world: credentials-based identity systems as a driver for economic inclusion. Front. Blockchain **2** (2020). https://doi.org/10.3389/fbloc.2019.00028
33. Zhang, P., Kuo, T.-T.: The feasibility and significance of employing blockchain-based identity solutions in health care. In: Patnaik, S., Wang, T.-S., Shen, T., Panigrahi, S.K. (eds.) Blockchain Technology and Innovations in Business Processes. SIST, vol. 219, pp. 189–208. Springer, Singapore (2021). https://doi.org/10.1007/978-981-33-6470-7_11

Usability Evaluation of SSI Digital Wallets

Abylay Satybaldy[✉]

Computer Science Department, NTNU, Gjøvik, Norway
abylay.satybaldy@ntnu.no

Abstract. Self-sovereign identity (SSI) is a new decentralized ecosystem for secure and private identity management. In contrast to most previous identity management systems where the service provider was at the center of the identity model, SSI is user-centric and eliminates the need for a central authority. It allows the user to own their identity and carry it around in a form of digital identity wallet, for example, on their mobile device or through a cloud service. The digital wallet supports mechanisms for key generation, backup, credential issuance and validation, as well as selective disclosure that protects the user from unintended sharing of user's personal data. In this article we evaluate the usability of existing SSI digital wallets: Trinsic, Connect.me, Esatus and Jolocom Smartwallet. We study how these early experiments with SSI address the usability challenges. We aim to identify the potential obstacles and usability issues, which might hinder wide-scale adoption of these wallets. Applying the analytical cognitive walkthrough usability inspection method, we analyse common usability issues with these mobile-based wallets. Our results reveal that wallets lack good usability in performing some fundamental tasks which can be improved significantly. We summarize our findings and point out the aspects where the issues exist so that improving those areas can result in better user experience and adoption.

Keywords: self-sovereign identity · digital wallet · usability study

1 Introduction

Identity management is the key component of information flow, provenance, information protection as well as enabler for many digital services. At present, identity data and credentials have become increasingly centralized by organizations and some of the larger corporations. The aggregation of personal data in centralized databases and data silos is undesirable for many reasons, including security, data lock-ins, as well as personal tracking and targeted advertising (e.g. for political influence). The security flaws in design incur an enormous risk of data breaches in the traditional systems. The latest evidence of such data breaches are the cases of Equifax [4], Cambridge Analytica [16], and First American Financial [8], where the identity information of millions of individuals was exposed. Moreover, identity data of users is fragmented among multiple providers. Consequently users must establish and manage a large number of

© IFIP International Federation for Information Processing 2023
Published by Springer Nature Switzerland AG 2023
F. Bieker et al. (Eds.): Privacy and Identity 2022, IFIP AICT 671, pp. 101–117, 2023.
https://doi.org/10.1007/978-3-031-31971-6_9

accounts, IDs and passwords to interact with the large number of repositories, service providers and verifiers. Lack of adequate privacy controls, and visibility to how user identity data is generated, managed and shared by third parties is yet another major concern.

These challenges have led the industry and the academia to explore innovative approaches to the management of digital identity information and cryptographic secrets. Self-sovereign identity (SSI) is a new architecture for privacy-preserving and user-centric identity management. Christopher Allen proposed a set of ten properties for SSI, which are often referred to in the literature, and are as follows: "existence, control, access, transparency, persistence, portability, interoperability, consent, minimization, and protection" [1]. SSI aims to avoid a single point of dependency and allows individuals to take ownership of their digital identities.

SSI is a set of technologies that move control of digital identity from third parties directly to individuals. The foundation concepts of SSI were officially brought to life when the Credentials Community Group was created under the umbrella of the international organization, the World Wide Web Consortium (W3C). The group defined two fundamental standards for the development of a new decentralized identity architecture: Decentralized Identifiers (DIDs) [38] and Verifiable Credentials (VCs) [39]. DIDs are a new type of identifier that is decentralized, resolvable and cryptographically verifiable. It differs from other types of identifiers in that it can exist without the involvement of any certificate authorities, third parties, providers, or centralized identity registers. VCs are typically used in conjunction with DIDs and are used to build trust between the involved parties in an SSI ecosystem, which includes an issuer, a holder, and a verifier as shown in Fig. 1.

In SSI, there is no central authority, so users hold their own digital keys and have full control over their personal information. This information is typically carried around by the user in the digital identity wallet on their mobile device. A digital wallet, in the context of SSI, is a software application and encrypted database that stores credentials, keys, and other secrets necessary for self-sovereign identity management to operate. It enables the user to have data sovereignty and complete control as well as data portability. A user can establish relationships and interact with third parties in a trusted manner. The digital identity wallet contains public-private key pairs that can be used to sign transactions, statements, credentials, documents or claims. Each participant in the SSI ecosystem needs a digital wallet in order to issue, hold, and verify VCs.

Users use a personal digital wallet to manage their keys and data which means that unlike typical systems that store data centrally, credentials and identity data would be saved in digital wallets that would be distributed all over the edges of the network giving individual users full control over their personal data. This would also vastly increase the complexity of any kind of attack, and even if certain systems were penetrated, it would no longer be a massive honeypot containing millions of individuals' personal information. The data can be delegated and managed by a third party service, and in the ideal case it is up to the user to choose the provider of those services. Even though the delegation models will be the most convenient for novice users, in this research we focus on

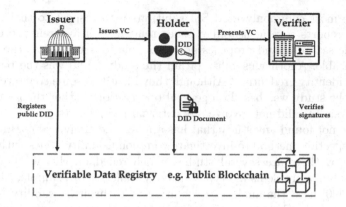

Fig. 1. Self-Sovereign Identity Architecture.

the case in which the users hold the identity data directly themselves on their mobile devices.

The concept of European Digital Identity Wallet was published by the European Commission in 2022 [12]. This initiative from the EU resulted in an enormous increase in interest in SSI, decentralized identity and wallet-based systems. In this paper we aim to contribute to this novel technology by evaluating usability of existing digital identity wallets.

1.1 Problem Statement

Self-sovereign identity systems should be designed to solve the challenges faced by end users. So far, we have seen that the existing implementations mainly focus on the underlying technology, not the user interaction [28,36]. Usable interface and privacy implications for users are not addressed yet in sufficient depth [29]. The future SSI schemes with a novel technological underpinning but developed with impractical end user interaction are unlikely to create widespread uptake.

1.2 Research Objectives

The research objectives are following:

- To evaluate the usability of digital identity wallet apps among its users.
- To derive recommendations from the user study to enhance the usability of digital identity wallets.

2 Related Work

Several researchers have pointed out that usability remains a pressing unknown in the existing SSI solutions [6,35]. However, there have been a few existing works which studied the usability issues related to SSI systems [7]. Zaeem et al. [42]

studied the most commonly used SSI solutions with respect to their usability. The paper reports several usability issues related to heavy reliance of wallets on QR code scanning and proposes potential solutions to replace the QR code when applicable. Another usability pitfall the study found was the backup and recovery of identity credentials. Although they identified some concrete usability problems, the study was based on general observations rather than any quantitative analysis and did not involve any external participants.

We have not found any study that has applied the analytical cognitive walkthrough inspection method to investigate common usability issues with SSI wallets. However, there are several studies which relied on this methodology to examine usability problems in cryptocurrency wallets. For example, Moniruzzaman et al. [20] used the analytical cognitive walk-through usability inspection method to show that both desktop and mobile-based cryptocurrency wallets lack good usability in performing the fundamental tasks. The usability study identified several common usability issues with wallets such as the use of difficult technical language, lack of interface cues and action guides, and user restrictions due to abstractions. Eskandari et al. [11] also applied a cognitive walk-through inspection method to evaluate the usability and security issues in several bitcoin wallets and found that users performing tasks involving key management can be stuck with complex security issues. Moreover, the study revealed that the metaphors and abstractions used in the analysed wallets are subject to misinterpretations, and that the wallets do not do enough to support their users.

As there are significant differences in terms of core functionalities between cryptocurrency and identity wallets, we aim to fill in this gap in this study and evaluate the usability of identity wallets by applying an analytical usability inspection method, the cognitive walkthrough method.

3   Methodology

There exist different usability inspection methods such as the heuristic evaluation (HE) [2], the cognitive walkthrough (CW) [32], the pluralistic walkthrough (PW) [26], and the formal usability inspections [15]. HE is done by expert evaluators examining the design of a user interface and judging its compliance with a list of predefined principles (heuristics). HE is a low-cost and intuitive method for evaluating the user interface early in the design process. On the other hand, CW is a task-oriented and structured method that focuses on the learnability of a system for new users and can be performed on an interface at any time during the development process, from the original mock-ups through the final release [25]. It rests on the assumption that evaluators are capable of taking the perspective of the user and can apply this user perspective to a task scenario to identify user-interface problems. PW adapted the traditional usability walkthrough to incorporate representative users, product developers, members of the product team, and usability experts in the process. This approach offers feedback from users even if the interface is not fully developed and enables rapid iteration of the design cycle [15]. Formal usability inspections are structured activities with defined steps and trained inspectors. This method is most appropriate for more complex software where product teams want to track usability defects and establish a process to detect and eliminate major usability bugs [41].

Our main goal was to investigate the usability issues digital identity wallet users face. Considering that the main focus of the study is on new users and the selected wallet applications for testing are all already released, the cognitive walkthrough method has been selected for evaluating the usability of wallets.

3.1 Procedure

The cognitive walkthrough is conducted following the procedure summarized below:

1. Determine what tasks are most appropriate for the walkthrough.
2. Select a group of evaluators and give them basic training on the process.
3. Evaluators walk through the action sequences for each task and answer the following four standard questions which were first mentioned in the usability book by C. Wharton et al. [40] and currently is considered as a standard procedure in the cognitive walkthrough questionnaires. These questions essentially require each participant to answer in a binary yes/no fashion where a yes signifies that the user has been able to perform the respective task whereas a no signifies the user has failed.
   Q1. Will the user understand how to start the task?
   Q2. Is the control (e.g. button) for the action clearly visible?
   Q3. Will the user associate the correct action with the outcome they expect to achieve? (link of the control with the action).
   Q4. If the correct action is performed, will the user see that progress is being made towards their intended outcome?
4. If the evaluator fails to complete the task, the short interview was conducted to identify the exact problem.
5. Record issues and design suggestions that were not the direct output of the walkthrough, assumptions about users, comments about the tasks, and other information that may be useful in improving the usability of wallet apps.

3.2 Usability Evaluation

The study collected qualitative (interview notes) and quantitative (questionnaire results) data during the cognitive walkthrough usability evaluation. The main focus of the study was to identify usability issues users encounter when using digital wallets. Therefore short interviews were conducted whenever the evaluator failed or struggled to perform the task during the cognitive walkthrough.

The data from the questionnaire results was used to measure the effectiveness and the number of errors per task. Errors are defined as mistakes that are made by the participant when attempting a task. Effectiveness can be measured using the completion rate of tasks and can be defined as a percentage by utilising the simple equation represented below [3].

$$Effectiveness = \frac{Number\ of\ tasks\ completed\ successfully}{Total\ number\ of\ tasks\ undertaken} * 100\%$$

3.3 Tasks and Scenario

For our experiment, we have selected five major tasks (Table 1) based on the core functions of an SSI wallet specified in the literature [21,23,24]. To make it easy for evaluators, we focus on a scenario where a user (Alice) will receive a college diploma and will prove to her new employer she graduated college to get a job.

> *T1: Configure.* User installs a wallet for the first time in a new device, creates a new account and saves his/her wallet recovery phrase.
>
> *T2: Establish a connection with third parties.* The SSI wallet can create an encrypted communication channel to exchange information between a user and a third party (issuer, verifier or another user). This communication channel is based on a unique identifier, which the user controls. The user receives connection invitations which are usually transmitted through QR codes or deeplinks. The user scans the QR code and accepts the connection invitation that shows up in the wallet. The connection will be added to the user's wallet.
>
> *T3: Receive a credential from issuer and store it in a wallet.* Issuer offers a credential to the user. The user opens the credential offer and inspects the attributes. If everything looks correct, the user accepts the offer. The credential will be issued to the user's wallet, and can be viewed in the corresponding tab.
>
> *T4: Share a credential with verifier and complete the verification process.* The user gets the verification request from the verifier. From the home screen, the user selects the verification request to respond, customizes the information and shares only required attributes (if a wallet supports the selective disclosure). If the information looks correct, the user shares the credential and gets confirmation whether the credential proof was successful or not.
>
> *T5: Backup and restore a wallet.* This task will require the user to set up a backup for the wallet and then restore it. The recovery phrase is usually used to recover the encrypted wallet in case the device is lost or destroyed.

Table 1. Fundamental tasks and sub-tasks for the experiment.

T1: Configure	T1.1 Download and install the wallet app T1.2 View and save wallet recovery phrase
T2: Establish a connection with third parties	T2.1 Scan QR code and accept the invitation T1.2 View the added connection in the wallet
T3: Receive a credential from issuer and store it in the wallet	T3.1 Inspect the attributes and accept the credential offer T3.2 View the new credential in the wallet
T4: Share a credential with verifier and complete the verification process	T4.1 Select the verification request to respond and present the credential that can satisfy the request
T5: Backup and restore the wallet	T5.1 Set up a local or cloud backup for the wallet T5.2 Restore the wallet

3.4 Selected Wallets

Table 2 presents an overview of the eight analysed SSI wallet providers. The study results show that all except Civic base their development work on open SSI standards and specifications by W3C and DIF. This highlights the positive development in SSI space as following common standards considerably help achieving interoperability between existing SSI systems. The three of the reviewed SSI systems does not provide a mobile application for wallet. To meet the study's goal of examining usability issues, four different digital identity wallet applications that satisfy our requirements (Table 2) were selected. The wallets selected for this study are Trinsic [37], Connect.me (Sovrin) [13], Esatus [10] and Jolocom Smartwallet [17]. We selected these wallets because they follow the SSI principles and common standards. They provide mobile wallet applications on both iOS and Android platforms and regularly maintain them. The selected wallets support core SSI functionalities with minimum feature sets maturity of level 1 (*basic*) as presented by Rosendahl (2022) [27] and can be used to conduct usability tests. Additionally, they support several distributed ledgers, have sizable online communities, and provide tutorials and documentation with the most technical details of their designs.

3.5 Participant Requirement

The participants were recruited via project advert asking their interest and engagement. Upon receiving expression of interest from the participants, we contacted them via email to book a time as per their availability. Prior to the evaluation, each participant was supplied with the documentation of our designed cognitive walk-through method and other necessary tutorials.

The main focus of study was to test new users who have not used identity wallet apps before. Therefore, we have excluded users with prior experience. According to the literature [14,15], it is best to narrow down the target audience to the users most likely to use the product. As identity wallets are at early stage of development and there is no data available on user base, we looked into similar mobile applications like Apple Wallet app and cryptocurrency wallets. Based on our analysis, Apple Wallet usage is the highest among Millenials and Generation Z consumers [19,30] and cryptocurrency wallets are most popular with young adults [5,34]. Therefore, we have selected graduate students and young professionals within the age group of 20 to 35 years.

Table 2. Overview of the SSI wallet providers.

Characteristics	Esatus	Civic	Jolocom	Trinsic	Sovrin	Spruce	Affinidi	Veramo
Aligns with SSI standards (W3C and DIF)	Yes	No	Yes	Yes	Yes	Yes	Yes	Yes
Mobile application for wallet (iOS and Android)	Yes	Yes	Yes	Yes	Yes	No	No	No
Regularly maintained (mobile wallet app)	Yes	Yes	Yes	Yes	Yes	–	–	–
Core SSI features maturity (mobile wallet app)	Rich	Rich	Basic	Rich	Basic	–	–	–
Supported distributed ledgers	Esatus, Sovrin, IDunion	Ethereum, Solana	Jolocom	Sovrin, BCGov, Indy	Sovrin	ION, Tezos, Ethereum	Ethereum	Ethereum

It is widely accepted that testing with small group of users is capable of finding almost as many usability issues as testing with many users, specifically when the study focuses on one target group as in our case [18,22]. Moreover, we aim to conduct a case study for a relatively new concept and carry out an in-depth investigation employing quantitative and qualitative methods. Therefore, a small group of five participants were recruited. Each experiment lasted between 60 to 80 min in average and was conducted with mobile wallet apps on Apple iPhone powered by iOS 15.

4   Results

In this section, we describe the qualitative and quantitative results obtained from the study. As part of the qualitative analysis short interviews were conducted whenever the evaluator failed or struggled to perform the task during the cognitive walkthrough. Overall, 35 different usability problems were captured from evaluation sessions.

4.1   Qualitative Analysis

1. Trinsic

T1: Configure. Trinsic app uses onboarding screens to introduce users with various features of the app and to inform them that their identity data is encrypted and stored locally. The welcome page also contains *Recover wallet* button that enables existing users to restore their wallet. Evaluators reported that the onboarding process was smooth and informative. The app does not offer a password or passcode options and only relies on biometric authentication to protect the wallet. However, although all participants enabled a biometric security during the configuration phase, the app has not shown a biometric authentication dialog afterwards and basically allows anyone to access the app.

T2: Establish a connection. All participants were able to scan QR code and accept the invitation (T2.1) as the app's home page contains a large *Scan code* button with additional animation on top. Two evaluators could not find the *Connections* (failed Q1 and Q2) to view the added connection (T2.2) from the first attempt. The *Connections* tab is two taps away from the home page which features three primary tabs (Home, Credentials, and Settings) but these tabs are represented by descriptive icons only. It might be helpful to add texts under icons to avoid confusion among end users.

T3 and T4: Receive and share a credential. The app allows a user to scan a QR code, inspect the attributes and accept the credential offer from a issuer. If the user does not choose the correct blockchain network before accepting the credential, "A network mismatch has occurred. Please select the correct network" message shows up. It would be helpful if the message also notifies the user which network to choose as Trinsic supports five different blockchain networks. Moreover, Trinsic users have to use QR code scanning each time they receive and share a credential.

T5: Backup and restore a wallet. Users can navigate to *Backup and restore* tab under *Settings* menu and can choose local or cloud backup options. Trinsic supports a wallet recovery phrase which is displayed as a 12-word phrase. The app uses in-app notification to confirm that the user has already written down his/her phrase and warns that it is not possible to recover the wallet without this phrase. If the wallet was successfully backed up, it shows a notification to the user that this has occurred. All evaluators answered with *Yes* to Q4 and confirmed it. To restore the wallet users need to enter their recovery phrase into the box and click "Recover wallet" button. The app does not explain the correct format the phrases should be entered.

2. Jolocom

T1: Configure. Passcode protection is mandatory in Jolocom, and the user is notified about the importance of securing the wallet on first run. Finding the generated recovery phrase was not challenging for evaluators and T1.2 was accomplished successfully by all evaluators. The user must navigate to the *Settings* tab located in the navigation bar. The interface displays a warning about the importance of saving the secret phrase. However, the app allows only one opportunity to view and write down the phrase. Although there is a warning about this feature, it might not be the best practice as users might easily make a mistake during the process or lose it afterwards.

T2: Establish a connection. Although the QR code scan button is represented by only icon, all evaluators reported that it is clearly visible and they understand how to start the task. When the connection is added to the user's wallet, the app shows the notification "Success! Your interaction was successful" to let the user know that the process is complete. But the app gave the same notification message for all other processes. Participants found it too generic and less informative. Moreover, there is no a separate tab for connections. Once the user establish a connection, it will show up under *History* tab with other processes such as issuance and verification requests. The organization of information on this screen was not very clear to the study participants.

T3 and T4: Receive and share a credential. The app uses in-app pop-up notifications to show the incoming credential offers. The notification message shows a sender, credential and corresponding attribute names, and provides the user with *Accept* and *Ignore* options. However, the attribute values are hidden which does not allow the user to fully inspect the credential before accepting it. The issued credential can be viewed from the *Documents* tab.

T5: Backup and restore a wallet. Jolocom wallet supports seed phrases for private key recovery. To recover the wallet users need to click *Import identity* button and insert 12-word recovery phrase one by one. Evaluators reported that the recovery option is only available during the configuration phase. However, restoring the wallet content was not possible as the app does not backup properly.

3. **Esatus**

T1: Configure. Esatus does not have onboarding screens that guide users on how to use an app's various features as in other wallets. The apps only requires the user to create a PIN and enable notifications. Biometrics could be enabled from *Settings* menu. Esatus generates a new set of seed phrases during the setup of wallet, but shows no notification to the user that this has occurred. The wallet recovery phrase can be found under the *Create/Export backup* tab in *Settings* menu. One participant struggled to find the correct tab (failed Q2).

T2: Establish a connection. Evaluators reported that all the tabs for primary functions (Connections, Credentials, Scan, and Settings) can be easily accessed from the home screen and represented by recognizable icon and text. When the user establish a connection with a third party it shows up in *Connections* tab. For each connection the app provides a transparent history of interactions between parties. Participants have not experienced issues with T2.2.

T3 and T4: Receive and share a credential. All received credentials are visible in *Credentials* tab which is also the home page of the app. The app uses horizontal scrolling list to display credentials. However, horizontal scroll works best only when there are few credentials available and is not very convenient when the wallet stores many credentials. *Info* section displays some redundant information such as credential definition and schema (e.g. KuXsPLZAsxgjbaAeQd4rr8:2:schema:2.0) which are useful for developers but not for the average app users. There is also *Proofs* tab in the home screen which allows to create proofs but the app does not provide any explanation about this feature and how to use it. The *Proofs* screen just displays "No Gateways found" when the user opens it first time. The terminology is too technical for users.

T5: Backup and restore a wallet. As with other wallets, recovery is not possible if no backup of the wallet file was made. Creating a backup is straightforward by using the *Create/Export backup* menu and then following the instructions. The app also verifies that users saved the recovery phrase correctly.

4. **Connect.me**

T1: Configure. The evaluators claimed that the onboarding process is very limited and features only user approval for enabling biometrics and notifications. Connect.me generates private keys for its users, but the process is hidden and abstracted from users. Moreover, the study participants could not view their recovery phrases.

T2: Establish a connection. Connect.me features a separate *My connections* tab for displaying the list of added connections. The app gave clear error messages when the process of establishing a connection failed. The wallet relies on QR code scanning to initially connect an identity owner with other entities. But the app heavily relies on QR code scanning and requires it for every interaction such as receiving issuance and verification requests which might hinder the user experience. Moreover, it was reported that the *Scan* button is too small and its icon's colour is same as its background (white) which makes it hardly visible.

T3 and T4: Receive and share a credential. Credential offer notification message displays the name of the issuer and all attributes which can be inspected by simply scrolling down. After inspection the user can *Accept* or *Reject* the credential. Users also get notified when the process is complete and the credential is issued. The verification request transparently shows the name of the verifier and which attributes is being requested. Users can view added credentials under the tab *My Credentials* which has a colorful and graphical user interface. The study participants agreed that it was easy to use the wallet for receiving and sharing the credential.

T5: Backup and restore a wallet. It was found that Connect.me wallet app still does not support this fundamental feature and it was recorded as a failure in our experiment. Users of this wallet will not be able to restore their personal data, credentials and connections in case of mobile device loss or theft.

4.2 Quantitative Analysis

Analysis of the results is performed mainly on the metrics such as user's effectiveness performance and the number of errors made per task. There were 5 main tasks (T1-T5) with a total of 9 sub-tasks (Table 1). For each sub-task evaluators had to complete 4 steps (total 36 steps) and answer usability questions (Q1-Q4) mentioned in Sect. 3.1. During the experiment a total of 36 *yes-no* answers from each evaluator were recorded. A *yes* signifies that the user has been able to perform the respective step for sub-task whereas a *no* signifies the user has failed. We assumed that a task is successful if the user was able to perform all four steps (answered Q1-Q4 with *yes*).

Table 3 shows the effectiveness performance average for selected wallet applications. The methodology for calculating the effectiveness is described in Sect. 3.2. The average effectiveness for Connect.me and Jolocom wallets were quite low, 56.11% and 75.00% respectively. Users had much smoother experience with Esatus and Trinsic mobile wallets and consequently higher effectiveness performance was observed, 91.11% and 90.56% respectively. As we can see, users

Table 3. Effectiveness average for the selected wallets.

Wallets	Esatus	Connect.me	Jolocom	Trinsic
Effectiveness average (%)	91.11	56.11	75.00	90.56

failed to complete some fundamental tasks in every examined digital identity wallet.

Figure 2 better represents the difficulties faced while completing the tasks for all the selected wallets where the graphs illustrate the average number of failed steps per task (signified by a *no* answer) by participants. We can observe that receiving a credential (T3) and sharing it with verifier (T4) were the most easy tasks to accomplish by the participants as the lowest number of steps were failed. For every selected wallet, users struggled with task T5 most - backing up and restoring a wallet.

5   Discussion

In this section, we summarize and discuss the main usability issues that were identified from our study and propose recommendations to enhance the usability of digital identity wallets.

All the four studied SSI wallet apps rely on QR code scanning to initially connect an identity owner with an issuer or a verifier. One of the major advantages of using QR code in SSI wallet apps is its ease of use and mobile friendliness which was again confirmed by our study participants. However, several participants reported that some examined wallets heavily rely on QR code scanning and require it for every interaction such as receiving issuance and verification requests which might hinder the user experience. This issue was also reported by Zaeem et al. [42] and our results confirm it. Based on this feedback, we recommend using QR code scanning for only opening a private and secure channel between the two parties. Then for further interactions use message exchange through already established secure connection (i.e. using DIDComm Messaging [9]) and in-app notifications to show incoming requests to the user.

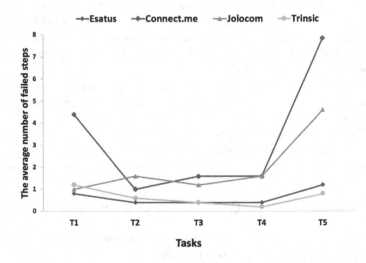

Fig. 2. The average number of failed steps per each task for the selected wallets.

SSI digital wallets do not support third-party centralized authentication methods and do not require a new user to create a login with password for the app during the configuration phase which was confirmed in this study. Instead wallets allow a user to create its own DIDs, receive credentials from different issuers and form his digital identity. Users will be using their wallets to authenticate to other services. Therefore it is important to ensure that only authorized users can access the wallet and its data. The study revealed that some wallets do not support passcodes/passwords and in one of the evaluated wallets the biometrics authentication was not working properly. Digital identity wallets should support both the passcode and biometrics authentication to protect the sensitive personal data stored in the wallet.

Several participants observed a little longer delays when retrieving or verifying credentials and it was not very clear to them why it usually happens. The reason behind this is that identity wallet apps in most cases need to synchronize with a public blockchain network and update the state in the ledger. Therefore, in some cases, decentralized apps[1] like wallets might be slower than traditional apps which we use daily. Moreover, all of the selected wallets support several blockchain networks. Setting the correct network before retrieving or verifying the credential is important and was a challenge for some participants. Wallets should have more intuitive interfaces with the interface cues enabling non-technical users to get comfortable with the app.

On first run, all of the evaluated wallets generate the recovery phrase without informing the user and do not provide any information on it. The abstractions made in identity wallets are sometimes beneficial for users, such as in the case of hiding the credential definition and schemas. However, the recovery phrase is the key to the wallet and the user should understand it and be warned about the importance of not forgetting the secret phrase. This information could be included in onboarding screens.

The study participants reported that some wallets used difficult technical languages. Examples of such languages are "out of sync", "no gateways found", and some others mentioned in Sect. 4.1. Highly technical language often becomes incomprehensible to average users due to the unfamiliar terminology that's simply part of the technical domain. These technical terms should be replaced by simpler instructions.

Traditional identity management models provide a key management protocol that rely on a trusted third party, while in the context of the SSI model the responsibility of key management is assigned to the identity owners themselves. The three wallets out of four presented here support seed phrases which enables the user to recover his/her wallet account (a private key). However, if you lose your device you may still lose all your existing credentials and connections stored in a wallet, even if you have recovered the private key. Thus, users are advised to backup encrypted wallet data. Our study reveals that only two of examined wallets (Trinsic and Esatus) allow the user to restore his/her personal data stored

---

[1] Decentralized applications (DApps) are applications that run on top of blockchain networks.

Table 4. Problems and recommendations

Usability Issues	Recommendations
The wallet app heavily relies on QR code scanning	Use QR code scanning for only opening a private and secure channel between two parties. Then for further interactions use message exchange through already established secure channel
Users experience longer delays when a wallet interacts with a blockchain	Use a graphical view indicator that displays the status of work being done. The visual cue allows users to see progress, which encourages them to wait
The user faces difficulty in setting the correct blockchain network	Wallets should have more intuitive interfaces with the interface cues and instructions enabling non-technical users to get comfortable with the app
The wallet app uses a difficult technical language	Replace highly technical terms with simpler instructions
The user is unable to backup the wallet content	The app should offer cloud and local backup options for its users
Seed phrases are a single point of failure	Decentralized key recovery solutions should be considered.
The user has problem finding the location of the recovery phrase	The wallet should have a separate visible tab that allows to view and save the recovery phrase
The user is unable to understand the functionality of the recovery phrase	The wallet should provide an explanation as to why it is important to securely save the recovery phrase and how to use it. This message should be easily accessed (e.g. a welcome page), along with links to further instructions
The app uses only icons for primary tabs	It might be helpful to add texts under icons to avoid confusion among end users.
The mobile authentication is not working properly	The app should support mobile authentication methods that are secure, reliable and protect the sensitive personal data stored in the wallet

in the wallet through cloud or local backup. Jolocom does provide this feature but it does not work properly. Connect.me wallet does not provide any options to recover and restore the wallet. The wallets also should notify the user about the risks of not taking a backup. Based on experiment results, only one of four selected wallets has done it.

Although evaluators have not reported critical usability challenges regarding the use of seed phrases during the experiment, using these seeds is not the most safe way for recovery as it presents a single point of failure. To improve the usability of backup and recovery, decentralized key recovery solutions should be considered. For example, a social recovery method which employs entities trusted by the identity owner called 'trustees' who store recovery data on an identity owner's behalf typically in their own wallets. There are several research papers that proposed decentralized key backup and recovery solutions for SSI wallets based on Shamir's Secret Sharing algorithm [31, 33] which could be potentially implemented in existing identity wallets.

Table 4 contains examples of usability problems frequently encountered in our evaluation and the recommendations from us to resolve them.

6   Conclusions

In this paper we presented the usability study of some existing digital identity wallets focusing on a series of tasks. The cognitive walkthrough inspection method has been used to identify the usability issues and to measure the effectiveness performance of users. Based on the review of the current state-of-the-art and comparison analysis, several wallets were selected. In our evaluation, we have observed that some existing digital identity wallets already provide a decent level of user experience and are good in terms of effectiveness, however there are still a number of usability issues in fundamental tasks that need improvements. We summarized the main challenges and proposed recommendations that may be helpful to improve the overall usability and accessibility among the users. Our findings suggest that the key management and wallet recovery methods need to be improved. It is crucial for digital identity wallets to have a secure and usable management of keys and personal data. Wallets should have more intuitive interfaces with the interface cues enabling new users to get comfortable with the app. Resolving these issues will considerably improve the user acceptance and global adoption of digital identity wallets.

All of the participants in this study were young adults employed/studying within the same university. While this likely introduces bias, our subjects were from different departments and well fit for the existing user base of digital wallets. Nonetheless, one future direction from this work would be to perform similar evaluations with older participants from different sectors. As the SSI technology matures and gains traction digital wallets might become integral part of the general population in near future.

References

1. Allen, C.: The path to SSI (2016), bit.ly/3W7KXV0. Accessed 20 May 2022
2. Alonso-Ríos, D., Mosqueira-Rey, E., Moret-Bonillo, V.: A systematic and generalizable approach to the heuristic evaluation of user interfaces. Int. J. Human-Comput. Interact. **34**(12), 1169–1182 (2018)
3. Alturki, R., Gay, V.: Usability testing of fitness mobile application: case study aded surat app. Int. J. Comput. Sci. Inform. Technol. (IJCSIT) **9**, (2017)
4. Berghel, H.: Equifax and the latest round of identity theft roulette. Computer **50**(12), 72–76 (2017)
5. Bohr, J., Bashir, M.: Who uses bitcoin? an exploration of the bitcoin community. In: 12th Annual International Conference on Privacy, Security and Trust, pp. 94–101. IEEE (2014)
6. Čučko, Š, Bećirović, Š, Kamišalić, A., Mrdović, S., Turkanović, M.: Towards the classification of SSI properties. IEEE Access **10**, 88306–88329 (2022)
7. Čučko, Š, Turkanović, M.: Decentralized and self-sovereign identity: Systematic mapping study. IEEE Access **9**, 139009–139027 (2021)
8. Dellinger, A.: Understanding the first american financial data leak: How did it happen and what does it mean? https://bit.ly/3QvjRG2 Accessed 1 May 2022
9. DIF: DIDComm Messaging.https://bit.ly/3CBJlMk Accessed 23 June 2022
10. Esatus: Esatus wallet, https://esatus.com/ Accessed 20 June 2022
11. Eskandari, S., Clark, J., Barrera, D., Stobert, E.: A first look at the usability of bitcoin key management. arXiv preprint arXiv:1802.04351 (2018)
12. European Commission: European Digital Identity Architecture and Reference Framework. Tech. rep. (2022), https://bit.ly/3kaFIXe
13. Evernym: Connect.me wallet, https://connect.me, Accessed 27 June 2022
14. Edmunds, M., Hass, C., Holve, E. (eds.): Springer, Cham (2019). https://doi.org/10.1007/978-3-319-96906-0

15. Hollingsed, T., Novick, D.G.: Usability inspection methods after 15 years of research and practice. In: Proceedings of the 25th Annual ACM Conference on Design of Communication, pp. 249–255 (2007)
16. Isaak, J., Hanna, M.J.: User data privacy: Facebook, cambridge analytica, and privacy protection. Computer **51**(8), 56–59 (2018)
17. Jolocom: Jolocom SmartWallet, https://jolocom.io/ Accessed 20 May 2022
18. Khajouei, R., Zahiri Esfahani, M., Jahani, Y.: Comparison of heuristic and cognitive walkthrough usability methods for evaluating health information systems. J. Am. Med. Inform. Assoc. **24**(e1), e55–e60 (2017)
19. Liébana-Cabanillas, F., García-Maroto, I., Muñoz-Leiva, F., Ramos-de Luna, I.: Mobile payment adoption in the age of digital transformation: The case of apple pay. Sustainability **12**(13), 5443 (2020)
20. Moniruzzaman, Md., Chowdhury, F., Ferdous, M.S.: Examining Usability Issues in Blockchain-Based Cryptocurrency Wallets. In: Bhuiyan, T., Rahman, M.M., Ali, M.A. (eds.) ICONCS 2020. LNICST, vol. 325, pp. 631–643. Springer, Cham (2020). https://doi.org/10.1007/978-3-030-52856-0_50
21. Mühle, A., Grüner, A., Gayvoronskaya, T., Meinel, C.: A survey on essential components of a self-sovereign identity. Comput. Sci. Rev. **30**, 80–86 (2018)
22. Nielsen, J.: How many test users in a usability study?, https://www.nngroup.com/articles/how-many-test-users Accessed 1 May 2022
23. Podgorelec, B., Alber, L., Zefferer, T.: What is a (digital) identity wallet? a systematic literature review. In: 2022 IEEE 46th Annual Computers, Software, and Applications Conference (COMPSAC). pp. 809–818. IEEE (2022)
24. Preukschat, A., Reed, D.: Self-sovereign identity. Manning Publications (2021)
25. Privitera, M.B.: Heuristic analysis, cognitive walkthroughs & expert reviews. In: Applied Human Factors in Medical Device Design, pp. 165–180. Elsevier (2019)
26. Riihiaho, S.: The pluralistic usability walk-through method. Ergonom. Design **10**(3), 23–27 (2002)
27. Rosendahl, R.: Understand your application's feature set maturity (2022), bit.ly/3XlABSn, Accessed 24 November 2022
28. Satybaldy, A., Nowostawski, M., Ellingsen, J.: SSI systems. In: IFIP International Summer School on Privacy and Identity Management. pp. 447–461. Springer (2019)
29. Schardong, F., Custódio, R.: Self-sovereign identity: a systematic review, mapping and taxonomy. Sensors **22**(15), 5641 (2022)
30. Shopify: How many people use apple pay in us?, https://bit.ly/3Xmtt8l, Accessed 23 November 2022
31. Singh, H.P., Stefanidis, K., Kirstein, F.: A private key recovery scheme using partial knowledge. In: 2021 11th IFIP International Conference on New Technologies, Mobility and Security (NTMS), pp. 1–5. IEEE (2021)
32. Smith-Jackson, T.L.: Cognitive walk-through method (CWM). In: Handbook of Human Factors and Ergonomics Methods, pp. 785–793. CRC Press (2004)
33. Soltani, R., Nguyen, U.T., An, A.: Practical key recovery model for self-sovereign identity based digital wallets. In: 2019 IEEE Intl Conf on Dependable, Autonomic and Secure Computing, pp. 320–325. IEEE (2019)
34. Statista: Crypto ownership among consumers in the united states, by age and gender, https://bit.ly/3Zu0eC Accessed 13 November 2022
35. Stokkink, Q., Ishmaev, G., Epema, D., Pouwelse, J.: A truly SSI system. In: 2021 IEEE 46th Conference on Local Computer Networks (LCN), pp. 1–8. IEEE (2021)
36. Toth, K.C., Anderson-Priddy, A.: Self-sovereign digital identity: a paradigm shift for identity. IEEE Secur. Privacy **17**(3), 17–27 (2019)

37. Trinsic: A full-stack SSI platform, https://trinsic.id/, Accessed 23 November 2022
38. W3C: Decentralized Identifiers (2022), bit.ly/3GXbCj9 Accessed 13 June 2022
39. W3C: Verifiable Credentials (2022), bit.ly/3XpGv5g, Accessed 8 June 2022
40. Wharton, C., Rieman, J., Lewis, C., Polson, P.: The cognitive walkthrough method: A practitioner's guide. In: Usability inspection methods, pp. 105–140 (1994)
41. Wilson, C.: User Interface Inspection Methods. O'Reilly, Morgan Kaufmann (2013)
42. Zaeem, R.N., Khalil, M.M., Lamison, M.R., Pandey, S., Barber, K.S.: On the usability of SSI solutions. Tech. rep. (2021). https://bit.ly/3ivOzCt

Influence of Privacy Knowledge
on Privacy Attitudes in the Domain
of Location-Based Services

Vera Schmitt(✉)

Technische Universität Berlin, Berlin, Germany
vera.schmitt@tu-berlin.de

Abstract. In our daily life, we make extensive use of location-based services when searching for a restaurant nearby, searching for an address we want to visit, or searching for the best route to drive. Location information is highly sensitive personal information that users share without the awareness of being continuously tracked by various apps on their smartphones or smart devices. Privacy knowledge and overall privacy literacy facilitate gaining control over sharing personal information and adjusting privacy settings online. This research examines the influence of privacy literacy on privacy attitudes in the domain of location-based services. Hereby, privacy literacy is measured through four dimensions by asking the participants about various aspects of knowledge about institutional practices, technical aspects of data protection, data protection law, privacy policies, and also about possible data protection strategies. The overall privacy literacy score is examined in relation to various privacy attitudes such as tolerance of sharing personal information, perceived intrusion when using location-based services, and their perceived benefits. Overall, 155 participants took part in the questionnaire. A significant difference can be found between the overall privacy literacy score between German participants and those from other countries with German participants having a higher privacy literacy score. Furthermore, privacy literacy positively correlates with trust in the GDPR, and also with privacy concern about the secondary use of location information. Indicating, that the higher the privacy literacy level is, the more concerned participants seem to be.

Keywords: Privacy Literacy · Privacy Concern · Location-Based Services · Privacy Attitudes · GDPR

1 Introduction

The omnipresence of smartphones and wearables has increased the collection of personal data significantly. Most users carry their smartphones or smartwatches around constantly with location-based services (LBS) activated [7]. Often, users

The study has been conducted with the support of the DFG in the scope of the project MO 1038/28-1.

struggle to gain control over the sharing and collection of their personal data as privacy settings do not disclose which permissions for applications on smart-phones run in the background and access sensitive information such as camera, audio, and location information [15]. To gain control over privacy settings and understand permission requests during the installation process of apps, users need to be knowledgeable about their device settings, and the potential conse-quences of continuous data sharing and motivated to protect their personal data [7]. Especially in the context of location information, highly sensitive location traces can reveal information e.g. about the work or home location, movement patterns, health condition, and social status, which can be used to create a very precise profile of an individual [5,24,25].

Previous findings show that users with higher privacy literacy tend to be more aware of privacy risks but it does not result in improved data protection behaviour [3,7]. Previous research has shown contradicting findings on the influ-ence of privacy knowledge. It has been empirically shown that mobile protection behaviour is significantly influenced by security and privacy knowledge levels [17], but [8] examined that privacy knowledge is not the main driver of privacy behaviour but rather peer influence. To further shed light on these contradicting findings, this research focuses on a specific data-sharing scenario in the LBS con-text, to provide further empirical evidence for the examination of the influence of privacy knowledge. Not much research has been done to examine the relation between LBS usage, privacy literacy and privacy attitudes [7,25] for German participants. Hereby, this research examines the relationship between usage pat-terns of LBS on privacy literacy, privacy attitudes towards LBS, and trust in the General Data Protection Directive (GDPR) from 155 smartphone users.

This research answers the following research questions:

RQ1: What is the influence of privacy literacy on privacy attitudes?
RQ2: What is the influence of privacy attitudes on LBS usage frequency?
RQ3: Does privacy literacy significantly differ between Germany and other coun-
tries?

The remainder of the paper is organized as follows: Sect. 2 discusses related work while Sect. 3 describes the design of the experiments. In Sect. 4, the results are presented and discussed. Finally, in Sect. 5 a conclusion is drawn from the analysis.

2 Related Work

Previous research has explored users' privacy literacy of data collection and their perception of security and privacy threats in various domains and contexts. Most previous research has focused either on online contexts [3,13], mobile technolo-gies [28], digital apps, and social media [9]. Fewer studies have been done in the domain of LBS [7,12]. LBS provide enhanced functionalities and are conve-nient to use e.g. for navigating to various locations and tracking relatives and objects. They are also of great importance in the domain of fitness trackers [11].

The control over location sharing in the domain of LBS is difficult to monitor for users, as applications often request location information without the users being aware of it. Often the risks and consequences of location sharing and information which can be abstracted from location traces remain mostly hidden from the user [7].

Users' location can be disclosed through various LBS-based applications such as Facebook Places and Foursquare or it can be tracked by inbuilt smartphone features such as GPS, IP address, or RFID. Irrespective of the means by which the information is generated, when the user shares his or her content, the generated content normally contains information about the geographical location and other information such as device type, date, time, operating system, and related key details which enable precise user profiling [10]. Thus, LBS open up new vulnerabilities and the leakage of location information of users has drawn significant attention from academia and industry, recently [15]. Hereby, users find themselves often in an information-demanding environment and the complexities in technologies can hinder their abilities to make privacy decisions that reflect their privacy concerns [11]. Moreover, different devices have various privacy settings which make the matter of controlling information access and release even more complex [2].

In this context, privacy literacy plays an important role in preventing the leakage of private location data within LBS and in turn enhances the adoption of LBS applications by users [6,7]. A general lack of privacy literacy may result in users keeping the LBS function turned on while performing tasks that may not even require location data [2]. Empirical research has shown disparities between users' online privacy behaviour and privacy attitudes, even though they express concern about sharing personal data online [29]. These discrepancies gave rise to the *knowledge-gap hypothesis* which describes the phenomenon that users are concerned about their privacy and would like to behave in accordance but lack adequate knowledge of how they can protect their personal information [14,18].

However, there are also contradicting findings. According to [17], mobile protection behaviour varies significantly based on different privacy and security knowledge levels. Moreover, [8] examined that privacy knowledge is not the main driver of privacy behaviour but rather peer influence. Furthermore, [14], [16], and [19] found that participants with higher privacy knowledge and literacy can perceive potential threats much better than lay participants. However, it did not affect privacy concern or privacy behaviour significantly. Further distinctions are made by [30] who divide participants into *privacy vulnerable* and *privacy resilient* categories based on the notion that privacy decisions are based on individual perceptions, experiences, and the knowledge about protection strategies. Nonetheless, most previous approaches did not examine privacy literacy, privacy knowledge, and general privacy perception in a specific domain where participants can relate to the personal information to be shared [1], [26].

To further explore the relationship between privacy literacy and attitudes with respect to a specific domain, the following section examines the methodological framework to study the relationship between privacy knowledge and privacy attitudes toward LBS.

3 Methodology

Various approaches have been proposed in previous literature to measure privacy knowledge. Hereby, privacy knowledge has been mainly measured by asking about data collection strategies and the duration of data storage [4]. More recent approaches rely on the concept of privacy literacy which is described as the "principle to support, encourage, and empower users to undertake informed control of their digital identities" [22]. Deliberate and informed decision-making about online privacy needs to be based on online privacy literacy and, therefore, can be understood as an important basis of privacy-aware decision-making [23].

Based on the concept of privacy literacy [29] have developed a validated Online Privacy Literacy Scale (OPLIS), which is based on an exhaustive analysis of prior literature and profound content analysis. The scale is composed of four dimensions (the full questionnaire can be found in Appendix B):

1. Knowledge about institutional practices; internet users visit multiple websites and use different online services in their daily lives. Thus internet users need to know about data-sharing practices and how their personal information is handled by the different service providers. This dimension focuses on knowledge about common practices of data collection from different service providers.
2. Knowledge about technical aspects of data protection; in the online world, users are often confronted with technical aspects of their privacy, thus, the dimension of technical data protection is an important requirement for effective online data protection and control.
3. Knowledge about data protection law; knowledge about privacy policies is a crucial component of privacy literacy, as the understanding of legal regulation enables users to make informed decisions and control over personal information sharing.
4. Knowledge about data protection strategies: this dimension addresses *active* and *passive* actions of data protection. Whereas the *passive* actions incorporate strategies such as nondisclosure of personal information, *active* actions include knowledge about how to use encryption, anti-spyware and privacy enhancing technologies [29].

The questions concerning the four dimensions can be either answered as right or wrong and the correct answers can be summed up to a privacy literacy score. These five dimensions are used in our survey to measure online privacy literacy and examine the effects on privacy attitudes and LBS usage.

Various privacy attitudes in the domain of LBS have been examined by [4, 21, 27] in a previous experiment assessing privacy attitudes towards fitness trackers in the domain of LBS. Hereby, [27] assessed privacy attitudes such as tolerance of location information sharing and appreciation or benefits gained through LBS.

The questionnaire developed by [27] is used for this study as a basis to measure the following seven privacy attitudes:

1. Tolerance of sharing personal information
2. Appreciation and benefits of LBS
3. Secondary use of personal information
4. Perceived intrusion of LBS
5. Perceived surveillance through LBS
6. Perceived ease of use of LBS
7. Perceived usefulness

Additionally, further questions about trust in the GDPR are asked in order to assess if higher privacy literacy is associated with higher trust in the GDPR. Further questions have been asked about the general usage of LBS in various contexts. Questions about demographic properties finalize the survey.

The survey was conducted via Survey Sparrow[1]. Overall, 155 responses have been received with most of the participants being between 25-44 years old with a bias towards female participants (64%). The majority of participants were German (79%) while the other 21% participants mainly came from the United States, United Kingdom, Canada, India, and Pakistan. The study was conducted on a voluntary basis and the participants did not receive a reimbursement for their participation, thus a balanced sample with an equal number of participants from each country could not be gathered[2].

4   Results

The main focus of the analysis is examining the influence of privacy literacy on privacy concern, privacy attitudes, and trust in governmental regulations such as the GDPR. The comparison of Germany and other countries is carried out, but with caution due to the biased sample sizes between participants from other countries and Germany.

For the comparison of privacy literacy, the dimension addressing questions regarding the GDPR is only taken into account by participants from European countries. For each correct answer, the participants received a point. For wrong answers, no points are withdrawn or given, points are only given for correct answers. When comparing Germany and the other countries, the GDPR-related questions have been excluded for both groups, such that only 15 questions remained. A Mann-Whitney U test was conducted and shows significant differences between privacy literacy in other countries and Germany (U=2783.5, p= .0007). The median for privacy literacy in other countries is 12 out of 20 possible points and for Germany, the median is 14 (see Fig. 1). Furthermore, significant differences can be found when comparing the perceived usefulness of

---

[1] https://surveysparrow.com/.

[2] The study has been conducted in accordance with the guidelines proposed by the ethics committee of Faculty IV of the Technische Universität Berlin.

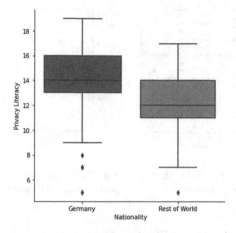

Fig. 1. Privacy literacy score Germany vs other countries.

LBS between Germany and other countries (U=1561, $p = 0.045$): The perceived usefulness is higher in other countries (median 3.6) than in Germany (median 3.3). Further significant differences can be found for the perceived intrusion (U=2551.5, p= .017) where German participants have a significantly higher perception of intrusion (median 4.0) than in other countries (median 3.5).

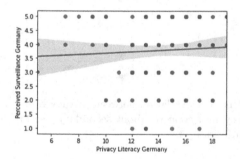
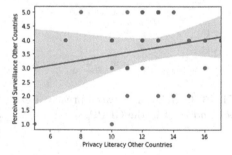

Fig. 2. Perceived surveillance and privacy literacy in Germany.

Fig. 3. Perceived surveillance and privacy literacy in other countries.

Additionally, in Fig. 2 and in Fig. 3 it can be observed that privacy literacy is more positively correlated with perceived surveillance in other countries than Germany. This indicates that with higher privacy literacy perceived surveillance increases as well in other countries whereas in Germany, there seems to be no association between privacy literacy and perceived surveillance.

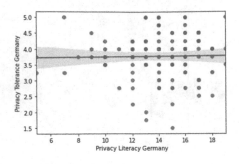

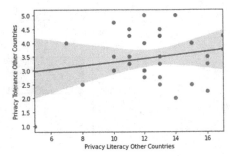

Fig. 4. Tolerance towards data sharing and privacy literacy in Germany.

Fig. 5. Tolerance towards data sharing and privacy literacy in other countries.

Similarly, this can be seen in Fig. 4 and in Fig. 5 where privacy literacy seems to have no association with the tolerance of data sharing compared to other countries. Further positive correlations can be observed between privacy literacy and trust in the GDPR and privacy concern (see Figs. 6 and 7).

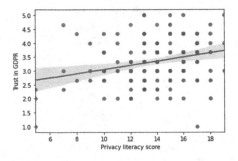

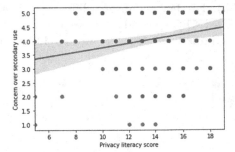

Fig. 6. Correlation between privacy literacy and trust in the GDPR.

Fig. 7. Correlation between privacy literacy and concern about secondary use of information.

Here, it is visible that higher privacy literacy influences trust in the GDPR but also results in higher privacy concern. In Fig. 8 the strength of the association between privacy literacy and privacy attitudes can be observed. Significant correlations between privacy literacy and privacy attitudes are also summarized in Table 1.

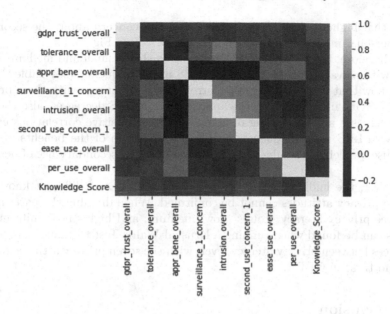

Fig. 8. Correlation plot between privacy literacy and privacy attitudes.

The analysis of the responses shows that there is a significant positive correlation between privacy literacy and trust in the GDPR (Spearman rank correlation: $r(153) = .27$, p $= .0006$), indicating if privacy literacy increases also trust in the GDPR increases (see Fig. 6). A further positive correlation can be observed between privacy literacy and concern about the secondary use of personal information (Spearman rank correlation: $r(153) = .89$, p $= .018$). Therefore, we can

Table 1. Correlation Analysis of Privacy Attitudes and Demographics (DF $= 153$)

Variable 1	Variable 2	Corr. Coef	P-value	Strength
Appreciation	Age	−.30	.001	Small
Appreciation	LBS usage frequency	.37	.001	Medium
Concern over secondary use	Age	.23	.003	Small
Ease of use	Age	−.19	.013	Small
Ease of use	LBS usage frequency	.23	.003	Small
Intrusion	LBS usage frequency	−.25	.002	Small
Intrusion	Age	.26	.001	Small
Perceived usefulness of LBS	LBS usage frequency	.23	.003	Small
Surveillance	LBS usage frequency	−.19	.016	Small
Surveillance	Age	.23	.004	Small
Tolerance	Age	.26	.001	Small

assume that higher privacy literacy leads to more concern about the secondary use of personal information in the domain of LBS (see Fig. 7).

Furthermore, the Spearman rank correlation shows small and medium correlations with privacy attitudes, age, and LBS usage frequency (see Table 1). The results show that there is a negative correlation between age with three privacy attitudes. With increasing age, the appreciation of LBS decreases, also the ease of use decreases and the feeling of being observed. Positive correlations can be found with LBS usage frequency with an appreciation of the benefits of LBS, ease of use, perceived usefulness, and concern over the secondary use of personal data.

However, the findings of [17] regarding the influence of different knowledge levels on privacy attitudes cannot be confirmed. When dividing the participants into three privacy literacy groups - low, medium, and high - no significant differences can be found when running a Kruskal-Wallis-Test to examine potential differences between privacy literacy levels with the seven privacy attitude dimensions and trust in GDPR.

5   Conclusion

In this study, we conducted a survey with 155 participants to examine the influence of privacy literacy on privacy attitudes towards LBS and the usage frequency of LBS. Overall, the analysis showed that there are significant differences between Germany and other countries with respect to privacy literacy and privacy literacy has an effect on certain privacy attitudes. Moreover, we can observe that privacy literacy does not have a considerable influence on privacy attitudes, except trust in the GDPR, and privacy concern of secondary use of personal information. The privacy attitudes showed small and medium correlations, especially with age and LBS usage frequency. Thus the research question can be answered as follows:

RQ1: What is the influence of privacy literacy on privacy attitudes? Privacy literacy can be positively associated with higher trust in the GDPR and the privacy attitude concern over the secondary use of information. However, the influence on the other privacy attitudes is very low and does not show any significant results.

RQ2: What is the influence of privacy attitudes on LBS usage frequency? The perceived usefulness of LBS is positively correlated with the appreciation of LBS and perceived ease of use. Interestingly, the higher the LBS usage frequency the lower participants perceive intrusion and surveillance.

RQ3: Does privacy literacy significantly differ between Germany and other countries? There are significant differences in privacy literacy between Germany and other countries whereas Germany has a significantly higher privacy literacy score. Further significant differences can be found in the perceived usefulness of LBS and perceived intrusion when using LBS between Germany and other countries.

However, previous findings from [17] cannot be confirmed as the analysis of privacy literacy levels did not show any significant differences with respect to the seven privacy attitudes and trust in GDPR. For future research, the influence of the context can be more closely examined, by considering concepts such as the theory of *contextual integrity, ch10nissenbaum2019contextual*, where five parameters need to be considered. Namely, (1) the sender, (2) the recipient, (3) the subject, (4) the information type, (5) and the transmission principle. Within this research, only the context parameter of information type (LBS) has been considered. Moreover, in further research larger sample sizes and more balanced samples from the countries of interest are required, which allows for more certainty to infer conclusions from the analysis.

Aknowledgments. Special thanks to Vinay Dev Mudgil for his support in implementing and running the survey.

Appendix

A: Privacy Attitudes Questionnaire

The questionnaire is based on questionnaires developed by [21], examining LBS and behavioural responses, [4] examining the privacy paradox about privacy and security behaviour in relation to privacy knowledge, and [27] assessing privacy perception for fitness trackers. The answers are given on a 5-point Likert scale, where 1 indicates *strongly disagree* and 5 *strongly agree*.

1. Tolerance
   (a) I need to disclose too much personal data for a useful use of location-based apps like maps, finding the nearest place of interest.
   (b) It is too easy for third parties to get access to my personal data when I use location-based apps.
   (c) There is a risk that the provider of location-based apps abuses my data for advertising/consumption purposes.
   (d) The use of location-based apps is related to a higher fraud risk than the use of other apps.
2. Appreciation
   (a) The benefits gained by using location-based services outweigh the privacy risks.
   (b) The benefits I get from using location-based services are worth giving away my personal information.
3. Secondary Use of Personal Information
   (a) I am concerned that mobile apps may use my personal information for other purposes without notifying me or getting my authorization
4. Perceived Intrusion
   (a) I feel that as a result of my using location-based services, others know about me more than I am comfortable with.

(b) I believe that as a result of my using location-based services, information about me that I consider private is now more readily available to others than I would want.
5. Perceived Surveillance
   (a) I am concerned that location-based services allow for monitoring my mobility patterns via smartphones.
6. Perceived Ease of Use
   (a) My interaction with the location-based services like finding directions or finding the nearest restaurant is clear and understandable.
   (b) Interacting with location-based services does not require a lot of mental effort. location-based services like maps, and finding the nearest restaurant are easy to use.
7. Perceived Usefulness
   (a) Using the location-based services, I find places of interest more quickly.
   (b) Using the location-based services, I receive personalized offers.
   (c) I like the apps that track my location to provide services like roadside assistance.
8. GDPR Perception
   (a) General Data Protection Regulation (GDPR) protects our online privacy and enables us to have greater control over, and ownership of, our personal data.
   (b) General Data Protection Regulation (GDPR) requires that organizations implement an appropriate level of security to prevent data loss, information leaks, and other unauthorized data processing operations.
   (c) We should trust GDPR while doing shopping and conducting all manner of information-baring tasks online.

B: Privacy Literacy Questionnaire

The OPLIS Questionnaire was developed by [29] and contains four dimensions (the correct answers are marked as bold):

1. Knowledge about institutional practices
   (a) The National Security Agency (NSA) accesses only public user data, which are visible for anyone. (True/**false**/don't know)
   (b) Social network site operators (e.g. Facebook) also collect and process information about non-users of the social network site. (**True**/false/don't know)
   (c) User data that are collected by social network site operators (e.g. Facebook) are deleted after five years. (True/**false**/don't know)
   (d) Companies combine users' data traces collected from different websites to create user profiles. (**True**/false/don't know)
   (e) E-mails are commonly passed over several computers before they reach the actual receiver. (**True**/false/don't know)
2. Knowledge about technical aspects of data protection

(a) What does the term "browsing history" stand for? In the browsing history...
   i. **...the URLs of visited websites are stored.**
   ii. ...cookies from visited websites are stored.
   iii. ...potentially infected websites are stored separately.
   iv. ..different information about the user are stored, depending on the browser type.

(b) What is a "cookie"?
   i. **A text file that enables websites to recognize a user when revisiting.**
   ii. A program to disable data collection from online operators.
   iii. A computer virus that can be transferred after connecting to a website.
   iv. A browser plugin that ensures safe online surfing.

(c) What does the term "cache" mean?
   i. **A buffer memory that accelerates surfing on the Internet.**
   ii. A program that specifically collects information about an Internet user and passes them on to third parties.
   iii. A program, that copies data on an external hard drive to protect against data theft.
   iv. A browser plugin that encrypts data transfer when surfing online.

(d) What is a "trojan"? A trojan is a computer program, that...
   i. **...is disguised as a useful application, but fulfills another function in the background.**
   ii. ... protects a computer from viruses and other malware.
   iii. ... was developed for fun and has no specific function
   iv. . .. caused damage as a computer virus in the 90ies but doesn't exist anymore.

(e) What is a "firewall"?
   i **A fallback system that will protect the computer from unwanted web attacks.**
   ii An outdated protection program against computer viruses.
   iii A browser plugin that ensures safe online surfing.
   iv A new technical development that prevents data loss in case of a short circuit.

3. Knowledge about data protection law
  (a) Forwarding anonymous user data for the purpose of market research is legal in the European Union. (**True**/false/don't know)
  (b) The EU-Directive on data protection...
    i. **... has to be implemented into national data protection acts by every member state.**
    ii. ... does not exist yet.
    iii. ... functions as a transnational EU-data protection act.
    iv. ... solely serves as a non-committal guideline for the data protection acts of the member states.

 (c) In Germany the same standard GTC applies to all SNS. Any deviations have to be indicated. (True/**false**/don't know)

 (d) According to German law, users of online applications that collect and process personal data have the right to inspect which information about them is stored. (**True**/false/don't know)

 (e) Informational self-determination is...

  i ...**a fundamental right of German citizens.**

  ii ... a philosophical term.

  iii ... the central claim of data processors.

  iv ...the central task of the German Federal Data Protection Commissioner...

4. Knowledge about data protection strategies

 (a) Tracking of one's own internet is made more difficult if one deletes browser information (e.g. cookies, cache, browser history) regularly. (**True**/false/don't know)

 (b) Surfing in the private browsing mode can prevent the reconstruction of your surfing behavior because no browser information is stored. (**True**/false/don't know)

 (c) Using false names or pseudonyms can make it difficult to identify someone on the Internet. (**True**/false/don't know)

 (d) Even though It-experts can crack difficult passwords, it is more sensible to use a combination of letters, numbers and signs as passwords than words, names, or simple combinations of numbers. (**True**/false/don't know)

 (e) In order to prevent access to personal data, one should use various passwords and user names for different online applications and change them frequently. (**True**/false/don't know)

References

1. Almuhimedi, H., et al.: Your location has been shared 5,398 times! a field study on mobile app privacy nudging. In: Proceedings of the 33rd Annual ACM Conference on Human Factors in Computing Systems, pp. 787–796 (2015)

2. Anderson, M.: More Americans using smartphones for getting directions, streaming tv (2016)

3. Barth, S., De Jong, M.D.: The privacy paradox-investigating discrepancies between expressed privacy concerns and actual online behavior-a systematic literature review. Telematics Inform. **34**(7), 1038–1058 (2017)

4. Barth, S., de Jong, M.D., Junger, M., Hartel, P.H., Roppelt, J.C.: Putting the privacy paradox to the test: online privacy and security behaviors among users with technical knowledge, privacy awareness, and financial resources. Telematics Inform. **41**, 55–69 (2019)

5. Chekol, A.G., Fufa, M.S.: A survey on next location prediction techniques, applications, and challenges. EURASIP J. Wirel. Commun. Netw. **2022**(1), 1–24 (2022). https://doi.org/10.1186/s13638-022-02114-6

6. Crossler, R.E., Bélanger, F.: The mobile privacy-security knowledge gap model: Understanding behaviors. Hawaii International Conference on System Sciences (2017)

7. Crossler, R.E., Bélanger, F.: Why would i use location-protective settings on my smartphone? motivating protective behaviors and the existence of the privacy knowledge-belief gap. Inf. Syst. Res. **30**(3), 995–1006 (2019)

8. De Luca, A., Das, S., Ortlieb, M., Ion, I., Laurie, B.: Expert and {Non-Expert} attitudes towards (secure) instant messaging. In: Twelfth Symposium on Usable Privacy and Security (SOUPS 2016), pp. 147–157 (2016)

9. Fiesler, C., et al.: What (or who) is public? privacy settings and social media content sharing. In: Proceedings of the 2017 ACM Conference on Computer Supported Cooperative Work and Social Computing, pp. 567–580 (2017)

10. Furini, M.: Users behavior in location-aware services: digital natives versus digital immigrants. Advances in Human-Computer Interaction 2014 (2014)

11. Gabriele, S., Chiasson, S.: Understanding fitness tracker users' security and privacy knowledge, attitudes and behaviours. In: Proceedings of the 2020 CHI Conference on Human Factors in Computing Systems, pp. 1–12 (2020)

12. Gamarra Acosta, M., et al.: Privacy perception in location-based services for mobile devices in the university community of the north coast of Colombia (2019)

13. Harborth, D., Pape, S.: How privacy concerns, trust and risk beliefs, and privacy literacy influence users' intentions to use privacy-enhancing technologies: The case of tor. ACM SIGMIS Database: DATABASE Adv. Inf. Syst. **51**(1), 51–69 (2020)

14. Hoofnagle, C.J., King, J., Li, S., Turow, J.: How different are young adults from older adults when it comes to information privacy attitudes and policies? Available at SSRN 1589864 (2010)

15. Jiang, H., Li, J., Zhao, P., Zeng, F., Xiao, Z., Iyengar, A.: Location privacy-preserving mechanisms in location-based services: a comprehensive survey. ACM Computing Surveys (CSUR) **54**(1), 1–36 (2021)

16. Kang, R., Dabbish, L., Fruchter, N., Kiesler, S.: {"My} data just goes {Everywhere:"} user mental models of the internet and implications for privacy and security. In: Eleventh Symposium on Usable Privacy and Security (SOUPS 2015), pp. 39–52 (2015)

17. Kraus, L., Wechsung, I., Möller, S.: A comparison of privacy and security knowledge and privacy concern as influencing factors for mobile protection behavior. In: Workshop on Privacy Personas and Segmentation, p. 2014 (2014)

18. Lind, F., Boomgaarden, H.G.: What we do and don't know: a meta-analysis of the knowledge gap hypothesis. Ann. Int. Commun. Assoc. **43**(3), 210–224 (2019)

19. Mekovec, R., Vrček, N.: Factors that influence internet users' privacy perception. In: Proceedings of the ITI 2011, 33rd International Conference on Information Technology Interfaces, pp. 227–232. IEEE (2011)

20. Nissenbaum, H.: Contextual integrity up and down the data food chain. Theoret. Inquir. Law **20**(1), 221–256 (2019)

21. Palos-Sanchez, P.R., Hernandez-Mogollon, J.M., Campon-Cerro, A.M.: The behavioral response to location based services: an examination of the influence of social and environmental benefits, and privacy. Sustainability **9**(11), 1988 (2017)

22. Park, Y.J.: Digital literacy and privacy behavior online. Commun. Res. **40**(2), 215–236 (2013)

23. Park, Y.J., Campbell, S.W., Kwak, N.: Affect, cognition and reward: predictors of privacy protection online. Comput. Hum. Behav. **28**(3), 1019–1027 (2012)

24. Pelet, J.É., Taieb, B.: Privacy protection on social networks: a scale for measuring users' attitudes in France and the USA. In: Rocha, Á., Correia, A.M., Adeli, H., Reis, L.P., Costanzo, S. (eds.) WorldCIST 2017. AISC, vol. 570, pp. 763–773. Springer, Cham (2017). https://doi.org/10.1007/978-3-319-56538-5_77

25. Poikela, M., Kaiser, F.: It is a topic that confuses me-privacy perceptions in usage of location-based applications. In: European Workshop on Usable Security (EuroUSEC) (2016)
26. Poikela, M.E.: Theoretical background to location privacy. In: Perceived Privacy in Location-Based Mobile System. TSTS, pp. 13–32. Springer, Cham (2020). https://doi.org/10.1007/978-3-030-34171-8_2
27. Sanchez, O.R., Torre, I., He, Y., Knijnenburg, B.P.: A recommendation approach for user privacy preferences in the fitness domain. User Model. User-Adap. Inter. **30**(3), 513–565 (2020)
28. Skirpan, M.W., Yeh, T., Fiesler, C.: What's at stake: characterizing risk perceptions of emerging technologies. In: Proceedings of the 2018 CHI Conference on Human Factors in Computing Systems, pp. 1–12 (2018)
29. Trepte, S., et al.: Do people know about privacy and data protection strategies? towards the "online privacy literacy scale"(oplis). In: Gutwirth, S., Leenes, R., de Hert, P. (eds.) Reforming European Data Protection Law. Law, Governance and Technology Series, vol. 20, pp. 333–365. Springer (2015). https://doi.org/10.1007/978-94-017-9385-8_14
30. Urban, J.M., Hoofnagle, C.J.: The privacy pragmatic as privacy vulnerable. In: Symposium on Usable Privacy and Security (SOUPS 2014) Workshop on Privacy Personas and Segmentation (PPS) (2014)

Privacy and Data Protection in the Era of Recommendation Systems: A Postphenomenological Approach

Ana Fernández Inguanzo(✉) 🆔

Law, Science, Technology and Society Research Group (LSTS), Brussels School of Governance,
Vrije Universiteit Brussel, Bd de la Plaine 2, 1050 Ixelles Brussels, Belgium
ana.fernandez.inguanzo@vub.be

Abstract. Privacy and data protection are two fundamental rights. As complex concepts, they lend themselves to various interpretations aimed at protecting individuals. In this paper, I explore the concepts of 'privacy' and 'data protection' directly related to the protection of 'identity'. I argue that the ability for privacy and data protection law to protect identity is being challenged by recommendation systems. In particular, I explore how recommendation systems are continuously *influencing* people based on what can be predicted about them, while the legal tools that we have do not fully protect individuals in this regard. This paper aims at breaching this gap, by focusing on the study of Porcedda, who examines four different notions of privacy related to identity under article 7 of the European Charter of Fundamental Rights. Through the huge capacity for analytics that draws on a lawful combination of consent and non-personal data, this paper examines why data protection regulation does not, in fact, fully protect individuals. In this paper it is explored how the notion of privacy, understood as the protection of identity, is especially relevant to understand the limitations of data protection law, and I explore postphenomenology to help us better contextualize the relationship between identity and recommendation systems.

Keywords: privacy · data protection · identity · philosophy · postphenomenology

1 Introduction: The Negative *Influence* of Recommendation Systems

Digital developments in the 21st century that use Big Data Technologies to display content – especially the use of algorithms (Machine Learning or Artificial Intelligence) in social networks – are challenging current privacy and data protection laws. They are labelled 'recommendation systems' and refer to technologies that categorize and recommend content based on massive amounts of data. Their increased capacity, power, and analysis in recent years poses new risks to the privacy field. This is not new, but in recent years, the impact of recommendation systems has proven to be increasingly

© IFIP International Federation for Information Processing 2023
Published by Springer Nature Switzerland AG 2023
F. Bieker et al. (Eds.): Privacy and Identity 2022, IFIP AICT 671, pp. 133–147, 2023.
https://doi.org/10.1007/978-3-031-31971-6_11

powerful with the potential for significant negative consequences to individuals and to society. In 2001, Sunstein argued how the Internet creates 'echo chambers' [1], where individuals are constantly exposed to conforming opinions, thus creating a feedback loop that reinforce pre-established views. A decade later, Pariser coined the term 'filter bubble' [2] to denominate how previous behaviours online determine the information that will be shown in the future, thus similarly reproducing circular content. For example, in politics individuals receive information explicitly about one political party or ideology that is determined by previous searches, which leads to content polarisation and reducing the capacity to make informed decisions in elections. The highly popular and controversial company of Cambridge Analytica [3] was able to retrieve information of millions of Facebook users to target personalised advertisements, and influence their opinions in elections. This is what Christopher Wylie, former employee of Cambridge Analytica [4], refers in his book as 'computer psychology', the use of psychology and software engineering that create tools to influence groups in social networks through algorithmic recommendations.

These types of recommendations (based on data) influence people's views through algorithmic and profiling systems that, by gathering (big) amounts of data, *control* or *influence* what people see by categorising and classifying the order of newsfeeds. Researchers have shown how Facebook algorithms were responsible for spreading 'divisive' content that helped the growth of German extremists' groups [5]. Even more, these systems have accelerated the creation of misinformation and fake news, even more problematic today with the prevalence of Covid misinformation [6, 7]. Yet, some of these issues are not only related to the gathering of data, but also to content-moderation in social networks. Although these issues are not only limited to the gathering of data, they are also always related to it. In fact, the algorithms used in recommendation systems are based on personalization, where individuals' data is necessary. These systems *influence* or at the very least *steer* people's opinions, as well as affect groups and communities, by for example reinforcing certain stereotypes [8], and this is only possible through the gathering of data. There are increasingly more personalized websites that use recommendation systems such as Spotify, Amazon, or Netflix, the latter uses algorithms to study groups and communities for content production [9]. Not only individuals are affected by these systems also group analysis reinforce or steer individuals. And thus, the vicious circle continues.

This so-called *influence* is broader than politics and runs deep in every recommendation system that uses data for content delivery. The Facebook Contagion Study [10] conducted by the platform in 2012 allowed to test manipulative effects on news feeds. The result proved that it is possible to influence emotions of a person by tailoring specific content – both negative or positive – in user's newsfeeds, where the more positive content led to a more positive emotions and shared content, and equally the negative content led to a more depressing and negative content-sharing.

Another example is found with YouTube's algorithms [11], which among other things, analyse data to maintain users engagement, and one of the variables was found to give 'speculation' a high rank, thus prioritizing these types of videos on the newsfeed due to its ability to keep users interested. The result was that YouTube was promoting or recommending conspiracy-theory videos, such as those claiming that the earth is flat [12].

There are plenty of examples in which algorithms and recommendation systems have a negative influence in society by spreading misinformation and polarizing content. These harms also include the exploitation of user's interests and vulnerabilities to sell products [13] such as the development of misleading patterns, sometimes referred to as 'dark patterns' [14], that make users take certain pre-determined actions. These algorithms take a step further, rather than merely analyzing present behavior they also try to predict the future, as if they could analyze our future thoughts, aiming to *influence* future actions:

> "Instead of merely offering advertisers the ability to target people based on demographics and consumer preferences, Facebook instead offers the ability to target them based on how they will behave, what they will buy, and what they will think" [15].

In this paper, I do not focus on the benefits of these technologies that classify and share content – which are in fact necessary to categorize the huge amount of content produced every day in the digital world [16]. I focus on the negative implications, where I study how recommendation systems can lead to negative consequences for individuals. For example, by retrieving gender data, it has been proven how algorithms exclude women from seeing similar job opportunities than men in social network's newsfeeds [17]; other studies also show a more subliminal *influence* of advertisements on how women see themselves, represented as sexual objects, based on the continuous ads or content/recommendations they receive [18], and the list goes on.

Algorithmic recommendation systems do not only influence the advertisement industry (e.g., what people buy), but also far more sensitive choices such as people's political views, the jobs they have access to, or how they perceive themselves (e.g., their body image, their gender) with implications for society and culture (e.g., TV content-creation, or health information). Nevertheless, the main regulatory tool in the European Union that protects against the misuse of personal data is the General Data Protection Regulation (hereafter GDPR). In practice, the examples above are lawful under the GDPR, thus proves limited to account for these intrusions or influences in the era of recommendation systems. Nonetheless, the European Data Protection Board (EDPB) an independent organism that contributes to the consistent application of data protection rules, considers dark patterns a violation of the regulation [14]. Yet, the issues are more profound than tricking people (e.g., with language or misleading pop-up boxes) to accept cookies. It affects opinions and thoughts of individuals constantly interacting with recommendation systems. In this paper, I aim to clarify the gap between data protection law and the lack of protection to this negative *influence* of recommendation systems over individuals. In the next sections I study what is this *influence* – how it is produced, why it is important and why it should be protected in the legal field.

The paper is structured as follows: Sect. 2 gives an overview of the fundamental rights to privacy and data protection, of their differences, and the limitations to protect individuals with recommendation systems. Section 3 focuses on the necessity to look at a definition of the right to privacy, understood as the protection of identity. Section 4 begins to explore the concept of identity as interconnected, following postphenomenologist, and the importance to include individuals in how recommendation systems co-shape their identities, and the necessity to build legal tools to that protects them in this respect. Section 5 offers a discussion and conclusion on these issues.

2 Privacy and Data Protection: Two Separate Fundamental Rights

Privacy and data protection are two different, but connected, fundamental rights in the European Union. Historically, these two rights are interconnected [19]. Privacy as a human right appeared first in 1948 when the term 'privacy' took a legal dimension with the Universal Declaration of Human Rights (UDHR) under article 12[1] Table 1. Privacy also emerged as a fundamental right under the European Charter of Fundamental Rights in 2009 (hereafter EU Charter), that was a legally binding instrument in the EU[2]. The right to *personal* data protection was also given a separate status as a human right under article 8 [20]. The latter was a process evolving from different national laws[3], leading to the GDPR that was put into effect in 2018 [23], where questions regarding privacy in the digital world are directed towards the protection of personal data. Nonetheless, these two rights are connected, if only historically, such as the Directive 95/46/EC[4] of 1995 commonly known as the 'Data Protection Directive' that was after replaced by the GDPR, aimed at protecting individuals "right to privacy with respect to the processing of personal data" (Art.1(1)). On the contrary, in the GDPR there is no mention of the word 'privacy', which focuses on the right to data protection (Article 1(2)).

In practice, the separation of two fundamental rights creates a dichotomy where historically both concepts have also been interpreted separately. Privacy is explained by different scholars as a social value because it reduces the capacity of the government to influence or coerce individuals from external influence [21], understood as self-determination, autonomy and freedom of choice [22]. Going back to the famous 1890's article by Warren and Brandeis that first coined the term 'right to privacy', it was referred to as the right to 'be let alone', which at the time was threatened by the development of instant-cameras and gossip newspapers. Hardly would these scholars have imagined technologies that analyze your entire behavior and personality traits, such as people's political preferences, their IQ or emotions, or decide what movies or even jobs are good for you. Since then, the privacy field has changed significantly with new digital technologies. Nonetheless, one hundred years ago Warren and Brandeis were defending the importance to protect people's psychological traits, related to the protection of

---

[1] This gave 'privacy' the acknowledgement of a human right; and inspired the creation in 1950 of article 8 of the European Convention of Human Rights (ECHR). Article 17 of the International Covenant on Civil and Political Rights (ICCPR) of 1976 followed, which is the first legally binding instrument in Europe related to privacy, as it refers to an international treaty which was joined by 180 states, however it was not legally binding for the European Union.

[2] Specifically, the right to privacy in EU law was not legally binding until the Lisbon Treaty in the same year 2009.

[3] Broadly speaking, national laws started to emerge, not regarding the concept of privacy but data laws. In 1973 Sweden created the first national privacy law named 'Data Act', followed by the German Federal Data Protection Act of 1978.

[4] Directive 95/46/EC of the European Parliament and of the Council of 24 October 1995 on the protection of individuals with regard to the processing of personal data and on the free movement of such data, OJ L 281, 23.11.1995.

thoughts or feelings or as they put it "the protection afforded to thoughts, sentiments, and emotions, expressed through the medium of writing or of the arts [...] is merely an instance of the enforcement of the more general right of the individual to be let alone" [22].

The two concepts developed differently from the understanding of the 'protection of feelings and emotions', autonomy, self-determination or 'to be let alone', and as the fundamental right to privacy Table 1 to a modern conception of privacy in the digital world, understood as control over *personal information*. In 1967 Alan Westin conceived the modern notion of privacy as "the claim of individuals, groups, or institutions to determine for themselves when, how, and to what extent information about them is communicated to others" [23]. These two notions are different from each other, the latter being a more practical approach towards considering data something that can be exchanged and controlled, that led to the GDPR [24], while privacy has a broader scope and refers to the protection of "private, family life, home and communications".

There is a question that remains – why are the (negative) examples exposed in Sect. 1 linked to the use of data in recommendation systems, namely the negative impact on gender, filter bubbles, reinforcement of stereotypes etc., still lawful? The GDPR is the main regulation that exists today[5] to protect people in this regard, yet it is limited, as it only refers to *personal* data[6] and leaves every other data outside of the scope of the law. It is relevant to highlight that the GDPR still considers pseudonymized data personal (Article 4(5)), leading authors to consider that it has a broader scope of what 'personal' is therefore making GDPR applicable. However, in practical terms, it is all allowed by the legal basis[7] of 'consent'. The GDPR offers legal bases under which it is possible to gather personal data – one of them being 'consent'. According to the GDPR, consent must be: freely given, specific, informed, unambiguous and clear (Article 4(11)). Social Networks commonly gather consent to analyze data and create recommendations that are tailored and personalized to individuals. In practice, this is achieved through long statements in forms of Privacy Policies and Cookies. This is rather contradictory, as normally these are long pieces of text that people do not understand nor have time to read. Such as one sentence of Facebook's data policy warns users that it may "use the information we receive about you... for internal operations, including troubleshooting, data analysis, testing, research and service improvement" [26]. Language is complex, far from specific, and lacks clarity. Similarly, the examples in Sect. 1 of this paper where *influence* over ideologies, gender and circular content exist lawfully, this is achieved without protection, through GDPR's consent.

---

[5] There will be new EU regulations such as Data Act or AI Act that will deal with non-personal data, but these are not enforced yet and refer to a data transformation by 2030. [25] https://www.europarl.europa.eu/factsheets/en/sheet/64/digital-agenda-for-europe.Data Governance Act has been approved in 2022 but will only be enforced in 2023. And it only applies to the facilitation of public data sources. See: https://digital-strategy.ec.europa.eu/en/policies/data-governance-act. In addition, especially relevant for this paper is the Digital Service Package that contains two regulations: Digital Service Act (DSA) and Digital Markets Act (DMA), that will enter into force in 2024: https://digital-strategy.ec.europa.eu/en/policies/digital-services-act-package.

[6] Article 4(1) GDPR.

[7] Article 6 GDPR.

Table 1. Conceptual graphic of the concept of 'Privacy' as a fundamental right

Art 12 Universal Declaration of Human Rights (UDHR, 1948) 1. No one shall be subjected to arbitrary or unlawful interference with his privacy, family, home or correspondence, nor to unlawful attacks on his honour and reputation 2. Everyone has the right to the protection of the law against such interference or attacks	Art. 8 European Convention on Human Rights (ECHR, 1950) [overlaps to art.12 UDHR] 1. Everyone has the right to respect for his private and family life, his home and his correspondence 2. There shall be no interference by a public authority with the exercise of this right except such as is in accordance with the law and is necessary in a democratic society in the interests of national security, public safety or the economic well-being of the country, for the prevention of disorder or crime, for the protection of health or morals, or for the protection of the rights and freedoms of others
Art. 17 International Covenant on Civil and Political Rights (ICCPR, 1976) 1. No one shall be subjected to arbitrary or unlawful interference with his privacy, family, home or correspondence, nor to unlawful attacks on his honour and reputation 2. Everyone has the right to the protection of the law against such interference or attacks	European Charter of Fundamental Rights (EU Charter, 2009) [overlaps with art. 8 ECHR]: Article 7 - Everyone has the right to respect for his or her private and family life, home and communications Article 8, - 1. Everyone has the right to the protection of personal data concerning him or her. 2. Such data must be processed fairly for specified purposes and on the basis of the consent of the person concerned or some other legitimate basis laid down by law. Everyone has the right of access to data which has been collected concerning him or her, and the right to have it rectified. 3. Compliance with these rules shall be subject to control by an independent authority

In addition, many authors like Solove warn that privacy as a fundamental right and not only data protection is necessary to protect against the possible threats to new socio-economic and technological developments to protect human 'self-determination' from external influences and new developments. In this line, Solove explains the complexity of this term [27] highlighting the necessity to understand privacy as "the capacity of the human subject to keep and develop his personality in a manner that allows him to fully participate in society without however being induced to conform his thoughts, beliefs, behaviours and preferences to those thoughts, beliefs, behaviours and preferences held by the majority". Following this rationale, privacy protects against the misuse or *influence* over the thoughts of individuals[8]. In the next section, I will focus on the relation between privacy and thought processes with the concept of 'identity'. These two concepts are

---

[8] Herein lies another path, which merits further exploration in the future: could the fundamental right to 'freedom of thought, conscience and religion (Article 9, EU Charter) also be considered

interrelated, and I will clarify how the concept of privacy in the digital sphere refer to the protection of thoughts, and the necessity for data protection to also account for it.

3 Privacy and Identity

The fundamental right to personal data protection, and the GDPR, has proven to be limited to protect individuals against the *influence* of recommendation systems. This lack of protection has been explained in the literature as an issue with the limited scope, arguing that all types of data should be considered personal as it always relates to an individual [28]. This is also what has been accounted for the necessity for 'group privacy', advocates have claimed that groups (or group profiling) should also be part of a regulatory landscape [29], but also framed as discriminatory algorithms, and we should aim for anti-discrimination law in algorithmic profiling [30], the latter leading to algorithmic governance. Individual (personal) data protection is therefore not enough to protect us against the (negative) *influence* of recommendation systems.

The fundamental right to privacy shares more light on this issue. Porcedda [31] has coined the term the 'four limbs of privacy' to explain the fundamental right to privacy under article 7 of the EU Charter Table 1. She considers privacy as an "umbrella term" that contains 'four limbs' related to the protection of four different sections: (1) private life (2) family life, (3) home (4) communications. In her work, the author shows the importance of identity as an intrinsic value of privacy: "I ideally belong in a group of authors that consider privacy instrumental to the development of identity/personhood based on intimacy and leading to autonomy"[9]. Porcedda's analysis shows that protecting privacy is in fact, protecting people's identities, and her work supports the benefits of having two separate rights, a more practical approach of data protection[10] "both rights, in fact, are instrumental in fostering personhood, one's unique identity, protected as an expression of dignity, and enabling autonomy as the two rights emerged out of modernity"[11]. Porcedda names it 'one synergy', both rights supporting each other. However, the scholar does not explore[12] the lack of identity protection in practice with secondary law GDPR; and how it should change regarding new development of (big) data technologies, as exposed in Sect. 1 of this paper, especially with recommendation systems. The multiple dimensions of the right to privacy have also been exposed by several scholars and have been part of the EU Court of Justice decisions, yet Porcedda's analysis helps to frame the issue. In

---

applicable in protecting identity in the digital sphere? – However, in this paper I center the discussion on privacy and data protection as sufficient to understand this issue.

[9] Page 74 – Porcedda, M.G.: Cybersecurity and privacy rights in EU law: moving beyond the trade-off model to appraise the role of technology.

[10] The right to the protection of personal data as related to private life is also one at the core of the European culture of data protection since the German Constitutional Court claimed that we have the "right to informational self-determination".

[11] Page 80 – Porcedda, M.G.: Cybersecurity and privacy rights in EU law: moving beyond the trade-off model to appraise the role of technology.

[12] Although Porcedda's work mentions how the notion of 'personal data' does not account for new inventions of computerized systems and unprecedented (personal) data processing capabilities, such as transborder data flows (p.93).

the following paragraphs, I summarize Porcedda's analysis of the four limbs of privacy, and how these are related to protecting identity, and the limitations of this protection within recommendation systems.

(1)**The right to private life** refers to protect private life since the Greek Polis, where this life was outside the public eye, even claiming that it allowed to benefit male's domination at home [32]. Porcedda shows the change since the Greeks towards the modern concept of privacy, and how it now refers to protecting one's development and personality in a liberal democracy, to forge individual and their free thoughts without external interferences, arguing that privacy allows "… the development of one's personality by making sense of the different roles played by the individual in a community…"[13]. This is a modern consideration of privacy, protecting the freedom to decide and to act in private that can interfere with citizen's thoughts and ideas, and even more so with the importance to avoid fascists or totalitarian regimes in these instances. In this line, to protect private life is not to protect the private space but to protect 'personality or identity' in private spaces, however, this has proven challenging with a computerized society, especially regarding recommendation systems and analytics that decide what content an individual should see, or as it is claimed in a misleading form, it provides you with recommendations tailoring your interests but restraining others.

(2) **The right for family life** also relates to answering the question 'Who am I?'[14]. The author points out how family life must be protected to freely choose who you want to be (private life), but also to decide without external interference who an individual decides to marry, or what type of family you would like to have (family life). The latter is, according to the author, another crucial component to protect *identity*, as identity develops through different stages of socialization that starts with the family[15], and family life is a crucial element should be protected also against fascists or totalitarian systems that want to repress it, such as prohibiting interracial or gay marriages[16]. Following this, recommender systems that allow to *influence or coerce* individuals based on family status or relationship and suggest what movies a person should watch, or what news might be relevant (e.g., a single woman receives different content than a lesbian, different from a person that is gay, and another one from a person that is married), are, at the very least, in some degree of conflict with the right to privacy.

(3) **The right of home;** this should not be confused with the right of *a home*, in contrast, this is also shown to be a place to forge individual identity, a safe place to express one's identity and thoughts without repercussion or interference, far from authoritarian powers. In Porcedda's words "because Article 8 concerns rights of central importance to the individual's identity, self-determination, physical and moral integrity, maintenance

---

[13] Page 83 – Porcedda, M.G.: Cybersecurity and privacy rights in EU law: moving beyond the trade-off model to appraise the role of technology.

[14] Page 87 – Porcedda, M.G.: Cybersecurity and privacy rights in EU law: moving beyond the trade-off model to appraise the role of technology.

[15] Taylor (1989) in Sources of the self argues that the fundamental interaction of identity is of love and family "the increasing possibility to choose freely one's partners, which places love at the heart of the family, makes family life instrumental to the development of identity" (Idem).

[16] Page 88 – Porcedda, M.G.: Cybersecurity and privacy rights in EU law: moving beyond the trade-off model to appraise the role of technology.

of relationships with others and a settled and secure place in the community .... While this is threatened by new technologies, such as a form of 'self-surveillance'[17]. Indeed, this has been shown to be conflicting with new technologies such as recommendation systems that limit the capacity for individuals to have a 'home' due to profiling, analytics and data gathering, where they have little control over profiling.

Finally, (4) right of communications; refers to our thoughts expressed in (written) language, be it through the phone or chats. Identity is expressed through language and must be protected "and can prove particularly harmful for the creation of the individual's image of the self"[18]. This refers particularly to data protection, however new developments in algorithmic data analysis challenge this, where our desires are also based on clicks and likes. Every data point counts, even Facebook is able to gather what a user starts to type but deletes afterwards [33].

The value of Porcedda's work is shown in the intersection of the right to privacy, as in fact a right to identity, with the right to personal data protection. These two rights are important to protect individuals from an abusive intrusion in their *identity, personhood, and autonomy* in support of a "freely developed identity" [31]. Porcedda affirms that both rights act as a synergy and help to protect individuals (in different ways), where data protection allows to 'once this personality is expressed, its integrity can be protected against misuses, even allowing it to change'[19]. As analysed and demonstrated in these past two sections, however, not only is the right to data protection currently inadequate to address the *influence* of recommendation systems, but in addition the influence of recommendation systems threatens the right to privacy, seen as the right to identity.

4   Privacy as Interconnected – Postphenomenology and Identity

Recommendation systems have an influence over the identity of a person. It has been shown to, lawfully, modify through recommendation systems, culturally and individually, the thoughts and opinions of an individual. The extent to which this influence is exerted is up to interpretation. Let us imagine (although it has a similar real-life example [37]) a recommendation system that profiles a woman in her 30s as interested in baby products because of her age, where the recommendation system refers pregnancy products to her, as well as other articles or even videos referring to married people, kids, and the importance of being a mother in a variety of forms across platforms, romantic movies, family-oriented articles that explain the psychology of kids etc. On the contrary, a man in the same age is profiled by a recommendation system as a single-oriented, interested in articles about economy and work performance. There are two different identities, however one cannot be sure how these profiling or analysis affects them in their lives. As de Hert argues "'Being profiled" therefore supplement "being identified" as the real threat to identity.... Because profiles on us will be established on us without us knowing how and when and if they will be used..." [38]. It can be the case that the woman was not

---

[17] Page 90 – Porcedda, M.G.: Cybersecurity and privacy rights in EU law: moving beyond the trade-off model to appraise the role of technology.

[18] Page 91 – Idem.

[19] Page 97 – Porcedda, M.G.: Cybersecurity and privacy rights in EU law: moving beyond the trade-off model to appraise the role of technology.

sure she wanted to become a mother, with these recommendations constantly referring to this type of content, based on profiling, it will perhaps be convinced or feel pressure to become one, while the male in his 30s did not come across this content.

There are impositions or influences in our identity that modify individual thoughts and emotions, and that have repercussions over individuals' perceptions of themselves and their lives, but the nature of identity as something subjective and culturally constructed makes it difficult to pinpoint one single element. In this line, social networks and recommendation systems have created tools to remove dangerous content that can easily be perceived as alarming [39], but not to withdraw general instances such as those based on gender. In this section, I analyze why the nature of identity is a far more interrelated complex than merely understood as a separate digital form, where I consider that post-phenomenology helps to clarify this concept in this digital world of recommendation systems and social networks.

Scholars have warned about how information platforms are a 'massively intermediated environment' that must be addressed [21], and the necessity to control different forms of algorithms as "it configures life by tailoring its conditions of possibility" [36]. However, the concept of identity does not appear in their analysis. Other authors have also coined the term 'digital subject', and refer to a complex relation of human beings, although related to, still separated from the digital [35]. Cheney-Lippold [36] has advocated for a separated 'algorithmic identity' meaning "an identity formation that works through mathematical algorithms to infer categories of identity on otherwise anonymous beings". Similar is the view of scholars [34] that see the character of data protection as dynamic, detached from a person and susceptible to flow. Traditionally, the concept of identity as well as privacy has been explained as socially constructed, as a part of culture and public understanding; even considering social institutions part of the identity of a person [40], technology was also thought as socially constructed [41]. Similarly, authors have considered social networks or algorithms are mere representations of the society that we live in[20].

On the contrary, the field of postphenomenology [42, 43], a field of study in philosophy of technology, argues the necessity to understand technology as a mediated tool, that acts upon the world, influencing or creating (new) interconnected relations. Technology is, in view of postphenomenologists, a co-shaper (co-evolving) with society and with individuals. These authors strongly affirm that there is an agency of technology, and this is especially relevant to understand the influence of new technologies like recommendation systems over the identity of individuals. Following postphenomenologists, I argue that new technological tools, especially recommendation systems, challenge and co-modify the freedom to define the identity of individuals, and in its extent challenge the right to privacy.

Whereas it has been shown how the concept of 'identity' is central to understanding privacy [38], the threat to identity is only stronger in a world where the *influence* of (big) data to study and analyze people is increasing exponentially, and data protection law should account for it. However, there is still a long way until we have regulatory

---

[20] The field of Science and Technology Studies (STS) has traditionally considered technology as socially constructed e.g., Trevor Pich; Langdon Winner.

tools[21] that can protect individuals from this *influence over our identity*, thus making individual's data protection stronger.

Following postphenomenologica perspective, identity should be considered not solely socially constructed, but technologically co-modified: the technology also modifies our own views and relations to the world. While Porcedda argued that "profiling removes the power of individuals to make claims about who they are"[22], this is only one side of the problem, because profiles also co-modify the very own individuals. Identity is not separated from the individual, but is co-shaped by technologies, such as recommendation systems, that influence how we see ourselves and the world. This can lead to reflect of the necessity to give more autonomy of individuals over the profiles being made of them. Going back to the example of the woman in her 30s, perhaps this woman would like to know that she is being profiled as wanting kids and she is being denied of other type of content. But whereas Porcedda showed the importance to protect identity from interference, I also support the necessity to consider how identity is fluid, in constant co-modification by these technologies. People's identities are constantly being influenced by recommendation systems, against traditional social constructivism, individuals do not exist independently of these technologies that use data and algorithms to classify content.

Thus, the importance of data protection law to assess these type of classifications not as outside the individual, but co-modifying people in real life based on their data. Thus, data protection law should have tools to protect not only data, but also the inferences that a person has in real time. On the contrary, if one look at the problem as the necessity for group privacy or algorithmic discrimination become separate from the individual, discrimination is seen as a negative form that should be banned in certain instances or groups should be protected. While in fact, discrimination can vary from individuals, perhaps the 30-year-old woman wants to keep receiving kids' products and related pregnancy information, while other woman will find this to be limiting her possibility to find other career-oriented content. Discrimination can be in many different forms, and can change depending on how identities are developed, or who the person is. If we take the autonomy of individuals to see what is happening with their data, protecting people from discrimination without them being included is not very efficient. In the previous example, a woman in her 30s might be *influenced* to have a child just based on algorithmic profiles because (1) she is a woman (2) she is old enough (3) she likes couples' pictures (4) she likes romantic movies etc. Is she being discriminated based on gender? Is she aware that this is happening? The issue then is framed differently, it is not about discriminatory algorithms, but rather protecting people in the digital sphere from interference on their thoughts or emotions, and in its extent, to develop freely their identity, whereby the importance to give individuals more autonomy in social networks and recommendation systems becomes necessary.

---

[21] Further investigations should account for new regulatory tools such as the AI Act and the influence or manipulation of recommendation systems.

[22] Page 100 - Porcedda, M.G.: Cybersecurity and privacy rights in EU law: moving beyond the trade-off model to appraise the role of technology.

5 Conclusion

The right to privacy has been shown to protect thoughts and ideas of individuals from outside technological interference – their identity. Porcedda's work helps to clarify the definition of the right to privacy, explaining how each 'four limbs' relate to the protection of identity. The right to privacy has been distinguished from the right to data protection, highlighting how the two rights are different, whereas privacy allows for a much-needed protection from the external (negative) influence of recommendation systems over people's identities. However, data protection tools do not help people in this respect e.g., the legal basis of consent that led to (long) privacy policies that individuals do not read and even less understand, or anonymization where profiles are lawfully being made influencing people's identities.

In this paper, it has been shown how data protection is the main regulatory framework in EU to protect individuals' personal data, however limited. Here it lies the conflict, data protection does not protect individuals from the manipulation generated from data analytics in social networks and recommendation systems. It is necessary to discuss that the two rights should not protect the same values, as they are in fact two separate rights, however this line of arguments points towards the problem: privacy protects individuals' thoughts and identities, whereas in practical terms, data protection law is the only regulatory framework that protects people's data but does not consider these issues.

There is still a long path to improve the protection of people's data, but this paper intended to show the necessity for considering identity as co-modified by these technologies as a central concept, and through postphenomenology, propose to consider people continuously co-shaped by data (e.g., stereotypes, gender, age…). Identity is a complex process of co-modification with technologies, and this paper highlights the continuous influence of opinions and ideologies through recommendation systems. This helps to re-interpret the issue as broader than only discriminatory algorithms and illustrates the gaps between data protection and privacy.

How can we prosper/protect identity in the digital sphere? This paper helps to frame the issue of the intrinsic relation of people's identities as a dynamic character that evolves and co-exist with recommendation systems. It also clarifies the lack of tools among GDPR, and the necessity to create new tools that support inferences created by (big) data technologies, among social networks and recommendation systems. I argued the importance of giving people autonomy over the recommendations, as they are constantly co-modified, and they should have the freedom to decide what they would like to receive or how (or if) they are being steer or deprived from certain content.

Both rights cannot and should not protect the same issues, but it is possible to learn from the right to privacy. Data protection law, as it has developed, does not have the tools to protect from the negative influence over identity in recommendation systems, that have led to intrusions over people's ideas and thoughts, be it political or as common as the decision to have a kid, read poetry, or restrain to offer news about personal development. Individuals in our current digital society cannot and should not be considered outside the digital, but rather 'brought-up' and influenced through technologies. In this regard, data protection still has a lot to learn.

Acknowledgements. This paper has received valuable comments and support of my supervisors Rosamunde Van Brakel, Trisha Meyer and Rocco Bellanova; the previous work and inspiration of Maria Grazia Porcedda, and Paul de Hert.

This project has received funding from the European Union's Horizon 2020 research and innovation programme under grant agreement No 813497.

References

1. Sunstein, C.R.: Echo chambers: Bush v. Gore, impeachment, and beyond. Princeton University Press, Princeton (2001)
2. Pariser, E.: The Filter Bubble: What The Internet Is Hiding From You. Penguin UK (2011)
3. Cadwalladr, C., Graham-Harrison, E.: Revealed: 50 million Facebook profiles harvested for Cambridge Analytica in major data breach (2018). https://www.theguardian.com/news/2018/mar/17/cambridge-analytica-facebook-influence-us-election
4. Wylie, C.: Mindf*ck: Inside Cambridge Analytica's Plot to Break the World. Profile Books (2019)
5. Horwitz, J., Seetharaman, D.: Facebook Executives Shut Down Efforts to Make the Site Less Divisive (2020). https://www.wsj.com/articles/facebook-knows-it-encourages-division-top-executives-nixed-solutions-11590507499
6. Posetti, J.: News industry transformation: digital technology, social platforms and the spread of misinformation and disinformation. 15 (2018)
7. The online world still can't quit the 'Big Lie'. https://www.politico.com/news/2022/01/06/social-media-donald-trump-jan-6-526562. Accessed 11 Oct 2022
8. Bellanova, R., González Fuster, G.: No (Big) Data, no fiction? Thinking surveillance with/against Netflix. Presented at the February 9 (2018)
9. Hallinan, B., Striphas, T.: Recommended for you: the Netflix Prize and the production of algorithmic culture. New Media Soc. **18**, 117–137 (2016). https://doi.org/10.1177/1461444814538646
10. Meyer, M.N.: Everything You Need to Know About Facebook's Controversial Emotion Experiment. https://www.wired.com/2014/06/everything-you-need-to-know-about-facebooks-manipulative-experiment/
11. As algorithms take over, YouTube's recommendations highlight a human problem. https://www.nbcnews.com/tech/social-media/algorithms-take-over-youtube-s-recommendations-highlight-human-problem-n867596. Accessed 17 Mar 2022
12. Thompson, C.: YouTube's Plot to Silence Conspiracy Theories. https://www.wired.com/story/youtube-algorithm-silence-conspiracy-theories/
13. The Age of Surveillance Capitalism: The Fight for a Human Future at the New ... - Shoshana Zuboff - Google Libros. https://books.google.be/books?hl=es&lr=&id=W7ZEDgAAQBAJ&oi=fnd&pg=PT12&dq=surveillance+capitalism+book&ots=dpn6GTSDu0&sig=nlwmFMGAZqt2bwVPdNloOhCRSXQ&redir_esc=y. Accessed 10 Dec 2021
14. edpb_03-2022_guidelines_on_dark_patterns_in_social_media_platform_interfaces_en.pdf. https://edpb.europa.eu/system/files/2022-03/edpb_03-2022_guidelines_on_dark_patterns_in_social_media_platform_interfaces_en.pdf
15. Biddle, S.: Facebook Uses Artificial Intelligence to Predict Your Future Actions for Advertisers, Says Confidential Document. https://theintercept.com/2018/04/13/facebook-advertising-data-artificial-intelligence-ai/. Accessed 01 Mar 2022
16. How to clear your viewing history in Netflix. https://www.imore.com/how-clear-your-viewing-history-netflix. Accessed 19 Aug 2022

17. Facebook's ad algorithms are still excluding women from seeing jobs. https://www.techno logyreview.com/2021/04/09/1022217/facebook-ad-algorithm-sex-discrimination/. Accessed 10 Aug 2022
18. Nkem, F.U., Chima, O.A., Martins, O.P., Ifeanyi, A.L., Fiona, O.N.: Portrayal of Women in Advertising on Facebook and Instagram (2020). https://doi.org/10.5281/ZENODO.4006048
19. 20190513.Working_Paper_González_Fuster_Hijmans.pdf.   https://brusselsprivacyhub.eu/ events/20190513.Working_Paper_Gonza%CC%81lez_Fuster_Hijmans.pdf
20. EU Charter of Fundamental Rights. https://ec.europa.eu/info/aid-development-cooperation-fundamental-rights/your-rights-eu/eu-charter-fundamental-rights_en. Accessed 05 Aug 2022
21. Cohen, J.E.: What privacy is for symposium: privacy and technology. Harv. Law Rev. **126**, 1904–1933 (2012)
22. Gutwirth, S., De Hert, P.: Privacy, data protection and law enforcement. Opacity of the individual and transparency of power. Direito Público. 18 (2022). https://doi.org/10.11117/rdp.v18i100.6200
23. Warren, S.D., Brandeis, L.D.: The right to privacy. Harv. Law Rev. **4**, 193–220 (1890). https://doi.org/10.2307/1321160
24. Westin, A.F.: Special report: legal safeguards to insure privacy in a computer society. Commun. ACM. **10**, 533–537 (1967). https://doi.org/10.1145/363566.363579
25. GDPR EUR-Lex - 32016R0679 - EN - EUR-Lex, https://eur-lex.europa.eu/eli/reg/2016/679/oj. Accessed 01 Mar 2022
26. Digital Agenda for Europe | Fact Sheets on the European Union | European Parliament. https://www.europarl.europa.eu/factsheets/en/sheet/64/digital-agenda-for-europe. Accessed 13 Dec 2022
27. Meta Privacy Policy – How Meta collects and uses user data. https://www.facebook.com/privacy/policy/?entry_point=data_policy_redirect&entry=0. Accessed 05 Aug 2022
28. Solove, D.J.: A taxonomy of privacy. Univ. Pa. Law Rev. **154**, 477–564 (2005)
29. Bellanova, R.: Digital, politics, and algorithms: governing digital data through the lens of data protection. Eur. J. Soc. Theory **20**, 329–347 (2017). https://doi.org/10.1177/1368431016679167
30. Taylor, L., Floridi, L.: Group Privacy: New Challenges of Data Technologies. Group Priv. (2017)
31. O'Neil, C.: Weapons of Math Destruction: How Big Data Increases Inequality and Threatens Democracy. Crown (2016)
32. Porcedda, M.G.: Cybersecurity and privacy rights in EU law : moving beyond the trade-off model to appraise the role of technology (2017). http://hdl.handle.net/1814/26594. https://doi.org/10.2870/4605
33. Schoeman, F.D.: Philosophical Dimensions of Privacy: An Anthology. Cambridge University Press, Cambridge (1984)
34. Naughton, J.: Facebook Saves The Stuff You Type — Even If You Have Second Thoughts And Delete It BEFORE You Post. https://www.businessinsider.com/facebook-saves-stuff-you-start-typing-and-the-delete-2013-12. Accessed 14 Dec 2022
35. Hill, K.: How Target Figured Out A Teen Girl Was Pregnant Before Her Father Did. https://www.forbes.com/sites/kashmirhill/2012/02/16/how-target-figured-out-a-teen-girl-was-pregnant-before-her-father-did/. Accessed 12 Aug 2022
36. What's in a name?: identiteitsfraude en -diefstal. Maklu (2012)
37. How to Filter, Block, and Report Harmful Content on Social Media | RAINN. https://www.rainn.org/articles/how-filter-block-and-report-harmful-content-social-media. Accessed 12 Aug 2022
38. Cheney-Lippold, J.: A new algorithmic identity: soft biopolitics and the modulation of control. Theory Cult. Soc. **28**, 164–181 (2011). https://doi.org/10.1177/0263276411424420

39. The Digital Subject: People as Data as Persons. https://journals.sagepub.com/doi/epub/https:// doi.org/10.1177/0263276419840409. https://doi.org/10.1177/0263276419840409. Accessed 22 Oct 2022
40. Rodotà, S.: Data protection as a fundamental right. In: Gutwirth, S., Poullet, Y., De Hert, P., de Terwangne, C., Nouwt, S. (eds.) Reinventing Data Protection?, pp. 77–82. Springer, Dordrecht (2009). https://doi.org/10.1007/978-1-4020-9498-9_3
41. Agre, P.E.: The architecture of identity: embedding privacy in market institutions. Inf. Commun. Soc. **2**, 1–25 (1999). https://doi.org/10.1080/136911899359736
42. Winner, L.: Do artifacts have politics? Daedalus **109**, 121–136 (1980)
43. Ihde, D.: Postphenomenology: Essays in the Postmodern Context. Northwestern University Press (1995)
44. Verbeek, P.-P.: What Things Do: Philosophical Reflections on Technology, Agency, and Design. Penn State University Press (2021). https://doi.org/10.1515/9780271033228

The DMA and the GDPR: Making Sense of Data Accumulation, Cross-Use and Data Sharing Provisions

Muhammed Demircan[✉]

LSTS Research Group, Brussels Privacy Hub, Vrije Universiteit Brussel, Brussels, Belgium
`muhammed.demircan@vub.be`

Abstract. The Digital Markets Act aims to fix the inherited problems of the digital markets by imposing obligations on large online platforms, also known as the gatekeepers. Such obligations involve data accumulation, data cross-use prohibitions and data sharing related obligations that heavily interplay with the data protection rules, hence the GDPR. However, all of these three provisions are highly linked to the data subject consent in the sense of the GDPR. The academic literature heavily criticised consent as the legal basis, especially in the context of the digital markets. This article firstly criticises the legal policy choice of consent to keep the digital markets contested and then analyses the risks arising from the beforementioned provisions for the EU data protection law, especially from the angle of the GDPR principles. It also focuses on the security of data transfers. It then evaluates the possible legal frameworks in order to minimise the risks, such as the data sharing agreements. It finally calls for a sector-specific approach to the general "per se" mentality of the DMA, supported by "core platform service specific" guidelines to be issued in order to minimise the risks for effective data protection in the digital markets.

Keywords: Digital Markets Act · General Data Protection Regulation · Data Accumulation · Data Cross-Use · Data Sharing

1 Introduction

On 12 October 2022, the final version of the Digital Markets Act (hereafter: "DMA") was published in the Official Journal of the European Union [27]. Twenty years of underenforcement discussions in the competition law, arising from the neoliberal "laissez-faire" approach, have motivated European regulators to rethink and restructure the law of the digital markets [15]. DMA aims to fix the inherited problems of the digital markets by imposing obligations on large online platforms, also known as the gatekeepers. Such obligations involve data accumulation, data cross-use prohibitions and data sharing related obligations that heavily interplay with the data protection rules, hence the GDPR [26]. Nearly three years before the initial DMA proposal, the former head of the EDPS indicated that competition law and data protection law could no longer afford the

F. Bieker et al. (Eds.): Privacy and Identity 2022, IFIP AICT 671, pp. 148–164, 2023.
https://doi.org/10.1007/978-3-031-31971-6_12

bureaucratic, jurisprudential, and theoretical burdens which stand in the way of efficient collaboration in an age of digital economy [6]. However, due to the hypercomplex nature of digital regulations interplaying with each other, providing efficiency and coherence between different legal instruments remains an enormous challenge, despite the goodwill of authorities.

The DMA intends to regulate the digital markets in an ex-ante methodology with a "per se" approach[1] [1]. It can be claimed that one of the philosophical backgrounds of the DMA comes from a political attempt to face a legal-market problem that some have called data colonialism, big tech's extreme concentration of data wealth [9]. Therefore, regulating digital markets in the DMA, which are built on data-consuming business models, including personal data, creates an inevitable overlap between the GDPR and the DMA. Where numerous DMA provisions openly refer to the GDPR, others remain unclear in providing efficiency and coherence. Among other digital legislative initiatives, the DMA focuses solely on the most prominent players in the digital markets. Therefore, it holds a unique place for the protection of personal data.

The DMA openly acknowledges in Recital 12 that it shall not apply with prejudice to the GDPR. Considering that personal data protection is a fundamental right (Article 16 of the Treaty on the Functioning of the European Union and Article 8 of the Charter of Fundamental Rights of the European Union) and that protecting and promoting fundamental rights are both the core and the aims of the EU policies [13], the DMA should be carefully analysed within the scope of its effects on personal data protection since it aims to regulate the market behaviour of enormous data-driven companies. After all, both regulations aim for the healthy functioning of the internal market in the EU [1].

Accordingly, this article comprises three main sections focusing on the synergies and tensions between the GDPR and the DMA. Section 2 aims to analyse the data accumulation, data cross-use prohibitions and data sharing related obligations in the DMA within the scope of the lawfulness of the processing principle in GDPR. Section 3 aims to address the options to ensure maximum compliance with the GDPR principles (including the principle of security of processing (Articles 5 and 32 of the GDPR) [26]) in Article 5. Section 4 explores the ways forward, including a call for sector-specific guidelines regarding data classification and standardisation. Finally, the conclusion sums up the findings of the article by suggesting creating a consent-legality monitoring team in the Commission as well as explaining the need for a sector-specific guidelines approach for obligated business user-gatekeeper data sharing.

2   Data Accumulation, Data Cross-Use and Data Sharing in the DMA: Legal Basis and Lessons

The DMA has numerous clauses that interplay with the GDPR. However, within the scope of this article, the focus will be given to a few core provisions of the DMA.

---

[1] "Per se" in Latin means "by itself" or "in itself" and here refers to the DMA's presumed illegality over some commercial practices.

One of the most significant provisions relating to personal data in the DMA is about the data accumulation and cross-use capacities of the gatekeepers[2]. According to Recital 3 of the DMA, gatekeepers are a small number of large undertakings providing core platform services[3] with considerable economic power. Gatekeepers operate as multi-sided platforms, enabling two or more customer groups to engage with each other on their platforms by acting as a median in which the goods and services are offered to the end users by the business users[4] [4].

The capacity to process vast amounts of data gives gatekeepers potential advantages in terms of the accumulation of data, thereby raising barriers to entry, according to the Recital 36 of the DMA [27]. Therefore, established firms like Google and Facebook have a significant competitive advantage over rivals thanks to their vast data processing capacities, which also causes high entry costs for possible new entrants [17].

Article 5(2)(b) of the DMA forbids gatekeepers to "combine personal data from the relevant core platform service with personal data from any further core platform services or from any other services provided by the gatekeeper or with personal data from third-party services". Similarly, Article 5(2)(c) of the DMA prohibits to "cross-use personal data from the relevant core platform service in other services provided separately by the gatekeeper, including other core platform services, and vice-versa". However, gatekeepers are allowed to combine or cross-use datasets if the end-user grants consent in the meaning of Article 7 of the GDPR.

Another remarkable provision highlighting the importance of data, including personal data, for building a competitive business atmosphere in digital markets is Article 6(10) of the DMA[5]. This article regulates the need of business users to access the data that has been "generated in the context of the use of the relevant core platform services" by the end users. This data sharing provision aims to force the gatekeepers to share data that hold a business value, so that the business users can be better equipped for competition. According to Article 6(10) of the DMA, gatekeepers are obliged to grant

---

[2] According to Article 2(1) of the DMA and Recital 3 of the DMA indicates that gatekeepers are the biggest provider of online goods and services providing core platform services have emerged with considerable economic power that could qualify them. Similarly, some of those undertakings exercise control over whole platform ecosystems in the digital economy and are structurally extremely difficult to challenge or contest by existing, or new market operators, irrespective of how innovative and efficient those market operators may be.

[3] Core platform services include a variety of services or products that are offered by the gatekeepers, the most common ones being online intermediation services, online search engines, operating systems, web browsers and cloud computing services. A full list can be found in Article 2(2) of the DMA.

[4] 'Business user' means any natural or legal person acting in a commercial or professional capacity using core platform services for the purpose of or in the course of providing goods or services to end users, according to Article 2(21) of the DMA.

[5] Article 6(10) of the DMA creates an obligation on the side of the gatekeeper to provide business users access, free of charge, with effective, high-quality, continuous and real-time access to and use of aggregated and non-aggregated data, including personal data. With regard to personal data, the gatekeeper shall provide for such access to, and use of, personal data only where the data are directly connected with the use effectuated by the end users. This obligation is only triggered after the business users receive consent from the end users for such access.

access to those datasets that feature business value for business users. When it comes to the sharing of the datasets that involve personal data, the gatekeepers can only provide data that "are directly connected with the use effectuated by the end users in respect of the products or services offered by the relevant business user through the relevant core platform service" and when the end users opt-in for such sharing by giving their consent.

In order to interpret this article, the multiple layers of data processing in the context of Article 6(10) of the DMA shall be defined. First, the transfer of the datasets constitutes data processing by itself. Since the article brings an obligation for the gatekeepers to share these datasets, this transfer shall be based on the legal obligation legal basis of Article 6 of the GDPR. Second, the processing of these datasets by the business users shall only be based on consent, according to the wording of Article 6(10) of the DMA. Article 6(10) does not make this distinction by itself; however, it is essential to separate multiple layers of data processing since it makes a meaningful difference with regard to the legal basis of different layers.

Although not binding for EU data protection enforcement authorities, ICO's interpretation in its Data Sharing Code of Conduct also follows a similar approach to the above-mentioned interpretation. It is mentioned, with regards to the legal bases for processing and therefore the transfer of personal data, that "there is no need for the controller to seek individuals' consent for the sharing if the law clearly specifies that the sharing can take place without consent" [16]. In a similar context, the EDPS has mentioned that the draft Data Governance Act would not constitute a legal ground for data sharing by itself under the GDPR [12]. However, the DMA and the DGA are different in their aims. The DGA does not oblige any data sharing, whereas the DMA brings obligations to share datasets. Therefore, since Article 6(10) of the DMA constitutes a legal obligation, the initial transfer of the personal datasets shall be based on the legal obligation legal basis of the GDPR.

The first layer of the data processing (transfer of the datasets) in Article 6(10) of the DMA will be analysed in the later stages regarding the responsibility sharing between the gatekeeper and the business user in terms of the security of the processing. For the sake of clarity, the reference to consent in Article 6(10) of the DMA will be only analysed with respect to the second layer of the processing, the processing of the end user data by the business user, after the initial transfer.

These two provisions indicate a legal policy choice by requiring the end user's consent within the sense of the GDPR. The subsection of Sect. 2 will focus on this policy choice and analyse whether and how these provisions may actually achieve their objectives.

2.1   The Choice of Consent to Keep Digital Markets Contested: Is It the Right Approach?

The GDPR states various legal bases for personal data processing under Article 6[6]. One should first note that tying the data accumulation, data cross-use prohibitions and

---

[6] Legal bases for processing personal data in Article 6 of the GDPR are as follows; consent, performance of a contract, legal obligation, vital interests of a natural person, public interest and legitimate interest.

data sharing obligations to the end user's consent may be problematic and inefficient in tackling the competition issue in digital markets.

Before the very dynamic nature of the internet gave birth to very big digital companies in the world, the competition law theory has built on the assumption that every powerful company would be contested by new entrants with high innovation capacities [23]. This phenomenon was called the "creative destruction" of the dominant firms. Such reasoning had some empirical support twenty years ago. In fact, the early years of the internet saw a vibrant, open economy where startups were common, no internet corporation seemed to hold sway for very long, and competition was fierce [15]. It is now the case that some firms got so big that they hold every corner of the business-making process, from innovation to customer reach, from holding the marketplaces to buying prominent but small firms (killer acquisitions) [15]. To put it into an example, we can use the example of DuckDuckGo. Although DuckDuckGo claims to be much more privacy friendly than Google, its market share remains around %1. Therefore, no matter how innovative and customer-friendly DuckDuckGo becomes, it can not beat the data-consuming algorithmic business model of Google.

The EU regulatory choice of relying on the individual's consent may seem to empower citizens by giving them ultimate control over their data. This policy choice is based on an idealistic scenario that individuals are capable and willing to customise their data policy choices. However, it mostly neglects informational asymmetry[7] [10] and consent fatigue. Consent fatigue refers to the emotional state of mind of the data subjects when a high number of standard form requests, with are full of legal technicalities, are submitted to them [18]. In an age of consent boxes, bundling the hopes of improving digital market competition to weakened individuals might prove wrong.

The consent legal basis has been subject to discussions in the EU data protection literature as well. A main criticism of the central position of consent in data protection is based on the reliance on consent for processing activities that would otherwise constitute a violation of the GDPR (when based on other legal bases of the GDPR, such as legitimate interest) [24]. On top of that, in the context of digital markets, such consents are mostly reduced to a rubber-stamping process, where consent is obtained with a tick, and individuals give their consent to move on to the following web window [5].

The choice of consent as the legal basis within the scope of Article 5(2)(b) and Article 5(2)(c) of the DMA, which focuses on the possibility of accumulating or cross-using personal data by the gatekeepers from various services that it provides or the services that the third parties give on the gatekeeper platform, is highly problematic due to the power imbalances, on top of other reasons such as the consent fatigue. The power imbalance between the gatekeeper, which holds incredible importance in modern daily life, and the end user, whose utilisation of such services is nearly inevitable, prevents consent from being freely given.

Graef [14], who is criticising the consent legal policy choice in the DMA, suggests that the legal ground for the DMA obligations should go beyond the consent and rely

---

[7] According to Recital 43 of the GDPR, when there is a clear imbalance (of power and therefore information) between the data subject and the controller, consent is unlikely to be legal (See also *"Press release: Advocate General's Opinion C-252/21 | Meta Platforms and Others (General terms of use of a social network"* for a similar interpretation)).

on stricter grounds such as Article 6(1)(b) GDPR, which states that the processing of personal data is lawful when it is "necessary for the performance of a contract". Contractual necessity as a legal basis could protect the end users in two ways. Firstly, the combination or cross-use of the datasets would be only possible if it is indispensable for the performance of a contract, such as the provision of a service [14]. Secondly, the end user's interest would be automatically protected by a necessity test required on this legal basis. In such a policy choice, the end user would not be dealing with an increasing number of consent boxes when browsing through the internet and acquiring services or goods from the gatekeeper. Contractual necessity is only of the legal bases provided in the GDPR and only mentioned here as an alternative to strict consent legal policy choice in the DMA.

Considering all the different possibilities of legal bases in the GDPR, we claim that consent within the scope of the DMA, due to the power imbalance, informational asymmetry and consent fatigue, would always be flawed in the relationship between the gatekeeper and the end-user. A possible end user consent creates the situation that combining or cross-using datasets that are not necessary for a performance of a contract would be legal in the context of the DMA. However, such processing would be illegal within the contractual necessity legal basis due to the result of the necessity test that has to be conducted.

However, in line with the concerns shared by academics and civil society [3] in relation to issues of consent, Article 5(2) of the DMA has been added to the final text of the DMA. This subparagraph of Article 5 regulates that "where the consent given (...) has been refused or withdrawn by the end user, the gatekeeper shall not repeat its request for consent for the same purpose more than once within a period of one year". The time limit is linked to the frequency of the consent requests. Hence, this provision only addresses the issue of consent fatigue rather than focusing on the core issues such as power imbalance and informational asymmetry, by ignoring the theoretical validity conditions of the consent in the sense of the GDPR.

Article 5(2)(3) of the DMA openly states that the combination or cross-use of personal datasets by the gatekeeper can also be performed based on Article 6(1)(c), Article 6(1)(d), Article 6(1)(e) of the GDPR, respectively, the legal obligation, vital interest and the public interest legal bases. Nevertheless, the situations in that these legal bases would apply are very limited in number. Plus, such extra grounds were not foreseen for business users within the scope of Article 6(10) of the DMA. The reason for adding these additional legal bases only to Article 5(2)(3) can be that these are only intended to force gatekeepers to share information where it is deemed necessary by authorities. Since consent is openly referred to as the main gate for combining or cross-using personal datasets within the legislative text itself, we understand that the legal obligation clause can only be triggered when the Commission gives a related decision ordering such conduct to combine or cross-use datasets.

On top of all the issues linked to the notion of consent, business users are already in a disadvantaged position in the DMA. They have to receive consent in the gatekeepers' core platform service interface based on the DMA provisions. A privacy-sensitive end user will likely refuse such requests, although it would enable a more competitive digital market since the request for consent is asked at the gatekeeper platform.

As mentioned in the last paragraphs of Sect. 2, a similar methodology to Article 5(2)(3) of the DMA could have also been accepted for Article 6(10). If Article 6(10) would not refer only to the consent legal basis but would state that the business users can process the data based on any legal basis stated in the Article 6 of the GDPR, the aim of the DMA, which is to increase competition in the digital markets by sharing the power of gatekeepers with the business users would be achieved.

Alternatively, the DMA could avoid openly referring to the consent of the end-user (by stating that any legal basis in the GDPR would be possible) in both Articles 5 and 6 of the DMA, and it could focus more on the GDPR principles such as data minimisation and purpose limitation as well as security measures when it comes to data sharing under a different legal ground. Although data minimisation seems to be in conflict with the sharing of data among business users and gatekeepers, limiting the data points to be shared to an absolute minimum by a more clear legal framework on which data points shall be absolutely necessary to ensure more competition in the digital markets could help to achieve DMA's goals. A suggestion relating to this is made in the following sections and especially in Sect. 4 of this article.

Since the policy choice has been concluded by requiring consent for such activities, in order to fix the flaws of the DMA and ensure that the data protection law is not negatively affected in digital markets, extra scrutiny for GDPR principles in the interpretation and enforcement of the DMA is vital. The following section will address the effective interpretation of GDPR principles in the context of related articles.

3   Data Accumulation, Cross-Use and Data Sharing in the DMA: Detecting Risks by the GDPR Principles

The European legislators are aware of the risks of the DMA. That is why there are many references to the protection of personal data and full compliance with the GDPR (and other relevant regulations) in the DMA. Recital 12 openly acknowledges that the DMA "should also apply without prejudice to the rules resulting from other acts of Union (…) in particular Regulation (EU) 2016/6791 (GDPR)". Recital 35 even claims that one of the reasons why the DMA was necessary was to "protect privacy". Similarly, Recital 72 indicates that "the data protection and privacy interests of end users are relevant to any assessment of potential negative effects of the observed practice of gatekeepers".

This section will address the risks arising mainly from the data sharing obligation (Article 6(10)) of the DMA, as well as noting the concerns about the data accumulation and cross-use prohibition, Article 5(2) of the DMA, in the light of the GDPR principles. Such an analysis will help the DMA to be interpreted in a way to achieve one of its aims, protect personal data and ensure that such obligations do not provide legal uncertainty that the subjects of the DMA can abuse. This is especially crucial in an age when business models of online giants tend to circumvent the laws through fluid commercial structures and liability models [22].

3.1 The Principle of "Purpose Limitation" in the Context of Article 5(2) and Article 6(10) of the DMA

According to Article 5(1)(b) of the GDPR, controllers must only use data for "specified, explicit, and legitimate purposes". The purpose limitation principle remains one of the core principles of the GDPR for a strong and coherent data protection framework in the EU, according to Recital 7 of the GDPR [26]. Purpose limitation also has a crucial role in the context of the DMA since the DMA regulates commercial behaviour linking to online advertising, which relies on the multi-layered processing of personal data.

One of the most significant critiques of the DMA concerns Articles 5(2)(a) and 5(2)(2) of the DMA[8]. The wording of the second paragraph of Article 5(2) has been criticised by a group of well-known European scholars and EU ex-officials since the wording "suggests advertising is a single data processing purpose, whereas there are plenty of data processing activities behind displaying an ad" [3]. However, the text remained the same in the final version. In their response to the concerns, the EU Parliament members have stated that the GDPR already contains the provisions that consent must be presented for each individual processing purpose, and it is unnecessary to reiterate the reference to "each processing purpose" in the DMA [14].

Purpose limitation also plays a vital role in the data sharing between the gatekeeper and the business user. According to Article 6(10) of the DMA, the gatekeeper should share with the business users only the personal data that are directly connected to the end user's use of the products or services offered by the relevant business user when the end users give their consent.

One of the criticisms of this provision was that the gatekeeper would not be in a position to show that the data sharing would be compatible with the initial processing purposes since the business users may process personal data unrelated to the first processing purposes [8]. However, this criticism seems inaccurate. First of all, Article 6(10) requires business users to request consent for their processing activities, and such consent should be specific for the purposes of such processing. Therefore, the gatekeeper would not be responsible after the data subject consents to such sharing. Even if the gatekeeper might be in a position to worry about the effects of data sharing on its own compliance with the GDPR, weaponising data protection rules in order to deny access to business users is openly forbidden in Recital 60 of the DMA. Recital 60 forbids the gatekeepers from using "any contractual or other restrictions to prevent business users from accessing relevant data".

On top of this, Article 6(4) of the GDPR openly acknowledges that new consent with new approvals on additional or different processing purposes overrules the compatibility assessment that should be conducted if the initial purpose for collecting and processing data is not in line with a new processing activity. Therefore, complying with the purpose limitation principle remains under the sole responsibility of the business user in

---

[8] Article 5(2)(a) of the DMA: "The gatekeeper shall not do any of the following: (a) process, for the purpose of providing online advertising services, personal data of end users using services of third parties that make use of core platform services of the gatekeeper; (…)". Article 5(2)(2) of the DMA: "Where the consent given for the purposes of the first subparagraph has been refused or withdrawn by the end user, the gatekeeper shall not repeat its request for consent for the same purpose more than once within a period of one year.".

the context of Article 6(10) of the DMA. This point also has links to the responsibilities of gatekeepers and business users in terms of the specific obligated data transfers. Responsibility sharing between them is discussed under the "Security of the Processing" subsection of Sect. 3.

3.2 The Principle of "Data Minimisation" in the Context of Article 6(10) of the DMA

Article 5(1)(c) of the GDPR states that personal data must be adequate, relevant, and limited to what is necessary concerning the purposes for which it is processed. Data minimisation has great importance in the context of business users' access to the datasets that are generated on the gatekeeper platform. Article 6(10) obliges gatekeepers to share "personal data only where the data are directly connected with the use effectuated by the end users (…)". This wording implicitly refers to the data minimisation principle by limiting the shared data to those only directly connected with end users' use. However, how to define which data points would be directly connected with the use of the core platform service remains unclear.

The DMA covers core platform services from various sectors, from operating systems to online intermediation services, from cloud computing services to web browsers, according to Article 2(2) of the DMA. All these sectors have different dynamics with unique characteristics when it comes to the types of data points that are collected. Especially, defining what is directly connected with the use of the end user remains to be in the hand of the gatekeepers since they are the ones who will be implicitly deciding which data points to share by starting the process of data sharing. Considering that the DMA openly states that it will be without prejudice to the GDPR, it is highly likely that the gatekeepers would try to limit the shared data points to the minimum.

For instance, a navigation software application, which is a business user in the context of the DMA, that runs on an "operating system"[9] of a gatekeeper, can request access to the location data of the end user using the service. If this service is granted in a commercial context such as Uber or similar platforms, the location data inherently links to the driver's route as well [8]. The risks arising from such access, especially considering that the access is real-time, may also evolve into security risks. Sharing such data points reveals the activity of the driver, which can even bring the risk that the navigation apps can profile the drivers. Nevertheless, the DMA only allows the end user data to be shared with the business user. The gatekeepers may refuse to grant access to those datasets on the grounds of the impossibility of separating driver location data from passenger data.

Similar tensions arising from the obligated data sharing provision and the data protection standards may also occur in the context of other core platform services. Likely, the gatekeepers would also limit the shared data in the context of online intermediation services by blocking specific data points on the grounds of data minimisation. This might be the case primarily if the business user competes with the gatekeeper for that specific service.

---

[9] Based on Article 2(10) of the DMA, an operating system means a system software that controls the basic functions of the hardware or software and enables software applications to run on it.

For instance, the exact timing of a book sale, through which computer model and which browser may seem to be non-personal data. However, these data points can be important for the business users' marketing operations. Business users can also request access to those data points under Article 6(10). However, linking those data points in a large volume increases the risks of re-identification [20]. More information leads to indirect violation of the data minimisation principle. Mixed datasets that involve personal and non-personal data points, even where data is anonymised, are very unlikely to comply with the data minimisation principle of the GDPR since all combined can lead to new observed datasets [12]. The risks arise even more considering that the gatekeepers also process data relating to vulnerable individuals.

Another challenge to complying with the data minimisation principle is when a data point directly connected to the end user's use does not happen to have a meaningful business value for the business user. For example, the computer model used by the end user on which the transaction on the gatekeeper platform happens may not have any competitive advantage for the business user if the business user is selling a distinct product such as construction materials. However, the data point gets created with the direct use of the end user and therefore falls into the scope of Article 6(10). Under Article 6(10) of the DMA, such a data point must be shared with the business user. Therefore, the wording of the article contradicts the data minimisation principle of the GDPR.

The DMA, by nature, is a sector-specific law about competition, with secondary goals such as data protection and fairness in digital markets [19]. However, it differs from general competition law proceedings because the DMA does not integrate a case-by-case basis but incorporates general "per se" rules in digital markets [19]. This results in vagueness and legal uncertainty, the related data sharing provision in the DMA applies to an extensive range of business users from different sectors and to any kind of data directly connected to the end user's use.

Such vagueness raises risks for weak and unclear enforcement of the DMA. Under-enforcement or misapplication of the DMA also implies dangers for effective data protection. The possible ways to prevent it from happening will be discussed in Sect. 4.

3.3 The Principles of "Transparency, Accountability, Storage Limitation" and the Security of the Processing in the Context of Article 6(10) of the DMA

Transparency
Individuals must be informed about the use and processing of their data when it is collected directly from them or when it is received from other sources, according to GDPR Article 5(1)(a) and Articles 13 and 14. The EDPB/EDPS emphasise in their opinion on the DGA that each receiver in the data processing chain must give people access to transparent information about their data processing activity [12]. This would also apply in the context of the DMA.

Gatekeepers would need to inform the end users about their processing activities, including data sharing with the business users [8]. However, the data points to be shared would differentiate based on the use of the end user and the type of commercial activity of the business user (depending on which sector the business user is active in and what are data points to be shared in that regard). Therefore, it is likely that the information notice relating to data transfers should also be given based during the specific data sharing.

Gatekeepers may not know which data points would be shared with the business users since they would not know which goods or services the end user would acquire in the first place. Similarly, the business users would also need to provide such information to the end users. For business users, it would be easier to comply with the transparency obligation since they would be in a position to know what data points they would be getting.

3.4 Security of the Processing

According to Article 32 of the GDPR, organisations must take the proper organisational and technical steps to provide a level of security, commensurate with the risk. The GDPR acknowledges that organisations that are separately accountable for the protection and security of the data must work together to ensure adequate data protection and security. In the context of the DMA, the requirement to maintain an adequate level of security is still completely applicable.

Within the context of Article 6(10) of the DMA, there are two aspects to consider regarding the security of the processing. The first one is to clearly define the nature of the relationship between the gatekeeper and the business user with regard to the transfer of the end user datasets. In order to define the relationship, the GDPR mechanisms relating to data controllership and joint controllership shall be analysed.

The second one is to focus on the business user's responsibilities with regard to the accessed datasets. However, this is subject to a different research project in the future.

The Responsibility Sharing Between the Gatekeeper and the Business User in the Context of Article 6(10) of the DMA
As stated in Sect. 2, Article 6(10) of the DMA incorporates multiple data processing layers. The first one is the obligated transfer of the end user datasets to the business user by the gatekeeper. Without clearly splitting the responsibilities of gatekeepers and business users in terms of this specific data sharing scheme, the gatekeepers may weaponise data protection in order not to comply with the obligations and, therefore, indirectly leverage their market power. Similarly, examples have shown the weaponisation of privacy standards as a tool to block access to certain services or products, which hinders competition in a specific market [7]. It remains unclear to which scope the gatekeeper can claim that data-sharing may end up violating their GDPR obligations since the business user can not guarantee the safety of the personal data that are transferred to the business user [8].

Gatekeepers are surely classified as data controllers with regard to their relationship with the end users. On the other hand, business users also operate independently from the gatekeepers when defining the purposes and means of processing personal datasets in terms of Article 6(10) of the DMA. Therefore, they would not be classified as data processors according to Article 2(8) of the GDPR but rather as independent data controllers [26]. Although the GDPR regulates the joint controllership in Article 26, the relationship arising from Article 6(10) of the DMA may not constitute a joint controllership since the gatekeeper does not have a say in how and why the business user would process the end user data [11]. Following this speculative but not yet definitive interpretation, the transfer of datasets between the gatekeepers and the business users would constitute controller-to-controller data sharing [8]. The EDPB has not yet defined the responsibility sharing attached to this relationship.

However, important lessons can be taken from the responsibility sharing based on the data portability right in the GDPR. The GDPR regulates the data portability right for the data subjects in Article 20. The DMA also brings out data portability right for the end users in Article 6(9). The difference between Article 6(9) and Article 6(10) of the DMA is that Article 6(10) is triggered through the request of the business user, whereas the right to data portability in Article 6(9) and Article 20 of the GDPR is triggered upon the request of the data subject or the end user in the context of the DMA. Therefore, the Article 29 Working Party ("Article 29 WP") guidelines on the right to data portability can be handy in interpreting the responsibility sharing in the context of the DMA [2]. The guideline states that when data portability takes place, "the data controller is not responsible for compliance of the receiving data controller with data protection law, considering that it is not the sending data controller that chooses the recipient" [2]. Therefore, the gatekeeper's responsibility should end when the dataset is transferred to the business user. Such an interpretation would prevent gatekeepers not to share data with the business user based on concerns over the safety of the transfer.

Such an interpretation relating to the nature of the relationship between the gatekeeper and the business user would also be in line with the comments in Sect. 2, relating to the legal obligation and legal basis of the transfer, in the context of Article 6(10) of the DMA. Since the duty to share datasets is regulated as an obligation, the gatekeepers shall not have a say about the capacity of the business users in terms of the safety of the personal datasets that are shared with them. However, it shall be noted that business users are also subject to the GDPR as independent data controllers.

Relevant research suggestions in this regard include that the DMA guidelines shall include the appropriate security measures and obligations both for the gatekeeper and the business user in respect to the data sharing if needed, comprehensive and transparent security due diligence before the share of the data or clear guidelines for data sharing agreements within the scope of the DMA [8]. These will be analysed in Sect. 4.

4 The Way Forward

The European Data Strategy, published by the European Commission, aims to make the EU a leader in the data-driven society [25]. However, such an ambitious project holds risks for privacy and data protection rules. The Commission acknowledges such risks. The single market for the data will be built upon full compliance with the privacy and data protection rules [25]. The DMA, on the other hand, as explained above, despite its narrow focus on gatekeepers, will have a crucial place for the data protection standards in the EU since the gatekeepers are the most extensive data holders in the digital markets.

Section 2 has criticised the policy of consent both within the context of Article 5(2) and Article 6(10) of the DMA. However, this section will concentrate on making the best out of the final DMA text by suggesting the following steps to be taken.

Within the context of Article 5(2) of the DMA, the data accumulation and cross-use prohibitions, it will be imperative to closely monitor the quality of the consent by the end users. As stated, the consent legal basis has been heavily criticised regarding its inherited problems in the digital markets context. Therefore, we suggest that the Commission builds a team that will only focus on the consent requests arising from the DMA. Such a team may closely monitor the consent requests' quality, validity, transparency, fairness and clarity. This team would also follow up on the duties of the gatekeepers when the consent request is rejected, whether they would be providing the same quality of service to end users reject to grant consent within the meaning of Article 5(2) of the DMA, or whether the gatekeepers still accumulate or cross use datasets no matter the consent is positive or negative. Such dedication of the sources would be justified both by the inherited issues relating to consent and the unique dynamics of digital markets, which hurts the quality of consent even more than the traditional markets[10].

This would already be in line with the Commission's approach to the enforcement of the DMA. The commissioner for the internal market, Thierry Breton, has stated that the DMA will be enforced mainly by the DG CONNECT, a non-competition DG within the European Commission [28]. We welcome this approach by the Commission since the DMA is not a pure competition law but also focuses on important aspects of data-related business conduct, including personal datasets. The commissioner has also stated that the dedicated teams within the DG CONNECT will be organised around thematic domains, such as societal aspects, technical aspects and economic aspects [28]. One of the societal teams can be assigned to monitor and analyse the quality of the consent.

On the other hand, the DMA brings new "per se" rules for a wide variety of sectors, as explained in Sect. 3. This is particularly important with regard to the data sharing between the gatekeepers and the business users, Article 6(10) of the DMA. Consequently, these sectors have different realities regarding what constitutes data that will boost the competition by providing access to business users. It is crucial for the DMA to work to define which data points are relevant for which sectors clearly. Section 3 has explained the risks arising from the absence of a sector-specific approach in relation to the GDPR principles. Legal instruments to provide clarity in terms of the classification of datasets in different sectors, which amounts to possessing business value (so that the data minimisation principle is respected) are various.

The most prominent way to build a legal framework with respect to data sharing between businesses is the data sharing agreements. A broad typology of agreements and papers between two or more organisations or various divisions of an organisation are frequently referred to as "data sharing agreements" in the literature. The European Commission recently determined that it was unsuitable to take horizontal legislative action with regard to private sector data sharing after engaging in extensive stakeholder consultation and dialogue. However, civil society has discussed using the data sharing agreements within the context of the DMA [8].

Within the context of the DMA, data sharing agreements are highly flawed. This is caused due to information asymmetry and asymmetrical contractual dependency between the gatekeepers and the business users [21]. In digital markets, contracts are rarely negotiated, and standard contractual clauses are applied and dictated by the big players [21]. Consequently, data sharing agreements between the gatekeepers, and

---

[10] Please see Sect. 2, "The Choice of Consent to Keep Digital Markets Contested" for the reasons why digital markets are particularly risky for consent requests.

remarkably smaller companies, such as business users, end up being a largely unilateral contractual regime rather than being fair tools arising from legal negotiations [21]. The European Commission has taken a similar approach in its call for application relating to the business-to-business data sharing contracts expert group[11]. The expert group is entitled to develop a set of contractual clauses on model data sharing agreements in order to help the SMEs. However, it is stated in the call that the expert group will not deliver model contractual terms within the context of the DMA.

Similar thinking can be applied to any kind of legal instrument that will be subject to so-called negotiations between the gatekeepers and the business users. Therefore, to provide full efficiency and protect the interests of the business users, the European regulators should take charge by providing sector-specific guidelines in the context of data sharing obligations in the DMA.

Article 47 of the DMA grants the Commission authority to adopt guidelines on any aspects of the DMA to facilitate its effective enforcement. The Commission, therefore, shall issue guidelines based on a sector-specific (and/or core platform specific) guidelines, with the goals of;

- Defining which data points hold a business value for the specific core platform service so that only the necessary data points are transferred to the business user (data minimisation principle within the context of Article 6(10) of the DMA),
- Defining the obligations of the gatekeepers and the business users with regard to the transparency principle of the GDPR by providing guidelines on the limits of the gatekeeper's duties for informing the end users about possible data sharing in the future.

The Commission should also provide guidance on the non-sector-specific matters, with the goals of;

- Defining the responsibility sharing between the gatekeepers and the business users in terms of security of the data transfers, if appropriate, acknowledging the same thinking of the responsibility sharing relating to the GDPR data portability right guidelines,
- Making sure also that the business users have the capacity to keep the shared datasets secure and in line with the GDPR principles, such as the storage limitation principle of the GDPR.

The DMA, in Article 40, establishes a high-level group for the DMA. This high-level group includes both the EDPS and the EDPB. Therefore, such sector-specific guidelines can be developed in a hybrid way, both incorporating data protection principles and securing the aims of the DMA.

5   Conclusion

The rise of the internet and giant technology companies in the last decades has led to the saga relating to the interplay of the competition law and the data protection law.

---

[11] Please see the "Call for applications / Sub-group - stakeholders to Expert Group on B2B data sharing and cloud computing contracts" call of the European Commission.

Although several cooperation forums have been established, little has improved in the last years, both with respect to the competition and the data protection standards in the digital markets. That is why the DMA came with a novel approach, accepting general "per se" rules on top of the traditional competition law toolbox. Such a general approach will aim to fix the inherited and established problems of the digital markets.

As stated in the introduction, this article has aimed firstly to analyse the outcomes of the choice of consent as a legal policy in the context of data accumulation, data cross-use prohibitions (for gatekeepers) and data sharing scheme between the gatekeepers and the business users. Secondly, it has focused on detecting the risks arising from the vagueness of the beforementioned articles in relation to the GDPR principles.

The consent legal basis has been chosen to keep the digital markets contested, especially in relation to Article 5(2) and Article 6(10) of the DMA. Therefore Sect. 2 has mainly focused on the results of such a legal policy choice, explaining the inherited problems of the consent legal basis in the GDPR, and connecting it to the specific dynamics of the digital markets, such as informational asymmetry and power imbalances. Relating to this, Sect. 4 has advocated for a specialised consent task force to be created to provide maximum efficiency and coherence in the context of the DMA.

Since consent legal basis is likely to bring new issues, Sect. 3 has addressed the issues arising from the data sharing obligations between the gatekeepers and the business users, Article 6(10) of the DMA, in their relation to the GDPR principles. However, the DMA's general "per se" approach does not fit with the sector-specific nature of core platform services. In order to provide maximum efficiency and to protect the interests of the business users and the end users, a sector-specific approach to the enforcement of Article 6(10) shall be applied. Section 4, consequently, has advocated for sector-specific and/or core platform specific guidelines in the context of Article 6(10) of the DMA.

Although the DMA has the potential to ensure a fairer, more robust and open digital market within the EU, there are two very important challenges to focus upon: The legality of consent by end users shall be closely monitored by a specific team and the Commission shall provide sector-specific and/or core platform specific guidelines for data sharing between business users and gatekeepers in order to provide more certainty for business users to compete with the gatekeepers.

References

1. Akman, P.: Regulating Competition in Digital Platform Markets: A Critical Assessment of the Framework and Approach of the EU DMA, pp. 2–18 (2021). https://papers.ssrn.com/abstract=3978625. https://doi.org/10.2139/ssrn.3978625
2. Article 29 Data Protection Working Party: Guidelines on the right to data portability, p. 6 (2016)
3. Bertuzzi, L.: DMA: EU legislators resist pressure to change data provisions in the final text (2022). https://www.euractiv.com/section/digital/news/dma-eu-legislators-resist-pressure-to-change-data-provisions-in-the-final-text/
4. Brokaw, L.: How to Win With a Multisided Platform Business Model. https://sloanreview.mit.edu/article/how-to-win-with-a-multisided-platform-business-model/. Accessed 08 Aug 2022
5. Brownsword, R.: The cult of consent: fixation and fallacy. King's Law J. 15(2), 223–251 (2004). https://doi.org/10.1080/09615768.2004.11427572

6. Buttarelli, G.: Youth and Leaders Summit - Opening Speech (2019). https://edps.europa.eu/sites/edp/files/publication/19-01-21_speech_youth_and_leaders_en.pdf
7. Chee, F.Y.: EU's Vestager warns Apple against using privacy, security to limit competition (2021). https://www.reuters.com/technology/exclusive-eus-vestager-warns-apple-against-using-privacy-security-limit-2021-07-02/
8. CPIL: Bridging the DMA and the GDPR - Comments by the Centre for Information Policy Leadership on the Data Protection Implications of the Draft DMA, pp. 7–19. Centre for Information Policy Leadership (2021)
9. Decraene, D.: "Data Colonialism" and the ubiquitous appropriation of human life. https://www.law.kuleuven.be/citip/blog/data-colonialism-and-the-ubiquitous-appropriation-of-human-life/. Accessed 05 Aug 2022
10. Directorate for Competition Committee: Consumer Data Rights and Competition - Background note, p. 23. OECD (2020)
11. EDPB: Guidelines 07/2020 on the concepts of controller and processor in the GDPR Version 1.0, p. 48 (2020)
12. EDPB-EDPS: EDPB-EDPS Joint Opinion 03/2021 on the Proposal for a regulation of the European Parliament and of the Council on European data governance (Data Governance Act) Version 1.1. EDPS, pp. 47–49 (2021)
13. European Parliament. Directorate General for Parliamentary Research Services.: Fundamental rights in the European Union: the role of the Charter after the Lisbon Treaty: in depth analysis, p. 24. Publications Office, LU (2015)
14. Graef, I.: Why End-User Consent Cannot Keep Markets Contestable. https://verfassungsblog.de/power-dsa-dma-08/. Accessed 30 July 2022
15. Höppner, T.: From Creative Destruction to Destruction of the Creatives: Innovation in Walled-Off Ecosystems, pp. 9–15. SSRN Journal (2022). https://doi.org/10.2139/ssrn.4145216
16. ICO: Data sharing: a code of practice: Lawfulness. https://ico.org.uk/for-organisations/guide-to-data-protection/ico-codes-of-practice/data-sharing-a-code-of-practice/lawfulness/. Accessed 30 July 2022
17. Javeed, U.: Data and Competition Law: Introducing Data As Non-Monetary Consideration and Competition Concerns in Data-Driven Online Platforms (2021). https://papers.ssrn.com/abstract=3788178. https://doi.org/10.2139/ssrn.3788178
18. Matthan, R.: Beyond Consent: A New Paradigm for Data Protection, p. 3 (2017). https://takshashila.org.in/research/discussion-document-beyond-consent-new-paradigm-data-protection
19. Petit, N.: The Proposed DMA (DMA): A Legal and Policy Review, p. 2 (2021). https://papers.ssrn.com/abstract=3843497. https://doi.org/10.2139/ssrn.3843497
20. Rocher, L., et al.: Estimating the success of re-identifications in incomplete datasets using generative models. Nat. Commun. **10**(1), 3069 (2019). https://doi.org/10.1038/s41467-019-10933-3
21. Rutgers, J., Sauter, W.: Fair private governance for the platform economy: EU competition and contract law applied to standard terms, pp. 1–3 (2021)
22. Schrepel, T.: What to make of "business models eat law". https://www.networklawreview.org/business-models-eat-law/. Accessed 28 July 2022
23. Schumpeter, J.A., Swedberg, R.: Capitalism, socialism, and democracy, pp. 84–87. Routledge, London; New York (2014)
24. Zanfir-Fortuna, G.: Forgetting About Consent: Why the Focus Should Be on "Suitable Safeguards" in Data Protection Law, p. 9 (2013). https://papers.ssrn.com/abstract=2261973. https://doi.org/10.2139/ssrn.2261973
25. European Data Strategy. https://ec.europa.eu/info/strategy/priorities-2019-2024/europe-fit-digital-age/european-data-strategy_en. Accessed 10 Aug 2022

26. Regulation (EU) 2016/679 of the European Parliament and of the Council of 27 April 2016 on the protection of natural persons with regard to the processing of personal data and on the free movement of such data, and repealing Directive 95/46/EC (General Data Protection Regulation) (2016)
27. Regulation (EU) 2022/1925 of the European Parliament and of the Council of 14 September 2022 on contestable and fair markets in the digital sector and amending Directives (EU) 2019/1937 and (EU) 2020/1828 (DMA) (Text with EEA relevance) (2022)
28. Sneak peek: how the Commission will enforce the DSA & DMA. https://ec.europa.eu/commission/presscorner/detail/en/STATEMENT_22_4327. Accessed 10 Aug 2022

Towards Assessing Features of Dark Patterns in Cookie Consent Processes

Emre Kocyigit$^{(\boxtimes)}$ ⓘ, Arianna Rossi ⓘ, and Gabriele Lenzini ⓘ

SnT, University of Luxembourg, 4364 Esch-sur-Alzette, Luxembourg
{emre.kocyigit,arianna.rossi,gabriele.lenzini}@uni.lu

Abstract. There has been a burst of discussions about how to characterize and recognize online dark patterns — i.e., web design strategies that aim to steer user choices towards what favours service providers or third parties like advertisers rather than what is in the best interest of users. Dark patterns are common in cookie banners where they are used to influence users to accept being tracked for more purposes than a data protection by default principle would dictate. Despite all the discussions, an objective, transparent, and verifiable assessment of dark patterns' qualities is still missing. We contribute to bridging this gap by studying several cookie processes, in particular their multi-layered information flow —that we represent as message sequence charts—, and by identifying a list of observable and measurable features that we believe can help describing the presence of dark patterns in digital consent flows. We propose thirty one of such properties that can be operationalised into metrics and therefore into objective procedures for the detection of dark patterns.

Keywords: Dark patterns · Deceptive designs · Cookie consent · Features · Dark pattern detection

1 Introduction

Dark patterns are manipulative design techniques that aim to favour certain purposes of digital services at the price of user's autonomy, such as collecting as many personal data as possible, and are very often illegal. Discussions about what exactly dark patterns are have arisen from different perspectives, for instance user experience, data protection law, interaction design. Each view has added useful insights on their determining characteristics that can help researchers, legislators, regulators, product developers and designers alike to recognize them and avoid their use.

Dark patterns in cookie banners have been particularly studied [6,15–17] due to their ubiquitous presence, which has increased dramatically since the GDPR strengthened the consent and transparency requirements for personal data processing, therefore new ways of sidestepping the rules and extorting consent have been experimented. Still, even within this very specific domain, there is a lack of criteria capable of capturing the essence of dark patterns and that can be operationalised into measurable variables. Now, even if not all the characteristics of

F. Bieker et al. (Eds.): Privacy and Identity 2022, IFIP AICT 671, pp. 165–183, 2023.
https://doi.org/10.1007/978-3-031-31971-6_13

dark patterns can be measured, like the intentionality of the deception, this approach would offer a framework that can be leveraged to reliably discuss, argue, verify claims on the supposed presence of dark patterns on a digital service and, eventually, detect them.

Moreover, dark patterns are not only related with Human-Computer Interaction (HCI) layers, like the graphical user interface, but also with the back-end of applications. Even though inspecting the user interface level can help to determine some dark pattern characteristics such as unbalanced weight of options or hard-to-notice buttons, there are certain manipulative strategies that are hidden in the back-end and are therefore invisible without inspecting the elements of a web page such as the cookie content, the cookie size, etc. For example, some websites do not respect the user's consent refusal decision and continue to collect their data nevertheless, like Matte et al. indicated in [13]. Therefore, we consider both HCI and Machine-to-Machine Interaction (MMI) layers, like the Web Server, in this study.

Our Contribution. For the purpose of providing objective descriptions on whether there are dark patterns in cookie consent flows, we study different websites' cookie consent processes and extract their activity diagrams through HCI and MMI layers, i.e. User Action, User Interface, Browser and Web Server. Consequently, we propose thirty-one features of cookie consent processes that could be useful to recognize dark patterns via the objective assessment of their characteristics. We define such features based on the information flow layers like User Interface, Web Server etc. and label them according to their values, which can be quantitative or binary. By leveraging these objective descriptions which can be operationalised into metrics, automated detection and analysing tools can be developed to help different stakeholders to detect, prevent and avoid dark patterns.

2 Related Work

The history of deceptive designs influencing people's decisions dates back to the days when digital services did not exist. For instance, fake advertisements of store closings existed even before the internet with the goal of attracting customers and boosting purchases [14]. Today's online deceptive designs can be more complicated and hard to respond because digital services affect thousands, even millions of people, unlike a traditional store. Moreover, these designs are omnipresent: for example, 97% of the most common websites and applications exploit at least one deceptive design in the European Union [10].

Especially after 2010, when the UX expert Harry Brignull coined the term "dark pattern" [3], the approval of regulations like the GDPR, an increased public scrutiny and the visible pervasiveness of these design strategies prompted researchers to analyze dark patterns. Mathur et al. [11] defined dark patterns' attributes in seven categories: *"Sneaking", "Urgency", "Misdirection", "Social Proof", "Scarcity", "Obstruction", "Forced Action"*, after scraping 11K e-commerce websites and having examined their functionalities. In [5], M.C. Gray et al. categorized the dark patterns into five types as *"Nagging", "Obstruction", "Sneaking", "Interface Inference" and "Forced Action"* from an interface design and user experience perspective and covered all eleven types - e.g. *"Trick questions", "Sneak into basket", and "Roach motel"* - that were categorized in [1].

Even if many efforts have been made to create taxonomies where a strict categorization of different types of dark patterns is proposed, we believe it is more useful and objective to identify those attributes, i.e. functional characteristics, that can help detect a dark pattern, no matter the category to which it belongs. Mathur et al [11] defined dark pattern attributes as *"Asymmetric", "Restrictive", "Covert", "Deceptive", "Information Hiding", and "Disparate Treatment"*. Even though these definitions are helpful to describe some dark patterns, they are not yet measurable, actionable nor objectively portrayed. For example, the asymmetric attribute is defined as "unequal burden on options" provided to the user, but the burden is not explicitly measurable, also because it is not defined whether it concerns the amount of time, steps, cognitive effort, etc. that a user takes to perform a certain action.

Dark patterns can be faced in various parts of websites, applications, videogames, and other digital services. Researchers often focus on specific phases of the user experience, such as consent management flows, to analyze and understand their influence on users. For example, M. Nouwens et al. [15] found that dark patterns are ubiquitous in the designs of consent banners by scraping 10000 websites and their consent management platforms in the UK. In another work [13], Matte et al. detected legal violations related to dark patterns in cookie banners. For example, they proved that 141 websites behaved like they had user's positive consent though the user did not take any consent action. On the other hand, M.C. Gray et al. [6] highlighted that dark patterns in consent banners require an holistic approach due to their n-dimensional structure. C. Krisam et al. examined German websites and their cookies, and found that dark patterns that nudge users towards accepting cookies exist in most consent processes [8]. P. Hausner et al. also worked on the cookie banners of some German websites and inspected html and css elements of different examples as a first step of building automated detection tool for dark patterns [7].

In order to prevent and detect manipulative designs and legal violations in the cookie consent flow, developing automated detection tools is an emerging solution, like in [2]. However, there is still a long way to go in the automated detection studies. T.H. Soe et al. [17] used a data set [16] that contains 300 news websites, to train their machine learning model for automated detection of dark patterns in cookie banners such as "nagging, obstruction, sneaking" etc. They also pointed out the representation challenges and detection challenges of automated detection. For example, machine learning models can be quite successful for specific data types like image or text. Recent studies on image-based tasks or text-based tasks displayed promising results [4]. However, the image is usually not enough to understand if there is a dark pattern or not. Two banners that are visually similar but contain different textual contents can be classified under the same label by the model, even if one of them contains manipulative text, i.e., a dark pattern. Another challenge in automated detection is that data set bias can affect the model's decision-making mechanism [2], therefore data collection process and sources should be designed regarding real-life data and possible bias.

As a result, the automated detection of dark patterns is still an unsolved issue, and an objective definition of features, at date missing, can support automated detection processes.

3   Background

3.1   Cookie Consent Flow

In order to obtain measurable criteria of the cookie consent process that provide an objective description of the dark patterns presence in this process, we firstly studied the cookie consent flow and defined its phases as shown in Fig. 1. While the flows have different interface design elements such as buttons, banner size, text etc. or provide various user actions such as "Decline all", "Refuse unnecessary cookies" etc., they show a regular/common structure, probably also as a result of regulations like the GDPR.

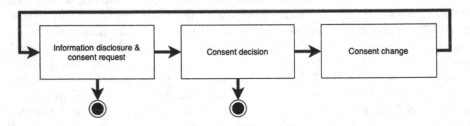

Fig. 1. Cookie consent flow phases

When users visit a website for the first time, they get informed about the presence of cookies and are asked to consent, following Article 7.3 of the GDPR and Article 6.3 and 6.4 of the ePrivacy Directive. This is why, we defined the first phase of the cookie consent flow as "Information disclosure and consent request". At this phase, cookie banners usually present links or buttons that redirect users towards a complete privacy policy, if they initiate that further action. Often there is also the possibility to customize consent options through user configuration.

After users are informed about the cookie policy, they usually have two options: leave the website without any further action or decide whether to grant or refuse consent. For this reason, the cookie consent process may end after the first phase or continue with the second phase, namely "Consent decision". At this stage, users can grant their consent for all data processing purposes, for some (with customization of consent option), or refuse consent. After the consent decision, user can surf the website without any further consent action. According to the user's decision, cookie-related requests and responses run between browser and web server. Thus, cookies which will be loaded and saved to the user's device are known when user revisit the website after the consent decision.

Finally, users may change their previous consent decision (i.e., right to consent withdrawal, Article 7 GDPR). Hence, we defined the third phase as "Consent decision change". At this stage, users may withdraw their consent, provide consent for previously refused processing purposes, or give consent for all or some of the previously refused purposes. This change reshapes cookie content which will be handled between the browser and web server for the user. Also, the third phase triggers the first phase as shown in Fig. 1.

We created a matrix to extract all possible cookie consent scenarios as shown in Appendix A. Because there is a loop from the third phase to the first phase, infinite scenarios are possible, but we ignored the last phase because it only determines if the loop is over or not. Eventually, we listed 14 possible scenarios in the consent management flow in terms of user actions and extracted the features by considering these scenarios.

3.2   Human-Computer and Machine-to-Machine Interaction Layers of the Cookie Consent Process

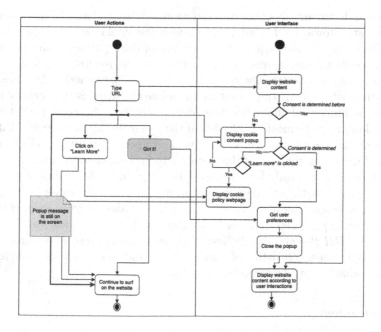

Fig. 2. User Action and User Interface layers of Cookie Consent Flow of Website 2

A web flow is performed via a harmony of different components by synchronous and asynchronous requests and responses online. We drew a Unified Modeling Language (UML) activity diagram which has different layers such as "User Action", "Browser - User Interface", "Browser - Engine" and "Server" as shown in Appendix B to inspect human-computer interaction and machine-to-machine interaction of consent management flows. While vertical flows display alternative cases level by level for each layer, horizontal flows show interactions between different layers. For example, request and response between web engine and web server can be seen in the horizontal flows.

Various consent management flows are available on websites, thus we selected 10 websites (see Appendix C) that provide different consent management flows to examine and drew a diagram for each to make a comparative study. This comparison contributed to define measurable features in the cookie consent flow which may be descriptive for Dark Patterns. For example, while the "User Action" layer of a website's cookie consent flow has 4 actions as shown in Fig. 2, another website's cookie consent flow is more complex because it has more than 20 actions as shown in Fig. 3. We focused on this type of differences to obtain the features. The feature extraction steps and the methodology are detailed in the next section.

4   Research Questions and Methodology

4.1   Research Questions

In our research, we aim to define the functional characteristics of dark patterns. As a first step towards this goal, we choose the cookie consent process as a use case to elaborate the objective assessment of dark patterns' characteristics. Thereby, our first research question is: *"What are the features in cookie consent processes to objectively describe the presence of dark patterns?"*. The answer to this question will be a starting point to formulate the metrics that can be helpful to define the functional characteristics of dark patterns. Secondly, most studies have only looked at the most visible side of the online world, like the user interface as we mentioned in Sect. 1, thus we have an imperfect understanding of dark patterns. Another motivation of this paper is to find out if there are features that are visible/measurable only by examining the HCI and MMI layers of the cookie consent flow. A holistic approach is essential to define a comprehensive feature list. Accordingly, another question is: *"Are there any dark pattern-related features of cookie consent processes that can be identified only by inspecting multiple layers of HCI and MMI flows?"*. We believe that answers to these questions will aid to formulate the characteristics of dark patterns and to extract suitable features for the automated detection models in future work.

4.2   Methodology

As a first step, we selected cookie consent flows of 10 different websites which are listed in Table 2. Some of them contain dark patterns like "Forced Action"

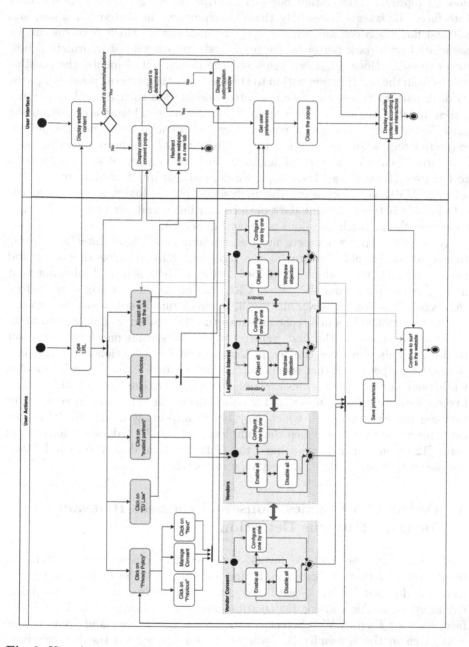

Fig. 3. User Action and User Interface layers of Cookie Consent Flow of Website 3

[5]. The second step is creating UML activity diagrams for each cookie consent flow to represent information flows in multiple layers as: User Action - User Interface - Browser - Server. By these diagrams, we inspected horizontal and vertical flows between and within layers to understand which patterns can be associated with dark patterns. We organized the analysis of information flow into two subsections. First, we inspected the number of elements, the possible routes from the starting user action to the final one, the patterns possibly related to dark pattern types, and cookie related information such as cookie size and cookie number of each cookie consent flow separately. Then, we compared the same layers of different cookie consent flows with each other. For example, we extracted routes for same action from different cookie consent processes and compared them to find their differences, such as number of actions required to the user. After the analysis steps, we defined features according to the HCI and the MMO layers by using the analysis outputs. Finally, we discussed the relationship between existing dark pattern attributes and our proposed features to answer the research questions presented in Sect. 4.

As a first step, we focused on "User Action" and "User Interface" layers to extract measurable features at the moment of information disclosure and consent request. For example, if we look at Fig. 2, there is a bold, blue line that highlights the path from the "Type URL" action to the "Continue to surf on the website" action. However, in Fig. 3, a direct line is not available between these two actions. This difference indicates that the user does not need to make a consent decision on the first website, while the second one forces the user to decide. This difference can be an indicator of forced action [5], which is a restrictive property [12] that is common in dark pattern examples. Additionally, while there are two user options available in Fig. 2 after the "Type URL" action, five options are present in Fig. 3. This also affects the difference in complexity between the two examples, which may be an important metric to define the asymmetric property, i.e., when the complexity of two flows does not have equal load [12]. Consequently, we defined the features "Forced decision" and "User options at first connection", respectively, in Sect. 5.

5   Features in Cookies Consent Processes Relevant for Dark Patterns Detection

After extracting the multiple layers of the cookie consent flows of ten different websites that are listed in B and carrying out the extraction process that was detailed in Sect. 3, we listed thirty one features according to different layers of cookie consent information flow – i.e., User Action, User Interface, Browser Engine, Web Server – and types – i.e., Binary and Quantitative – as given in the Appendix B. As a result, we categorized the features into: Human-Computer(User Action and User Interface) Interaction-based in Sect. 5.1 and Machine-to-Machine(Browser Engine and Web Server) Interaction-based in Sect. 5.2.

5.1   Human-Computer Interaction-Based Features

1. **Forced decision**: This feature describes if the cookie consent banner prevents website usage without a consent decision. In the UML activity diagram, if there is no direct link from the "Type URL" user action to the "Continue to surf on the website" user action, it means that the website forces the user to make a consent decision. The value of the feature would be "1" then. Some websites allow to navigate the website while keeping the consent banner on the screen without requiring a user action. In this case, the value would be "0".

2. **User options at first visit**: Consent banners vary in terms of the first possible actions available. While some of them provide three options such as "Agree", "Disagree" and "Customise", others can provide only one option like "Got it", or two options "Accept all" and "Learn more". This feature describes the number of user actions at the first connection.

Full consent

3. **Availability**: This feature describes if there is a full consent option that allows the user to accept all processing purposes at once, like an "Accept all" button. The value 1 is assigned when this option is available, while 0 is assigned when it is not. Generally, consent banners provide this option.

4. **Total number of routes**: This feature gives the total number of possible routes from the "Type URL" user action to the "Accept all/Agree all etc." user action. Some websites provide more than one way to consent to all cookies, while providing one or no way to reach the option of refusal.

5. **Minimum length of routes**: This feature describes the shortest route from the "Type URL" user action to the "Accept all" action, and can be helpful to define if a flow provides asymmetric options.

6. **Maximum length of routes**: This feature describes the longest route from the "Type URL" user action to the "Accept all" action and can be helpful to define if a flow provides asymmetric options. If loops exist, then only the first loop will be considered for this feature.

Full consent refusal

7. **Availability**: This feature describes if there is a full consent refusal option like the "Decline all" button, where 1 means that that option is available. While websites generally have a full cookie acceptance option, it is not always the case that they have a full consent refusal option on the first layer. Since websites may use various phrases to express consent refusal (for example, while one shows "Refuse unnecessary cookies", another one can show "Refuse all"), we accept all of these as full consent refusal indications.

8. **Total number of routes**: This feature gives the total number of all possible routes from the "Type URL" user action to "Decline all/Disagree all" user action. Therefore, this feature can be helpful to understand if both options are provided to user in a symmetric way.

9. **Minimum length of routes**: Users perform actions to complete a consent decision flow and this process contains a different number of steps. While

some websites provide shorter or easier ways to get to consenting, they may make the consent refusal path harder. This feature describes the shortest route from the "Type URL" user action to the "Decline all" action and can be helpful to define asymmetry within the website or comparatively with other websites.

10. **Maximum length of routes**: This feature describes the longest route from "Type URL" user action to "Decline all" action, and can be helpful to define if a flow provides asymmetric options. If loops exist, then only the first loop will be considered for this feature.

Customised consent Some websites provide the customization of consent preferences to users according to the data processing purposes. This process usually takes more time and requires more user actions than granting full consent.

11. **Availability**: This feature describes if the cookie consent flow contains a configuration or customization option concerning processing purposes and/or vendors, where 1 means that the customization is available on the cookie banner, while 0 signifies that it is not available.

12. **Total number of routes**: This feature gives the total number of all possible routes from "Type URL" user action to "Customize/preferences/options etc." user action. Therefore, this feature can be helpful to understand the complexity of the flow.

13. **Minimum length of routes**: This feature describes the shortest route from the "Type URL" user action to the "Partly accept/save and exit" action after configuring the consent settings. This feature can also be helpful to define if a flow provides asymmetric options.

14. **Maximum length of routes**: This feature describes the longest route from the "Type URL" user action to "Partly accept/save and exit" action. If loops exist, then only the first loop will be considered for this feature.

15. **Total user action options**: This feature describes the total number of actions on the User Actions layer of cookie consent flow. It can be helpful to express the complexity of consent management flow.

16. **Total consent flow routes**: This feature describes all possible routes from the first user action to the end on the User Actions layer. Website designs can provide different consent scenarios, where some of them offer "Accept all" scenarios more often than "Decline all" scenarios. This feature can be helpful to understand asymmetry through all possible scenarios.

17. **Total hyperlinks on user interface**: This feature concerns the Browser - User Interface layer, and describes the total number of hyperlinks (e.g. buttons) on it. It can be helpful to understand the complexity of interactions on the user interface.

18. **Consent decisions management availability**: This feature describes if there is a consent change button, link, dashboard etc. on the website to edit a previously given consent decision, e.g. withdrawing consent. If the value

of this feature is 1, that means that the consent decision can be updated by the user.

19. **Dead end**: This feature describes if there is a link or button which redirects user from the cookie consent flow to a new web page outside of the flow without providing the possibility to come back into the cookie consent flow. For example, a cookie banner can open a new window when a user clicks on the "privacy policy" link and the new page doesn't provide any "back" button.

5.2 Machine-to-Machine Interaction-Based Quality Features

In the network section of browser inspection, requests between browser and web server can be observed. The number of requests, the size and number of cookies, and the size of transferred files vary according to whether the visit is the first one or not and whether consent decisions are taken or not.

20. **Number of cookies at first visit**: The cookies that are installed on a device and their details can be unveiled when the web browsers are inspected. This feature describes the total number of cookies installed when a user visits a website for the first time.

21. **Number of cookies in full consent**: This feature describes the total number of cookies installed when a user visits the website after full consent grant.

22. **Number of cookies in full consent refusal**: This feature describes the total number of cookies when a user visits the website after full consent refusal.

23. **Cookie size at first visit**: This feature describes the total cookie size when a user visits the website for the first time. Each cookie has its own size value, but we obtain the total size to simplify the feature and generate a quantitative one.

24. **Cookie size in full consent**: The cookie size value should be associated with consent grant decision. This feature describes the total cookie size when consent is fully granted.

25. **Cookie size in full consent refusal**: This feature is the opposite of cookie size in consent grant feature, and describes the total cookie size when consent is refused. When user does not allow all cookies, this feature should be lower from the above one in most cases.

26. **Total requests at first visit**: This feature describes the total number of requests between browser and web server at the first stage, before the consent decision. Some of the requests are not related with consent but with functionality of the website, e.g., source files of the web page, while others are directly related with the consent management process or the consent decision. Therefore, this feature can be helpful when it is used with the below two to check if the consent decision is correctly implemented.

27. **Total requests in full consent**: This feature describes the total number of requests between browser and web server when consent is granted.

28. **Total requests in full consent refusal**: This feature describes the total number of requests between browser and web server when consent is refused.
29. **Transferred file size at first visit**: Transferred files between browser and web server can vary based on consent decision. This feature describes the total transferred file size in the first interaction between the user and the website.
30. **Transferred file size in full consent**: This feature describes the total transferred file size when the user types a URL after consent is granted.
31. **Transferred file size in full consent refusal**: This feature describes the total transferred file size when the user types a URL after consent is refused.

6   Discussion

We have listed 31 features which can be operationalizable into metrics to assess dark patterns after analysing the cookie consent processes in the previous section. One of the purposes of this work is to promote objective grounds to discuss qualities about online patterns and eventually provide evidence to discuss, confirm or refute claims on whether a particular design pattern is "Dark". To the best of our intention, the features that we have identified are all operationalizable. It is possible, in other words, to define measures for the features that can be evaluated on the layered message sequence charts that we have provided. Some of them can be already used to objectively capture certain qualities and characteristics that have been only informally described in the literature. For instance, in [12], Mathur et al. defined six attributes and two of them, i.e. asymmetric (unequal weights on the provided options to the user) and restrictive (discarding specific options that should be available to the user) can be described with the features we proposed. For example, asymmetric can be evaluated by comparing these features: "Total number of routes in full consent grant (#4)", "Total number of routes in full consent refusal (#8)", "Total number of routes in customized consent grant (#12)". If their values are not equal, we can conclude that the design is asymmetric in an objective way. The restrictive attribute can be described by the following ones: "Forced decision (#1)", "Full consent availability (#3)", "Full consent refusal availability (#7)", and "Customized consent availability (#11)". For instance, if the value of "Full consent refusal availability (#7)" is zero, then we can argue that users do not have the option to reject cookies in one action, i.e., the cookie consent flow contains a restrictive pattern.

The features can provide descriptions of dark patterns when they are used in different cookie consent flows, not only within one cookie consent flow. We believe that our proposals are not only providing direct description of dark patterns' attributes such as "asymmetric" or "restrictive", but also indirect metrics like "complexity". For example, the complexity of a large amount of different flows can be measured with the help of "Total consent flow routes (#16)", "Total user action options (#15)", and "Total buttons on User Interface (#17)". In this case, reasonable inferences can be made for individual samples after calculating the mean values. For example, "choice complexity", which is defined as required effort for an action or selection in [10], can be measured with these features.

Although dark patterns can be hidden in the back-end of the cookie consent flows, the MMI-based features can evaluate their presence since the features check the interaction within/between Browser and Web Server layers of the cookie consent flow. For example, when "Cookie size in full consent (#24)" and "Cookie size in full consent refusal (#25)" are assessed together, if they are equal we can deduce that the consent refusal option is not working or that the cookie consent flow is deceptive, as it shows to users the option of refusal but user's choice is not correctly registered. We measured these features of different websites when users firstly arrived to the website before consent decision and after full consent grant or full consent refusal as shown in the Fig. 4. As it can be observed, in most instances the values of the features are unsurprisingly lower, rather than equal, when a user refuses to consent comparing to the full consent grant.

Website	Cookie number			Cookie size			Request number			Transferred file size		
	in first visit	full consent	consent refusal	in first visit	full consent	consent refusal	in first visit	full consent	consent refusal	in first visit	full consent	consent refusal
w3schools.com	3	5	5	66	519	401	46	39	37	1.32 MB	144.01 KB	47.13 KB
researchgate.net	4	10	6	387	946	663	41	35	31	1.18 MB	15.31 KB	14.40 KB
stack overflow.com	5	6	6	360	379	403	44	36	33	609.51 KB	126.69 KB	104.17 KB
dropbox.com	10	65	46	677	2796	1757	108	405	90	1.80 MB	1.59 MB	375.26 KB

Fig. 4. Extracted values of machine-to-machine interaction-based cookie consent features

As we mentioned in Sect. 2, previous categorization and definition studies offer a variety of perspectives to examine dark patterns, but the literature on the topic still lacks objective and measurable criteria to assess the presence of dark patterns on online services. We believe that measurable metrics are not only needed for an objective evaluation, but also to develop automated detection tools, which require a concrete and measurable feature set and can be helpful for developers and designers during testing processes, and to regulators and researchers during evaluation and inspection processes. Automated detection tools like machine learning-based systems require structured data in the training process. These metrics can be helpful to constitute feature sets and data sets thanks to their measurable nature.

7 Limitations and Future Work

We examined the cookie consent flow as a use case of dark patterns and proposed thirty one features that can be operationalised into metrics based on our multi-layers interaction flow analyses. We provided clear descriptions for them, but we have not yet defined procedures, quality measures, nor guidelines to interpret them for any of the features that we have described. We have informally given a few exemplifying arguments to show that this exercise is possible, but its full development is left for future work.

We selected ten different websites and extracted the interaction flows of their cookie consent processes. We believe this sample is sufficiently representative for this initial analysis, but of course additional different examples may help to explore other features. We excluded the "legitimate interest" paths in the cookie consent flow and the flows that repeat over time, e.g., nagging users to consent in their later visits. Moreover, the choices we made in selecting certain elements of the process in the message sequence chart affect what features we can define. For instance the edges in our charts are unweighted. One could, for instance, consider the cost of a certain choice which can provide new features.

Furthermore, while studying multiple layers of interaction flows can contribute to obtain metrics describing dark pattern characteristics, we excluded the language. Therefore these features are not capable of describing examples like "confirmshaming" [9], which exploits human emotions like guilt to manipulate users. We also did not include visual elements such as button size, colour, contrast ratio etc. into this study but we intend to consider them in our future work.

The back-end of websites would need further investigations to cover other aspects of Dark Patterns and extend their features. For instance, we focused on the total cookie size in different consent conditions, but we did not extract the content of the cookies, and we observed the total number of requests between browser and web server, but we did not detect the ones that are directly related with cookies. Hence, the features can be elaborated into their breakdowns such as "Total cookie-based requests after full consent" or "Advertisement-based requests after full consent refusal". Since all cookies do not represent same mission, e.g., some can be designed the functionality of cookie consent mechanism.

8   Conclusion

We extracted the information flows of ten cookie consent processes and studied the multiple layers as "User Action", "Browser-User Interface", "Browser-Engine" and "Server" to obtain objective and measurable criteria to assess the presence of dark patterns. In this direction, we proposed thirty one features of dark patterns in the cookie consent flow. They can be operationalised into metrics not only to evaluate the presence of dark patterns on online services, but also to be build automated detection models.

Acknowledgement. This paper is published as a part of the project Decepticon (grant no. IS/14717072) supported by the Luxembourg National Research Fund (FNR). We would like to thank Nataliia Bielova for her helpful comments.

A   Appendix A

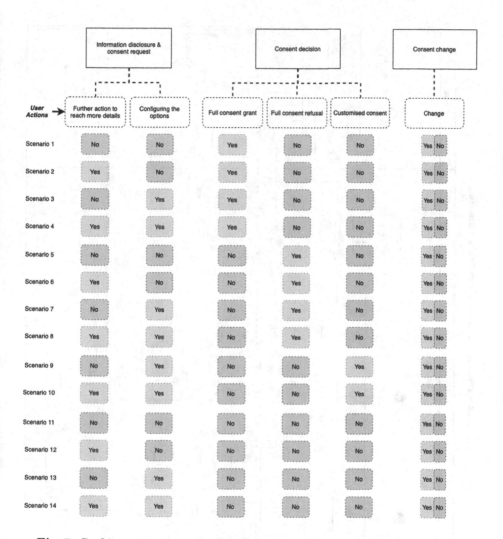

Fig. 5. Cookie consent scenarios based on user actions in the first two phases

B   Appendix B

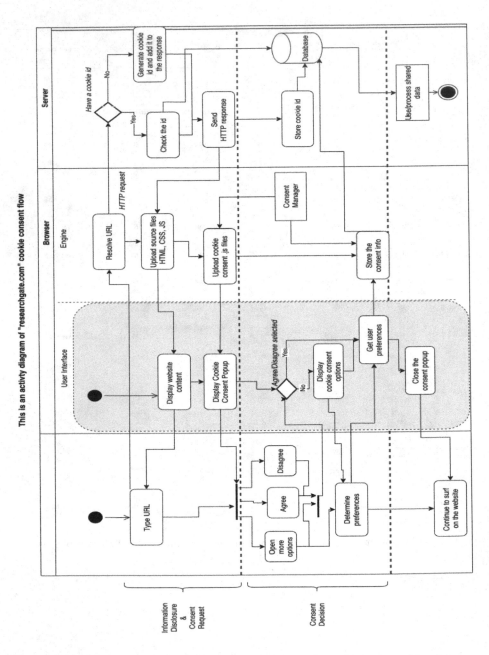

Fig. 6. Multi-layer presentation of human-computer and machine-to-machine interaction flow of cookie consent flow.

C   Appendix C

Table 1. Features of Cookie Consent Process Relevant for Dark Patterns Detection

No	Feature	Layer	Value
1	Forced decision	User Action	Binary
2	User options at first visit	User Action	Quantitative
3	Full consent availability	User Action	Binary
4	Total number of routes in full consent grant	User Action	Quantitative
5	Minimum length of routes in full consent grant	User Action	Quantitative
6	Maximum length of routes in full consent grant	User Action	Quantitative
7	Full consent refusal availability	User Action	Binary
8	Total number of routes in full consent refusal	User Action	Quantitative
9	Minimum length of routes in full consent refusal	User Action	Quantitative
10	Maximum length of routes in full consent refusal	User Action	Quantitative
11	Customised consent availability	User Action	Quantitative
12	Total number of routes in customised consent	User Action	Quantitative
13	Minimum length of routes in customised consent	User Action	Quantitative
14	Maximum length of routes in customised consent	User Action	Quantitative
15	Total user action options	User Action	Quantitative
16	Total consent flow routes	User Action	Quantitative
17	Total hyperlinks on user interface	User Interface	Quantitative
18	Consent decisions management availability	User Action	Binary
19	Dead end	User Action	Binary
20	Number of cookies at first visit	Web Engine	Quantitative
21	Number of cookies after full consent	Web Engine	Quantitative
22	Number of cookies after full consent refusal	Web Engine	Quantitative
23	Cookie size at first visit	Web Engine	Quantitative
24	Cookie size after full consent	Web Engine	Quantitative
25	Cookie size after full consent refusal	Web Engine	Quantitative
26	Total requests at first visit	Web Engine-Web Server	Quantitative
27	Total requests after full consent	Web Engine-Web Server	Quantitative
28	Total requests after full consent refusal	Web Engine-Web Server	Quantitative
29	Transferred file size at first visit	Web Engine-Web Server	Quantitative
30	Transferred file size after full consent	Web Engine-Web Server	Quantitative
31	Transferred file size after full consent refusal	Web Engine-Web Server	Quantitative

Table 2. Websites That Are Selected To Inspect Cookies Consent Processes

No	URL	No	URL
1	https://www.researchgate.net	6	https://twitter.com
2	https://www.kaggle.com	7	https://www.dropbox.com
3	https://www.w3schools.com	8	https://wwwfr.uni.lu
4	https://stackoverflow.com	9	https://github.com
5	https://www.linkedin.com	10	https://medium.com

References

1. Deceptive design - user interfaces crafted to trick you. https://www.deceptive.design/
2. Bollinger, D., Kubicek, K., Cotrini, C., Basin, D.: Automating cookie consent and gdpr violation detection. In: 31st USENIX Security Symposium (USENIX Security 22). USENIX Association (2022)
3. Brignull, H.: Dark patterns: dirty tricks designers use to make people do stuff. Retrieved Sept 29 2019 (2010)
4. Géron, A.: Hands-on machine learning with Scikit-Learn, Keras, and TensorFlow. "O'Reilly Media, Inc." (2022)
5. Gray, C.M., Kou, Y., Battles, B., Hoggatt, J., Toombs, A.L.: The dark (patterns) side of ux design. In: Proceedings of the 2018 CHI conference on human factors in computing systems. pp. 1–14 (2018)
6. Gray, C.M., Santos, C., Bielova, N., Toth, M., Clifford, D.: Dark patterns and the legal requirements of consent banners: An interaction criticism perspective. In: Proceedings of the 2021 CHI Conference on Human Factors in Computing Systems. pp. 1–18 (2021)
7. Hausner, P., Gertz, M.: Dark patterns in the interaction with cookie banners. arXiv preprint arXiv:2103.14956 (2021)
8. Krisam, C., Dietmann, H., Volkamer, M., Kulyk, O.: Dark patterns in the wild: Review of cookie disclaimer designs on top 500 german websites. In: European Symposium on Usable Security 2021, pp. 1–8 (2021)
9. Luguri, J., Strahilevitz, L.J.: Shining a light on dark patterns. Journal of Legal Analysis **13**(1), 43–109 (2021)
10. Lupiáñez-Villanueva, F., Boluda, A., Bogliacino, F., Liva, G., Lechardoy, L., de las Heras Ballell, T.R.: Behavioural study on unfair commercial practices in the digital environment: dark patterns and manipulative personalisation. European Commission, Directorate-General for Justice and Consumers, final report. May (2022)
11. Mathur, A., et al.: Dark patterns at scale: Findings from a crawl of 11k shopping websites. In: Proceedings of the ACM on Human-Computer Interaction 3(CSCW), pp. 1–32 (2019)
12. Mathur, A., Kshirsagar, M., Mayer, J.: What makes a dark pattern... dark? design attributes, normative considerations, and measurement methods. In: Proceedings of the 2021 CHI Conference on Human Factors in Systems, pp. 1–18 (2021)

13. Matte, C., Bielova, N., Santos, C.: Do cookie banners respect my choice?: Measuring legal compliance of banners from iab europe's transparency and consent framework. In: 2020 IEEE Symposium on Security and Privacy (SP), pp. 791–809. IEEE (2020)
14. Narayanan, A., Mathur, A., Chetty, M., Kshirsagar, M.: Dark patterns: past, present, and future: the evolution of tricky user interfaces. Queue **18**(2), 67–92 (2020)
15. Nouwens, M., Liccardi, I., Veale, M., Karger, D., Kagal, L.: Dark patterns after the gdpr: Scraping consent pop-ups and demonstrating their influence. In: Proceedings of the 2020 CHI Conference on Human Factors in Computing Systems, pp. 1–13 (2020)
16. Soe, T.H., Nordberg, O.E., Guribye, F., Slavkovik, M.: Circumvention by design-dark patterns in cookie consent for online news outlets. In: Proceedings of the 11th Nordic Conference on Human-Computer Interaction: Shaping Experiences, Shaping Society, pp. 1–12 (2020)
17. Soe, T.H., Santos, C.T., Slavkovik, M.: Automated detection of dark patterns in cookie banners: how to do it poorly and why it is hard to do it any other way. arXiv preprint arXiv:2204.11836 (2022)

Accessibility Statements and Data Protection Notices: What Can Data Protection Law Learn from the Concept of Accessibility?

Olga Gkotsopoulou(✉)

Vrije Universiteit Brussel, Pleinlaan 2, 1050 Brussels, Belgium
olga.gkotsopoulou@vub.be

Abstract. Terms and conditions, legal notices, banners and disclaimers are not new for websites, applications and products. However, with the ambitious legislative plan in the European Union to introduce accessibility features to several websites, applications, services and products, it becomes imperative to also consider the accessibility of the information included in such statements. In my paper, I specifically investigate data protection notices as opposed to accessibility statements and aim to answer whether the concept of accessibility can help us redefine the principle of transparency in EU data protection law. I conclude that accessibility can benefit the principle of transparency, by contextualizing it. However, at the same time it introduces a number of new challenges.

Keywords: Accessibility · Data Protection Law · Transparency · Data Subject Rights

1 Introduction

Terms and conditions, legal notices, banners and disclaimers are not new for websites, applications and products. They serve diverse functions and fulfil different legal obligations. The last two decades, worldwide we observe a rise in the use of such statements given the increase in regulation and enhanced requirements for transparency and user or consumer protection, especially in the European Union (EU) [1]. Often those statements are regarded by their drafters as disclaimers aiming to guard the concerned entities from liability (by lawyers for lawyers) [2], rather than serving an informative purpose ("a public announcement of internal practices") to the public, to the interested users and stakeholders, for the latter to be enabled to make informed choices [3, 4] or to even start a compliance investigation, if needed. In this regard, they have often been criticized for being opaque, lengthy and difficult to read, hard to locate or incomplete [3, 4, 5].

One case where such statements are used, is in the context of personal data protection law – specifically we look at the EU. The principle of transparency, as enshrined in Article 5(1)(a) of the General Data Protection Regulation (GDPR) Regulation (EU) 2016/679 of the European Parliament and of the Council of 27 April 2016 on the protection of

F. Bieker et al. (Eds.): Privacy and Identity 2022, IFIP AICT 671, pp. 184–197, 2023.
https://doi.org/10.1007/978-3-031-31971-6_14

natural persons with regard to the processing of personal data and on the free movement of such data, and repealing Directive 95/46/EC), calls (a) for internal transparency with the obligation to keep a record of processing activities and (b) for external transparency with the disclosure of certain information to the data subject regarding processing operations of personal data [6]. It requires for a minimum set of information to be provided in an easily accessible form and in clear, plain and age-appropriate language. One aspect of this transparency obligation is often understood by data controllers and national supervisory authorities as the provision of a public statement in the form of a data protection notice [7]. The interpretation of the obligation for transparency, however, has been a debatable concept, including voices that the transparency and choice model has substantially failed and other approaches are needed [8].

Several sets of guidelines have been issued by numerous researchers and stakeholders as to what it entails in practice and how those notices should be designed, drafted and communicated, for instance with the help of Transparency Enhancing Tools [9] or icon sets [10]. For example, Liepina et al. [11] have analysed the language of data protection notices in order to investigate their intelligibility, looking whether the information provided was comprehensible, substantive compliance was achieved and the expression was clear. Further research has been conducted by Rossi & Palmirani with respect to the potential of visualisation tools, icons and infographics as alternative means to 'small print' [10]. Schaub et al. [3] introduced the four-tier privacy notice design space, looking into timing, channel, modality and control.

Many issues remain unclear and contentious though, despite suggestions for effective notice design. Such issues include but are not limited to the inability of the European legislator to enforce evidence-based effective information communication [1], allowing the current situation to lead for instance to 'notice fatigue' [3] or the prevalence of 'dark patterns' [6].

Another context where statements are used is that of accessibility. The EU Web Accessibility Directive (WAD) (Directive (EU) 2016/2102 of the European Parliament and of the Council of 26 October 2016 on the accessibility of the websites and mobile applications of public sector bodies) - transposed in all the national jurisdictions of the Member States - requires public bodies to draft and make available accessibility statements on their websites and mobile applications. Another form of accessibility statement, even though not explicitly named as such is also foreseen in the European Accessibility Act (EAA) (Directive (EU) 2019/882 of the European Parliament and of the Council of 17 April 2019 on the accessibility requirements for products and services).

Despite the varying definitions of accessibility given that accessibility can mean many different things to many different people, in this particular context, according to Recital 2 WAD, accessibility should be understood as a set of "principles and techniques to be observed when designing, constructing, maintaining, and updating websites and mobile applications in order to make them more accessible to users, in particular persons with disabilities".

Like data protection notices, accessibility statements can vary in form and content, but they are expected to provide a mandatory minimum set of information. Again, in line with Article 7 WAD, this statement must include the specification of the applicable legislation and the clear indication of the website/application that the statement refers to, the compliance status thereof and a report about non-accessible content on the website or the application. Moreover, it must provide information as to how the statement was prepared (methods used), contact information for feedback and complaints, as well as information about the enforcement status. The accessibility statement is in principle anticipated to be also accessible.

In my paper, I raise the following question: Can the concept of accessibility help us improve the way data protection information and communications are provided? Can accessibility ultimately help us further define transparency? I decipher the purpose (and need) of such statements and notices providing the historical overview of those practices and their societal and legal justification. I argue that the concept of accessibility and of accessibility statements can be used to further explain the principle of transparency in the context of data protection law in four ways: linguistically, procedurally, technically and finally, substantively.

Chapter 2 specifically deals with the topic of information provision in the context of EU accessibility, whereas Chapter 3 demonstrates whether (and how) accessibility is relevant for data protection law, bringing forward ways to bridge the concept of accessibility with the principle of transparency in this particular context. Chapter 4 finally provides a brief overview of benefits and challenges for accessibility in transparency, and Chapter 5 concludes with some final thoughts.

2 Information and Communication Provision in the Context of Accessibility

2.1 Accessibility in the EU

Around 100 million persons in EU (1 out of 5) live with some form and degree of disability [12]. At the same time, the population is increasingly aging, with nearly 50% of persons with a disability being over 65 years old [12]. The EU acknowledging this situation, introduced its intention for a flagship initiative in the field in 2022, named *AccessibleEU*, a cooperation platform for the exchange of knowledge and good practice among accessibility experts across the EU Member States [12].

Accessibility, however, does not constitute a new concept *per se*. Discussions around accessibility coincide with the appearance and establishment of the civil rights movement and the disability rights movement in the 60s and 70s [13]. The discussion back then was primarily focused on the removal of physical barriers and soon also developed to embrace the removal of information and communication barriers [13]. With the ascend of the internet worldwide in 1996, the Web Accessibility Initiative was established within the auspices of the World Wide Web Consortium (W3C). The members of the initiative issued in 1999 the Web Content Accessibility Guidelines (WCAG) Version 1.0 to ensure that accessibility features are embedded on websites, allowing equal participation.

In 2006, the United Nations Convention on the Rights of Persons with Disabilities (UNCRPD) was adopted and the EU acceded to it in 2010. The EC Communication 'European Disability Strategy 2010–2020: A Renewed Commitment to a Barrier-Free Europe' was released shortly after and in 2012 it was followed by the Eurobarometer on Accessibility. In 2016, the Web Accessibility Directive (WAD), with 2 years of transposition time, was adopted. The main aim of this Directive was that, by June 2021, the websites and mobile applications of all public sector bodies are accessible to persons with disabilities and that they additionally include an accessibility statement. In 2019, the European Accessibility Act (EAA), with 3 years of transposition time, was adopted. The ambition of the latter is that by 2030 key services, products and tools to become fully accessible. Accessibility requirements can be found in other legal instruments as well, such as the European Electronic Communications Code, the Audiovisual Media Services Directive and the copyright legislation adopted under the Marrakesh Treaty.

2.2 What is Accessibility?

Article 9 of the UNCRPD provides a definition of accessibility: "[t]o enable persons with disabilities to live independently and participate fully in all aspects of life, States Parties shall take appropriate measures to ensure to persons with disabilities access, on an equal basis with others, to the physical environment, to transportation, to information and communications, [...]".

The two EU Directives also provide definitions. According to Recital 2 of the WAD: "[...] accessibility should be understood as principles and techniques to be observed when designing, constructing, maintaining, and updating websites and mobile applications in order to make them more accessible to users, in particular persons with disabilities." Moreover, according to Article 1 (2) of the Directive, the requirement for accessibility should be implemented "[...] independently of the device used for access thereto [...]".

According to the Recital 50 of the EAA: "Accessibility should be achieved by the systematic removal and prevention of barriers, preferably through a universal design or 'design for all' approach, which contributes to ensuring access for persons with disabilities on an equal basis with others. According to the UNCRPD, that approach 'means the design of products, environments, programmes and services to be usable by all people, to the greatest extent possible, without the need for adaptation or specialized design'. In line with the UNCRPD, 'universal design' shall not exclude assistive devices for particular groups of persons with disabilities where this is needed [...]".

Reading jointly the above definitions leads us to some initial observations. First, accessibility is often perceived as an umbrella concept. It can be used together or interchangeably with other terms, such as usability, barrier-free, universality, inclusion or inclusiveness, adaptation, integration, reasonable accommodation and so forth. Even though those terms can be related, most of them have received distinct definitions. For example, barrier-free refers to the removal of barriers (physical or otherwise) whereas according to the Digital Accessibility Glossary by the Harvard University, usability "[r]efers to how easily, effectively, and efficiently people, including people with disabilities, can use a product or system to achieve their goals, and how satisfied they are with the experience."[14] Universality or universal design is defined in Article 2 of the UNCRPD, as seen above and the definition is also adopted by the 2019 United Nations Disability Inclusion Strategy [15]. In Annex I of the latter report as well as in the World Health Organization policy on disability [16], (disability) inclusion is defined as "the meaningful participation of persons with disabilities in all their diversity, the promotion of their rights and the consideration of disability-related perspectives [...]" [15]. Reasonable accommodation is defined in Article 2 of the UNCRPD, as "[n]ecessary and appropriate modification and adjustments not imposing a disproportionate or undue burden, where needed in a particular case, [...]". Integration and adaptation appear to be older terms, which nowadays are usually replaced by inclusion and accessibility. The Council of Europe for instance used integration for its report 'Rehabilitation and integration of people with disabilities: policy and legislation', which was first published in 1973 and kept the term in the subsequent editions until 2003.

Second, accessibility is a by-default intersectoral notion, as it interferes with many different sectors – if not all sectors -, in order for persons to be provided with equal opportunities and to ensure non-discrimination. This by-default intersectionality of accessibility creates challenges. For instance, when we look into law and accessibility, Rink has characterised the grouping of legal communication and accessibility as 'oxymoron', in other words an 'implicit contradiction' [17]. Legal communication depends on a common ground between experts [18]. However, legal communication may also refer to a direct expert-lay person communication. In that case, the common ground required for successful communication between the expert and the lay person is reduced and it becomes even further reduced in the context of the communication between an expert and a lay person with a communication impairment [18]. The result is texts which are inappropriate for the intended audience, creating a "strong asymmetry in the communication process", even though the law requires that all parties stand an equal footing with respect to this information [18].

A third observation is that, technical or design accessibility of services and products cannot be complete without accessible information about those respective services and products. This information can be among others about safe use, personal data processing or the accessibility of the service or product itself.

2.3   Accessibility Statements

Accessibility statements were introduced with the WAD. All EU Member States appear to have transposed the Directive, whereas some of them already had relevant existing legislation (i.e. Czech Rep, Germany, Lithuania, Hungary, Austria, Portugal, Slovakia). According to Article 7 WAD:

1   "Member States shall ensure that public sector bodies provide and regularly update a detailed, comprehensive and clear accessibility statement on the compliance of their websites and mobile applications with this Directive.
2   . For websites, the accessibility statement shall be provided in an accessible format, using the model accessibility statement referred to in paragraph 2, and shall be published on the relevant website."

Accessibility statements must be made available using existing or future technologies (Recital 46 WAD). In line with the above and the Commission Implementing Decision 2018/1523, the accessibility statement must include mandatory information on the following matters:

• Specification of the applicable legislation and concerned website/application
• Compliance status

- Non-accessible content on the website

  - Is this lack of accessible content non-compliant?
  - Is the lack of accessible content due to disproportionate burden
  - Is the lack of accessible content because the content in question is outside the scope of the Directive?

- Preparation of the document (method used to prepare the statement)
- Feedback and contact information
- Enforcement

In the European Accessibility Act on the other hand, there is no direct obligation for an accessibility statement. However, Article 13 (2) of the EAA provides for a similar information obligation for service providers. Accordingly: "Service providers shall prepare the necessary information in accordance with Annex V and shall explain how the services meet the applicable accessibility requirements. The information shall be made available to the public in written and oral format, including in a manner which is accessible to persons with disabilities. Service providers shall keep that information for as long as the service is in operation." In the Table below, I compare the characteristics of the two types of statements.

Table 1. Comparison of requirements for accessibility statements in WAD and EAA

WAD	*EAA*
• Obligation of public bodies	• Obligation of all service providers
• Provision of a detailed, comprehensive and clear accessibility statement on compliance	• Provision of the necessary information and explain how the services meet the applicable accessibility requirements
• In accessible format	• In accessible format; in public and in written; for as long as the service is in operation
• On the website or when downloading the app	• In the general terms and conditions, or equivalent document
• Mandatory elements: o Specification of the applicable legislation and concerned website/application o Compliance status o Non-accessible content on the website: non-compliant, disproportionate burden or outside the scope o Preparation of the document (method used to prepare the statement) o Feedback and contact information o Enforcement	• Mandatory elements: o Consumer information requirements of Directive 2011/83/EU o A general description of the service in accessible formats o Descriptions and explanations necessary for the understanding of the operation of the service o A description of how the relevant accessibility requirements are met by the service

3 Accessibility in Transparency in Data Protection Law

3.1 Information and Communication Transparency in Data Protection Law

The principle of information and communication transparency is key in the EU data protection law and specifically in the General Data Protection Regulation (GDPR). According to the Article 29 Working Party Guidelines on transparency under Regulation 2016/679, "transparency is a long-established feature of the law of the EU. It is about engendering trust in the processes which affect the citizen by enabling them to understand, and if necessary, challenge those processes. It is also an expression of the principle of fairness [...]" [7] And it adds: "[t]he concept of transparency in the GDPR is user-centric rather than legalistic." [7] This means that "the quality, *accessibility* [emphasis by the author] and comprehensibility of the information is as important as the actual content of the transparency information" [7].

The transparency requirements are to be found in Articles 12 - 14 of the GDPR and apply irrespectively of the legal basis for processing. A popular way for providing information is through data protection notices on websites, applications and devices. Those notices include mainly information as described in Articles 13 and 14 depending on whether the personal data have been obtained or not from the data subject.

3.2 Is Accessibility Relevant for Data Protection Law?

Further I examine whether the concept of accessibility is present in the text of the data protection law. Accessibility according to the Oxford Learners' Dictionary is to be understood as: *how easy something is to reach, enter, use, see, etc. / how easy something is to reach, enter, use, etc. for somebody with a disability / how easy something is to understand.* The term 'accessibility' and the term 'accessible' in the GDPR appear in different articles and recitals as seen in the table below. In this table, the meaning of the terms has been interpreted to figure relevance and non-relevance, when the term signifies a different concept than the investigated one in the present paper, based on the above definitions. Specifically, by relevance, what is meant here is whether the terms that appear in the GDPR text are used within the meaning of *how easy something is to reach, enter, use, see, etc.* or they additionally leave space for interpretation in relation to information and communication accessibility. As seen in the table below, not all terms leave space for further interpretation in that latter context. The majority of the relevant terms as they appear in the text however could be argued to present a high relevance, whereas only one could be argued to have only low relevance.

Table 2. The term 'accessibility' in the GDPR

Accessibility	*Level of Relevance*
Recital 23 GDPR – *mere accessibility* of website/contact details	*Non-relevance*
Article 25(2) GDPR – *accessibility of personal data*	*Non-relevance*

Table 3. The term 'accessible' in the GDPR

Accessible	Level of Relevance
Recital 39 GDPR: any information and communication be *easily accessible*	*Relevance (High)*
Recital 42 GDPR: declaration of consent in *easily accessible form*	*Relevance (High)*
Recital 49 GDPR: services offered or *accessible*	*Non-relevance*
Recital 58 GDPR GDPR: any information addressed to the public or to the data subject be *easily accessible*	*Relevance (High)*
Recital 91 GDPR: monitoring publicly *accessible* areas	*Non-relevance*
Recital 154 GDPR: parts of documents *accessible*	*Non-relevance*
Article 4(6) GDPR: personal data which are *accessible*	*Non-relevance*
Article 7(2) GDPR: conditions for consent - *easily accessible form*	*Relevance (High)*
Article 12(1) GDPR: any information referred to in Articles 13 and 14 and any communication under Articles 15 to 22 and 34 *in easily accessible form*	*Relevance (High)*
Article 14(2)(f) GDPR: publicly *accessible* sources	*Non-relevance*
Article 25(2) GDPR: personal data made *accessible*	*Non-relevance*
Article 35(2)(c) GDPR: monitoring of a publicly *accessible* area	*Non-relevance*
Article 37(2) GDPR: a data protection officer is *easily accessible*	*Non-relevance*
Article 43(6) GDPR: certification requirements and mechanisms in *easily accessible form*	*Relevance (Low)*
Article 70(1)(y) GDPR: a publicly accessible electronic register of decisions	*Non-relevance*

Recitals 39 and 58 as well as Article 12(1) GDPR are of particularly high relevance for the present paper. Recital 58 GDPR specifically states: "The principle of transparency requires that any information addressed to the public or to the data subject be concise, easily accessible and easy to understand, and that clear and plain language and, additionally, where appropriate, visualisation be used. Such information could be provided in electronic form, for example, when addressed to the public, through a website. [...] Given that children merit specific protection, any information and communication, where processing is addressed to a child, should be in such a clear and plain language that the child can easily understand."

Recital 39 GDPR also states that "[t]he principle of transparency requires that any information and communication relating to the processing of those personal data be easily accessible and easy to understand, and that clear and plain language be used." Article 12(1) GDPR further provides that "any information referred to in Articles 13 and 14 and any communication under Articles 15 to 22 and 34 relating to processing to the data subject in a concise, transparent, intelligible and easily accessible form, using clear and plain language, in particular for any information addressed specifically to a child. The information shall be provided in writing, or by other means, including, where appropriate, by electronic means. When requested by the data subject, the information may be provided orally, provided that the identity of the data subject is proven by other means."

From the text above, it is noteworthy that the concept of accessibility goes beyond the reference to the term 'accessible'. Indeed, information and communication accessibility may also be present in the terms 'concise', 'easy-to-understand', 'clear language', 'plain language', 'visualisation', and so forth. All these terms interpreted under the light of the accessibility concept can take very specific meanings and become less vague and ambiguous. In other words, the concept of accessibility shows potential to help contextualise transparency under data protection law [19]. Further discussion and analysis on that is included in another forthcoming paper.

3.3 Is Accessibility Relevant for Transparency?

Consequently, the three sub-questions that arise next are to which extent accessibility is relevant for the principle of transparency:

- When is accessibility in transparency relevant?
- For what is accessibility in transparency relevant?
- For whom is accessibility in transparency relevant?

As for the first question, accessibility in transparency is relevant for information and communications. As seen earlier, Articles 13 and 14 cover the concept of information whereas Articles 15 to 22 and 34 the concept of communications. As to the second question, one could claim that accessibility is relevant as long as transparency itself is relevant. The A29WP confirms that transparency applies at the following stages of the data processing cycle:

- "before or at the start of the data processing cycle, i.e. when the personal data is being collected either from the data subject or otherwise obtained;
- throughout the whole processing period, i.e. when communicating with data subjects about their rights; and
- at specific points while processing is ongoing, for example when data breaches occur or in the case of material changes to the processing" [7]

Particularly, the first stage raises concerns. 'Before the data processing cycle' could also cover cases where an interested individual (not a data subject) is concerned. For instance, when an individual wishes to inform themselves before subscribing to a service or download an app (prospective transparency [20]). However, a recent decision from the Belgian data protection authority suggests that if one is not a data subject, does not have a direct interest to complain about the intelligibility of a data protection notice [21]. This decision seems to an extent in line with Recital 39 GDPR, "[i]t should be transparent to natural persons that personal data concerning them are collected, used, consulted or otherwise processed and to what extent the personal data are or will be processed." However, it appears to disregard the possibility that a person may be discouraged of using a service if they are not able to access the data protection notice or fully understand it before they contractually adhere to the service.

Concerning the third question, A29WP argues that: "[..] an accountable data controller will have knowledge about the people they collect information about and it can use this knowledge to determine what that audience would likely understand. For example, a controller collecting the personal data of working professionals can assume its audience has a higher level of understanding than a controller that obtains the personal data of children. If controllers are uncertain about the level of intelligibility and transparency of the information and effectiveness of user interfaces/ notices/ policies etc., they can test these, for example, through mechanisms such as user panels, readability testing, formal and informal interactions and dialogue with industry groups, consumer advocacy groups and regulatory bodies, where appropriate, amongst other things."[2] It also states that: [t]he requirement that information is "intelligible" means that it should be understood by an average member of the intended audience." [7].

The accessibility directives and the respective transposed law broaden by default the scope of the so-called 'intended audience' of all devices, services and applications – controllers/manufacturers cannot argue anymore that they do not know that their products or services are used by a wider audience. This will entail a fundamental redefinition of the 'average data subject' and enforcement of accessibility including in data protection related information and communication, to render the latter inclusive, taking into account definitions included in the two accessibility directives. Specifically, Article 3 (1) of the EAA states that: "persons with disabilities' means persons who have long-term physical, mental, intellectual or sensory impairments which in interaction with various barriers may hinder their full and effective participation in society on an equal basis with others;" And, Recital 4 EAA provides that: "'persons with functional limitations' [...] includes persons who have any physical, mental, intellectual or sensory impairments, age related impairments, or other human body performance related causes, permanent or temporary, which, in interaction with various barriers, result in their reduced access to products and services, leading to a situation that requires those products and services to be adapted to their particular needs."

4   Benefits and Challenges of Mainstreaming Accessibility in Data Protection Law

4.1   What is Currently Missing?

Several studies have shown that data protection notices are lengthy, difficult to locate or to understand. Some of those studies refer to this kind of problematic information representation as 'deceptive design patterns' which aim to interfere with a data subject's ability to make informed decisions about their personal data or be nudged into unwanted behavior [22]. There are even 'dark pattern tip lines', where a user can report dark patterns they come along [23]. In the accessibility context, this could mean that for instance, sections included in the footer of a website may not be always readable by screen readers, including links to data protection notices. The same could be also said for cookie banners for example in the form of pop-up windows.

A29WP appears to have grasped to an extent the potential and value of accessibility in the context of transparency. When comparing the first version of its guidelines on transparency for the public consultation as opposed to the final adopted version, there is an additional reference (paragraph 16) to 'other vulnerable members of society, including people with disabilities or people who have difficulties accessing information'[7]. The data controller is expected to assess its audience's likely level of understanding in combination with the vulnerabilities of such data subjects. However, condition for that remained that the data controller is aware that their product or service is used or is targeted to such audiences.

Acknowledging the complexity of the issue, the EDPB adopted for public consultation more recently in March 2022 the Guidelines 3/2022 on Dark patterns in social media platform interfaces: How to recognise and avoid them [6], which include a taxonomy and checklist of such patterns. Albeit in their current form, the EDPB seems to miss the opportunity to further discuss accessibility in data protection law using results of broader accessibility studies and evidence in legal communication. This would have been particularly beneficial, given that even though there are some exceptions, data protection notices appear to rarely follow accessibility requirements, not only content related but also technically speaking.

4.2 How Does Accessibility Benefit and Challenge EU Data Protection Law?

The concept of accessibility both benefits and challenges the EU data protection law. Existing and emerging accessibility principles can actually complement transparency, including for instance the POUR principles of digital transparency [24] standing for perceivable, operable, understandable and robust content and procedures.

Accordingly, the concept of accessibility and of accessibility statements can be used to further explain the principle of transparency in the context of data protection law in four ways: linguistically, procedurally, technically and at the end of the day, substantively. Linguistically, by taking into account diverse requirements, such as provision of easy-to-read versions, simple language versions, age-appropriate versions, sign language versions and so forth. Procedurally, because it ascertains that the different versions are user friendly and actually correspond to the needs of the addressees, through for instance evaluation mechanisms or the provision of contacts for feedback and requests. And technically, since data protection notices have to be compatible with different devices and applications, such as screen readers.

The structure of accessibility statements, can help improve intelligibility of data protection notices, by (a) establishing additional safeguards and mechanisms to request intelligible information or communication in data protection law, especially when not possible in the latter case due to lack of specific interest, for instance when the addressee of the information is not a data subject; (b) providing accessible information on accessibility statements about the data protection notice and in general the data protection features of the service or product, including compliance status (i.e. fully compliant, partially compliant, non-compliant) and audit info (i.e. how they verify the accuracy of their statement and consequently notice) and (c) inspiring or re-shaping the content of data protection notices.

Lastly, the concept of accessibility can substantively benefit data protection law, by ensuring that fundamental rights are taken into account in all phases of its implementation and that all data subjects are truly informed or at least have the chance to be informed about their rights and the respective obligations of the data controllers.

How does accessibility challenge data protection law? Below a non-exhaustive list of some considerations. First, accessibility is not one-size-fits-all. There is a wide ('infinite') concept of accessibility communities users [19], which means that achieving a fully compliant status may be very difficult in practice, given that the drafters or designers have to understand the requirements for each community and provide accordingly. This must also take into account the variance within each community, for instance [19]. Second, accessibility is always under construction. This is the so-called 'churn' effect [25]. It entails that accessibility features are often initially implemented but they do not remain maintained, sustained or updated, rendering them through time practically unusable. Third, any accessibility features implemented must be themselves privacy-friendly [19]. This is an explicit requirement envisaged in the Annex of the EAA. Fourth, in the specific case where accessibility is merely interpreted as reshaping data protection notices to correspond to accessibility statements, there is a risk to end up with an even larger information load for the user. Thus, intertwining the two types of notices/statements, requires utmost caution, to either completely replace the current design or to create a holistically new. Fifth, accessibility studies have emerged as a stand-alone, interdisciplinary field of research the last few decades, and accessibility in law is under-investigated.

5 Concluding Remarks

In a nutshell, in the previous chapters, we discussed the development of the concept of accessibility in the EU, as well as the adoption of respective legislation in the form of directives, which redefine the notion of the average consumer to include a wider audience. The requirement for different types of accessibility statements, as a form of notice describing the accessibility features of a website, product or service were analysed and their characteristics were compared. Consequently, it was examined whether the concept of accessibility has a place in the EU data protection law. The answer was yes, through the prism of transparency.

The concept of accessibility can help improve transparency in four ways: linguistically, procedurally, technically and ultimately, substantively. Nevertheless, it imposes further and new challenges to a data protection principle which has received a lot of criticism with respect to its practical implementation.

Concluding, it is argued that further research is needed to investigate practical ways in which accessibility can have a positive effect on the principle of transparency, empowering data subjects and enhancing equality.

References

1. Seizov, O., Wulf, A.J., Luzak, J.: The Transparent trap: a multidisciplinary perspective on the design of transparent online disclosures in the EU. J. Consum. Policy **42**(1), 149–173 (2018). https://doi.org/10.1007/s10603-018-9393-0

2. Anne Josephine Flanagan: Jen King, Sheila Warren: White Paper: Redesigning Data Privacy: Reimagining Notice & Consent for human- technology interaction. World Economic Forum, Geneva (2020)
3. Schaub, F., Balebako, R., Durity, A.L., Cranor, L.F.: A Design Space for Effective Privacy Notices*. In: Selinger, E., Polonetsky, J., and Tene, O. (eds.) The Cambridge Handbook of Consumer Privacy. pp. 365–393. Cambridge University Press (2018). https://doi.org/10.1017/9781316831960.021
4. Wulf, A.J., Seizov, O.: How to improve consumers' understanding of online legal information: insights from a behavioral experiment. Eur J Law Econ. (2022). https://doi.org/10.1007/s10657-022-09755-4
5. Oehler, A., Wendt, S.: Good consumer information: the information paradigm at its (Dead) end? J. Consum. Policy **40**(2), 179–191 (2016). https://doi.org/10.1007/s10603-016-9337-5
6. European Data Protection Board: Guidelines 03/2022 on dark patterns in social media platform interfaces: How to recognise and avoid them (Version 1.0). (2022)
7. Article 29 Data Protection Working Party: Guidelines on transparency under Regulation 2016/679, (2018)
8. Nissenbaum, H.: A Contextual approach to privacy online. Daedalus **140**, 32–48 (2011). https://doi.org/10.1162/DAED_a_00113
9. Spagnuelo, D., Ferreira, A., Lenzini, G.: Accomplishing Transparency within the General Data Protection Regulation: In: Proceedings of the 5th International Conference on Information Systems Security and Privacy. pp. 114–125. SCITEPRESS - Science and Technology Publications, Prague, Czech Republic (2019). https://doi.org/10.5220/0007366501140125
10. Rossi, A., Palmirani, M.: Can visual design provide legal transparency? the challenges for successful implementation of icons for data protection. Des. Issues **36**, 82–96 (2020). https://doi.org/10.1162/desi_a_00605
11. Liepiņa, R., et al.: GDPR Privacy Policies in CLAUDETTE: Challenges of Omission, Context and Multilingualism. Proceedings of the Third Workshop on Automated Semantic Analysis of Information in Legal Text (ASAIL 2019). 7 (2019)
12. European Commission: Union of Equality: Strategy for the Rights of Persons with Disabilities 2021–2030. , Brussels (2021)
13. Lazar, J., Goldstein, D., Taylor, A.: Chapter 2 - The history of access technology. In: Lazar, J., Goldstein, D., and Taylor, A. (eds.) Ensuring Digital Accessibility Through Process and Policy, pp. 21–40. Morgan Kaufmann, Boston (2015). https://doi.org/10.1016/B978-0-12-800646-7.00002-2
14. Digital Accessibility Glossary, https://accessibility.huit.harvard.edu/glossary, Accessed Dec 12 2022
15. Disability Inclusion Strategy. United Nations (2019)
16. World Health Organization: WHO policy on disability. World Health Organization, Geneva (2021)
17. Gutermuth, S.: Book review: Rink, I. (2020). Rechtskommunikation und Barrierefreiheit. Zur Übersetzung juristischer Informations- und Interaktionstexte in Leichter Sprache. Frank & Timme. Parallèles. 174–177 (2021). https://doi.org/10.17462/para.2021.01.11
18. Maaß, C., Rink, I.: Translating legal texts into easy language. J. Open Access Law. **9**, 10 (2021)
19. Wang, Y., et al.: Modern Socio-Technical Perspectives on Privacy. pp. 293–313. Springer International Publishing, Cham (2022). https://doi.org/10.1007/978-3-030-82786-1_13
20. Felzmann, H., Villaronga, E.F., Lutz, C., Tamò-Larrieux, A.: Transparency you can trust: transparency requirements for artificial intelligence between legal norms and contextual concerns. Big Data Soc. **6**, 2053951719860542 (2019). https://doi.org/10.1177/2053951719860542

21. Gegevensbeschermingsautoriteit: Beslissing ten gronde 106/2022 van 27 juni 2022. (2022)
22. Norwegian Consumer Council: Deceived by Design: How tech companies use dark patterns to discourage us from exercising our rights to privacy. (2018)
23. Welcome to the Dark Patterns Tip Line, https://darkpatternstipline.digitalimpact.io, Last Accessed 24 Dec 2022
24. Web Content Accessibility Guidelines (WCAG) 2.1, https://www.w3.org/TR/WCAG21/, Accessed Dec 24 2022
25. Cullen, K., Kubitschke, L.: Study on "Web accessibility in European countries: level of compliance with latest international accessibility specifications, notably WCAG 2.0, and approaches or plans to implement those specifications." European Commission (2009)

SeCCA: Towards Privacy-Preserving Biclustering Algorithm with Homomorphic Encryptions

Shokofeh VahidianSadegh[1]([✉]) [iD], Lena Wiese[1] [iD], and Michael Brenner[2] [iD]

[1] Institute of Computer Science, Goethe University Frankfurt, Frankfurt, Germany
VahidianSadegh@mathematik.uni-frankfurt.de lwiese@cs.uni-frankfurt.de
[2] Leibniz Universitaet Hannover, Hannover, Germany
brenner@luis.uni-hannover.de

Abstract. Massive amounts of newly generated gene expression data have been used to further enhance personalised health predictions. Machine learning algorithms prepare techniques to explore a group of genes with similar profiles. Biclustering algorithms were proposed to resolve key issues of traditional clustering techniques and are well-adapted to the nature of biological processes. Besides, the concept of genome data access should be socially acceptable for patients since they can then be assured that their data analysis will not be harmful to their privacy and ultimately achieve good outcomes for society [1]. Homomorphic encryption has shown considerable potential in securing complicated machine learning tasks. In this paper, we prove that homomorphic encryption operations can be applied directly on biclustering algorithm (Cheng and Church algorithm) to process gene expression data while keeping private data encrypted. This Secure Cheng and Church algorithm (SeCCA) includes nine steps, each providing encryption for a specific section of the algorithm. Because of the current limitations of homomorphic encryption operations in real applications, only four steps of SeCCA are implemented and tested with adjustable parameters on a real-world data set (yeast cell cycle) and synthetic data collection. As a proof of concept, we compare the result of biclusters from the original Cheng and Church algorithm with SeCCA to clarify the applicability of homomorphic encryption operations in biclustering algorithms. As the first study in this domain, our study demonstrates the feasibility of homomorphic encryption operations in gene expression analysis to achieve privacy-preserving biclustering algorithms.

Keywords: Gene Expression · Biclustering Algorithm · Privacy-Preserving AI · Homomorphic Encryption

Published by Springer Nature Switzerland AG 2023
F. Bieker et al. (Eds.): Privacy and Identity 2022, IFIP AICT 671, pp. 198–213, 2023.
https://doi.org/10.1007/978-3-031-31971-6_15

1   Introduction

Gene expression data are being generated through high-throughput technologies such as Microarray and RNA-seq. Biclustering algorithms – for instance, Cheng and Church [2] – have been used extensively in this regard for discovering meaningful groups and a link between sets of genes and sample traits [3]. Notwithstanding the importance of this analysis aspect, the rise in availability and use of genomic data raises a growing concern about its security and privacy [4]. Homomorphic encryption with certain operations (additions and/or multiplications) is able to handle sensitive genomic data by allowing data to remain encrypted even during computation. Accordingly, researchers have used the potential of homomorphic encryption operations in machine learning applications – particularly medical data analysis. To the best of our knowledge, existing recent studies have not addressed biclustering algorithms exclusively; this research gap leads to a lack of secure data processing in this area. We intend to realise the possibility of applying homomorphic encryption operations over biclustering algorithms, with our experimental results reported here showing promising results. Our Secure Cheng and Church algorithm (SeCCA) consists of nine different steps, each of which ensures partial security of the algorithm. In practice, due to the limitations of homomorphic operations discussed below, we benchmarked four of them successfully: we tested the computational performance of these four SeCCA steps and compared the result of them with the original algorithm without any encryption/decryption. The distinct contribution of this manuscript is to provide privacy-preserving steps for a biclustering algorithm, specifically Cheng and Church algorithm (SeCCA), as for the first time Cheng and Church introduced biclustering as a new paradigm to simultaneously cluster both genes and conditions. Since then, many other such algorithms have been published but mostly compare their works with this algorithm which has been a foundation and proof-of-concept implementation of biclustering. In this paper, we focus on the secure computation of the mean squared residue score that restricts access to sensitive private data by homomorphic encryption operations. Afterwards, we compare the biclusters obtained by non-encrypted with the ones obtained by the encrypted Cheng and Church algorithm by means of external evaluation measure (clustering error). All code and data sets are publicly available at https://github.com/ShokofehVS/SeCCA.

2   Related Work

Before approaching the core of our privacy-preserving procedure, we elaborate on concepts of biclustering algorithms. Further in this section, we mention relevant research on private genome data analysis applying cryptographic techniques.

2.1   Biclustering Algorithms

Traditional clustering algorithms are one-way clustering methods grouping observations according to similarities among all variables at the same time [5].

In addition, some studies elaborate that a biological process may be active only under subsets of genes as well as subsets of samples. There are also some genes or samples that may not participate in any cluster; hence it is of paramount importance to go beyond a traditional clustering prototype and apply a more adapted technique like the biclustering [6] which simultaneously clusters the rows and columns of a matrix for sorting heterogeneous data into homogeneous blocks [7].

2.2 Private Genomic Data Analysis

Numerous privacy-preserving clustering methods based on homomorphic encryption have been proposed; in the following, we survey some of these. The authors in [8] implemented a privacy-preserving evaluation algorithm for support vector clustering. By this model, the cluster label was allocated for new test data without decryption, which improved the clustering performance for non-convex data. A deep neural network with fully homomorphic encryption introduced in [9] adopted approximation methods and used bootstrapping to evaluate an arbitrary deep learning model on encrypted data. A secure K-means (CKKSKM) was developed in [10] to encrypt outsourcing data based on the CKKS scheme to prevent revealing private information. This scheme reduced the overhead of outsourcing data to the cloud for storage and calculation. In some experiments, clustering algorithms are represented with focus on multiple encryption techniques including homomorphic encryption and multiparty computation. [19] introduces the first practical and fully private density-based clustering scheme based on secure two-party computation. A scalable privacy-preserving clustering algorithm in [20] is designed for multi-party clustering in a modular approach which is five orders of magnitude faster than the current solutions. FHE-friendly K-Means-Algorithm on encrypted data by [21] presents a natural encoding that makes division by an encrypted value possible with some restrictions in terms of performance in practice. As opposed to the above approaches, in our paper, we present and analyse proof-of-concept implementations of biclustering (particularly Cheng and Church Algorithm) on homomorphically encrypted gene expression data – a use case for which no prior approaches could be found.

3 Theoretical Background

3.1 Cheng and Church Biclustering Algorithm

Biclustering algorithms – like Cheng and Church [2] – have been used extensively in gene expression analysis which results in a better understanding of diseases like cancer [22]. The concept of bicluster refers to a subset of genes and a subset of conditions with a high similarity score, which measures the coherence of the genes and conditions in the bicluster. It also returns the list of biclusters for the given data set. Important notations in the paper containing input parameters are summarised in Table 1. In addition, "enc" label at the beginning of each symbol like $enc\_maxValue$ indicates an encrypted expression which here is the encrypted maximum value of the data matrix. The residue of a cell in the bicluster (a_{ij}) over the subsets of the rows (I) and the columns (J) is defined by:

$$a_{ij} - a_{iJ} - a_{Ij} + a_{IJ}$$

where a_{iJ}, a_{Ij}, and a_{IJ} indicate the mean of the ith row, the mean of the jth column and that of all elements in the bicluster respectively. More precisely, a submatrix A_{IJ} is determined by the pair (I, J) where the row means are $a_{iJ} = \frac{1}{|J|} \sum_{j \in J} a_{i,j}$; and similarly, the column means are $a_{Ij} = \frac{1}{|I|} \sum_{i \in I} a_{i,j}$ along with the mean in the submatrix (I, J) as below:

$$a_{IJ} = \frac{1}{|I||J|} \sum_{i \in I, j \in J} a_{ij} = \frac{1}{|I|} \sum_{i \in I} a_{iJ} = \frac{1}{|J|} \sum_{j \in J} a_{Ij}$$

The mean squared residue score can be described as the variance of all elements in the bicluster, the mean of row variance, and the mean of column variance:

$$H(I, J) = \frac{1}{|I||J|} \sum_{i \in I, j \in J} (a_{ij} - a_{iJ} - a_{Ij} + a_{IJ})^2$$

The focus is on finding biclusters having low mean squared residue score and particularly large, maximal ones with scores below a predefined threshold. If $H(I, J) \leq \delta$ for $\delta \geq 0$, a submatrix A_{IJ} is referred to δ-bicluster. The algorithm starts with a large matrix (one with all the data) and then proceeds by removing the row or column to achieve the largest decrease in the score. Accordingly, the computation of the score of all the submatrices is needed after removing any row or column. First, a step for the simultaneous deletion of multiple rows/columns is performed over the input data set; this is followed by a single row/column deletion step (see Algorithms 2 and 3). In the next step, the result of applying node deletion may not be maximal, so some rows and columns can be added without increasing the mean squared residue score (see Algorithm 4). Add that, in the original study, Cheng and Church attempted to find α (a threshold for multiple node deletion) as large as possible and run the algorithm on 100 biclusters in less than 10 min as well. Steps 3 and 4 (refer to Sect. 4.2) won't be applied when the number of conditions is less than 100 for the yeast data set; therefore, only Algorithm 1 is called by starting deleting conditions.

3.2   Homomorphic Encryption

Homomorphic Encryption (HE) was coined first by Rivest in 1978 with the concept of "privacy homomorphism". Homomorphic encryption is considered a secure computation method on encrypted data (ciphertext) in which the result of the computation is also ciphertext. By decrypting the result in ciphertext, the decrypted result should be identical to the output of operations on non-encrypted (plaintext) data [11]. We apply Pyfhel as a python wrapper for the Microsoft SEAL library in our project because of its convenience to use and higher-level

---

Algorithm 1. Finding a Given Number of Biclusters

Require: A Matrix of real numbers with possible missing elements, $\delta \geq 0$ the maximum acceptable mean squared residue score, $\alpha \geq 1$ a parameter for multiple node deletion and n the number of δ-biclusters to be found

Ensure: Replacing missing elements in A with random numbers, A' a copy of matrix A

1: Apply multiple node deletion algorithm on A', δ, and α for rows (columns) greater than or equal to 100 (the result matrix B)
2: Apply single node deletion algorithm on B, and δ (the result matrix C)
3: Apply node addition algorithm on A and C (the result bicluster D)
4: Report D, and replace the elements in A' that are also in D with random numbers

---

Algorithm 2. Single Node Deletion

Require: A Matrix of real numbers, $\delta \geq 0$ the maximum acceptable mean squared residue score

Ensure: $A_{IJ} = A$ where I and J are initialised to the gene and condition sets in the data

1: Compute a_{iJ} for all $i \in I, a_{Ij}$ for all $j \in J, a_{IJ}$ and $H(I, J)$. If $H(I, J) \leq \delta$ return A_{IJ}
2: Find the row $i \in I$ with the largest $d(i) = \frac{1}{|J|} \sum_{j \in J} (a_{ij} - a_{iJ} - a_{Ij} + a_{IJ})^2$
3: Find the column $j \in J$ with the largest $d(j) = \frac{1}{|I|} \sum_{i \in I} (a_{ij} - a_{iJ} - a_{Ij} + a_{IJ})^2$
4: Remove the row or column having the larger d value by updating I or J

Algorithm 3. Multiple Node Deletion

Require: A Matrix of real numbers, $\delta \geq 0$ the maximum acceptable mean squared residue score, $\alpha > 1$ a threshold for multiple node deletion

Ensure: $A_{IJ} = A$ where I and J are initialised to the gene and condition sets in the data

1: Compute a_{iJ} for all $i \in I, a_{Ij}$ for all $j \in J, a_{IJ}$ and $H(I, J)$. If $H(I, J) \leq \delta$ return A_{IJ}
2: Remove the rows $i \in I$ with $\frac{1}{|J|} \sum_{j \in J} (a_{ij} - a_{iJ} - a_{Ij} + a_{IJ})^2 > \alpha H(I, J)$
3: Recompute a_{Ij}, a_{IJ} and $H(I, J)$
4: Remove the columns $j \in J$ with $\frac{1}{|I|} \sum_{i \in I} (a_{ij} - a_{iJ} - a_{Ij} + a_{IJ})^2 > \alpha H(I, J)$
5: If nothing has been removed in the iteration, switch to Algorithm 2

Algorithm 4. Node Addition

Require: A Matrix of real numbers, I and J signify a δ-bicluster

1: Compute a_{iJ} for all i, a_{Ij} for all j, a_{IJ} and $H(I, J)$
2: Add the columns $j \notin J$ with $\frac{1}{|I|} \sum_{i \in I} (a_{ij} - a_{iJ} - a_{Ij} + a_{IJ})^2 \leq H(I, J)$
3: Recompute a_{iJ}, a_{IJ} and $H(I, J)$
4: Add the rows $i \notin I$ with $\frac{1}{|J|} \sum_{j \in J} (a_{ij} - a_{iJ} - a_{Ij} + a_{IJ})^2 \leq H(I, J)$
5: For each row i still not in I, add its inverse if $\frac{1}{|J|} \sum_{j \in J} (-a_{ij} + a_{iJ} - a_{Ij} + a_{IJ})^2 \leq H(I, J)$
6: If nothing is added in the iteration, return the final I and J as I' and J'

Table 1. Notation and Symbols

Symbols	Description
a_{ij}	Element of expression matrix
a_{iJ}	Mean of the ith row
a_{Ij}	Mean of the jth column
a_{IJ}	Mean of all elements
$H(I, J)$	Mean squared residue of submatrix I and J
$\delta \geq 0$	Maximum acceptable mean squared residue score
$\alpha \geq 1$	Parameter for multiple node deletion
n	number of δ-biclusters to be found
enc_a_{ij}	Encrypted element of expression matrix

API. We use BFV [13] as a highly efficient fully homomorphic encryption scheme for applications working over larger amounts of data with the following settings that are chosen based on a number of examinations and according to the suggested setting parameters in creating context:

- The plaintext modulus p specifies the prime number applied on the polynomial's coefficients that determines how large encrypted values can get before wrap-around; we set $p = 1964769281$.
- The polynomial modulus m specifies the degree of the irreducible polynomial $x^m + 1$ of the underlying polynomial ring R; this ring is defined in BFV to be a cyclotomic ring $R = \mathbb{Z}[x]/(x^m + 1)$, where m is a power of 2; we set $m = 8192$.
- In addition, we set Pyfhel's security level parameter to 192 bit.
- We set the encoding scheme to fractional; in addition, 64 bits for integer and 4096 bits for the decimal part are adjusted.
- For BFV scheme, q is determined utilising the largest value that achieves 192-bit security for the given polynomial degree (parameter sec) [12]. Consequently, $logq$ is 152 according to the setup and parameters.

4   Secured CCA (SeCCA)

In this section, firstly, we describe a possible message flow for secure processing of the Cheng and Church algorithm consisting of two agents (data owner and storage system). Afterwards, we clarify how a homomorphic encryption scheme could be utilised to ensure the security of gene expression data analysis by biclustering algorithms (particularly the Cheng and Church algorithm).

4.1   Workflow

In our threat model, the gene expression data are privately kept by the data owner. We assume the server to be semi-honest ("honest but curious" [14]);

hence, by processing encrypted data we aim to ensure that any data cannot be leaked on the server side. In addition, the biclustering algorithm that we have used (Cheng and Church's) is public and we trust the cloud server to do computations correctly. It is worth mentioning the message flow which is inspired by [15] consisting of two agents such as the data owner (patient) and storage system (cloud) for secure processing in our scenario (Fig. 1).

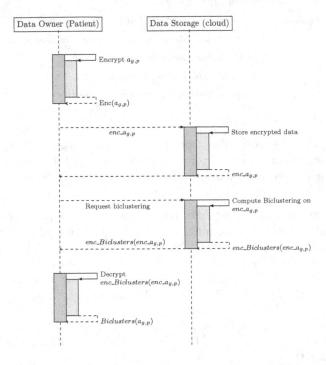

Fig. 1. Message Flow for Secure Processing of CCA

Our Secured CCA (SeCCA) proceeds along the same steps as the original non-secured biclustering algorithm [2]; however, in our approach, any computation – in particular, the mean squared residue score – is performed over encrypted data. It takes an input matrix (encrypted homomorphically on the cell level $a_{g,p}$), number of biclusters, MSR threshold (maximum mean squared residue accepted (δ parameter in the original study)), scaling factor, and minimum number of columns. It returns the list of biclusters for the given data set.

4.2 Implementation

We here represent our proposed secure analysis of Cheng and Church biclustering algorithm based on homomorphic encryption as the main contribution to a project done by Padilha et al. [16] which provides us by the implementation of the original algorithm, yeast cell cycle data set and Clustering Error

Table 2. SeCCA Steps

Step	Main Idea/Description
1	HE over maximum mean squared residue accepted $(((enc\_maxValue - enc\_minValue)^2)/12) \cdot 0.005$
2	Computation of mean squared residue score of rows, columns and full data matrix: $\frac{1}{|I||J|} \sum_{i \in I, j \in J}((enc\_a_{ij}) - (enc\_a_{iJ}) - (enc\_a_{Ij}) + (enc\_a_{IJ}))^2$
3	Computation of mean squared residue score of columns for node addition step $\frac{1}{|I|} \sum_{i \in I}((enc\_a_{ij}) - (enc\_a_{iJ}) - (enc\_a_{Ij}) + (enc\_a_{IJ}))^2$
4	Computation of mean squared residue score of the rows and the inverse of the rows for node addition step: $\frac{1}{|J|} \sum_{j \in J}((enc\_a_{ij}) - (enc\_a_{iJ}) - (enc\_a_{Ij}) + (enc\_a_{IJ}))^2$ and $\frac{1}{|J|} \sum_{j \in J}(-(enc\_a_{ij}) + (enc\_a_{iJ}) - (enc\_a_{Ij}) + (enc\_a_{IJ}))^2$
5	HE over rows to remove in multiple node deletion step $\frac{1}{|J|} \sum_{j \in J}((enc\_a_{ij}) - (enc\_a_{iJ}) - (enc\_a_{Ij}) + (enc\_a_{IJ}))^2 > \alpha(enc\_H(I,J))$
6	HE over columns to remove in multiple node deletion step $\frac{1}{|I|} \sum_{i \in I}((enc\_a_{ij}) - (enc\_a_{iJ}) - (enc\_a_{Ij}) + (enc\_a_{IJ}))^2 > \alpha(enc\_H(I,J))$
7	HE over rows to add in node addition step $\frac{1}{|J|} \sum_{j \in J}((enc\_a_{ij}) - (enc\_a_{iJ}) - (enc\_a_{Ij}) + (enc\_a_{IJ}))^2 \leq (enc\_H(I,J))$
8	HE over the inverse of the rows to add in node addition step $\frac{1}{|J|} \sum_{j \in J}(-(enc\_a_{ij}) + (enc\_a_{iJ}) - (enc\_a_{Ij}) + (enc\_a_{IJ}))^2 \leq (enc\_H(I,J))$
9	HE over the columns to add in node addition step $\frac{1}{|I|} \sum_{i \in I}((enc\_a_{ij}) - (enc\_a_{iJ}) - (enc\_a_{Ij}) + (enc\_a_{IJ}))^2 \leq (enc\_H(I,J))$

(CE). Our procedure provides an encrypted version of the algorithm in which the efficient node-deletion algorithm was introduced to search for submatrices in expression data with low mean squared residue score [2]. Based on different types of computations needed in the procedure that can potentially be transferred to the public cloud services, we summarise the required steps of SeCCA with homomorphic encryption operations in Table 2; therefore, one can choose an appropriate computation step for a desired task. Our main focus is on steps 1 to 4 to find out how to secure the calculation of mean squared residue in different stages. Although homomorphic encryption provides an elegant solution in machine learning in theory, however, several limitations hamper its implementation; a particular limitation in real-world platforms is the lack of evaluating comparisons and conditional selections [17] on encrypted data – this limitation also applies to the Pyfhel platform we used in our experiments. We propose a multi-round interactive execution of the conditional checking part by involving the data owner to decrypt a small integer and compare it to the plaintext 0. The workflow is interactive due to restrictions of the chosen framework in support of full workflow. While it will be the main goal of our future to obtain a non-interactive evaluation of the branching conditionals, we would like to emphasise that the non-interactive workflow can also cause computational overhead and be more expensive to follow compared to the interactive fashion (e.g., employing optimised CPU). Besides, division homomorphically into a plaintext in Pyfhel is possible for fractional encoding. In this study, we rewrite steps 5 to 9 having conditional statements to remove/add nodes into a non-encrypted approach (executed on the data owner side) and present schematic diagrams of these steps in Figs. 2, 3 and 4 that is similar to the workflow (depicted in Fig. 1).

Step 1. In step 1, encrypted versions of minimum and maximum values of the input data matrix are utilised for further computation of the maximum mean squared residue accepted. Here in this step, the data owner sends encrypted minimum and maximum values of the data matrix (similar to message 2 in Fig. 1) to the public cloud service because of the problems mentioned earlier. Then, computation of step 1 occurs in the storage system by having encrypted input parameters (i.e., enc_maxValue and enc_minValue); the result can be returned to the data owner or can be reused by the cloud storage for further computation:

$$enc\_MSR\_thr = (((enc\_maxValue - enc\_minValue)^2)/12) \cdot 0.005$$

The data owner can decrypt and obtain the result by private key: $Dec_{sk}(enc\_MSR\_thr)$.

Step 2. To measure the mean squared residue score (step 2), first, we need to compute the mean of the rows, the columns, and the submatrix over encrypted values. The data owner defines a submatrix of the input data ($submatrix_{ij}$) and passes it after encryption within a NumPy array to the storage system; there, the mean value of the rows (axis=1 of encrypted submatrix), the columns (axis=0 of encrypted submatrix) and the submatrix are determined by homomorphic encryption over NumPy arrays. Hence, predefined arithmetic operations (e.g., $-$, $+$) to calculate residue ($enc\_residue_{ij}$) and squared residue ($enc\_squaredResidue_{ij}$) of elements in the data matrix are applied in the ciphertext. For each submatrix cell $a_{i,j}$ we hence obtain its encrypted residue as well as squared residue (confer the plaintext counterparts in Sect. 3.1):

$$enc\_residue_{ij} = enc\_submatrix_{ij} - enc\_rowMeans_i - enc\_colMeans_j$$
$$+enc\_submatrixMean$$
$$enc\_squaredResidue_{ij} = (enc\_residue_{ij})^2$$

Afterwards, the storage system continues the process of finding the mean value of the squared residue (enc_MSR) of the elements by taking the sum of the encrypted squared residue (a NumPy operation)and its length to further divide a ciphertext (sum value of the encrypted squared residue) into a plaintext (length of the encrypted squared residue) and sends back the final result to the data owner: $enc\_MSR = mean(enc\_squaredResidue_{ij})$ over all rows i and all columns j in the submatrix. Then decryption can be performed by the data owner: $Dec_{sk}(enc\_MSR)$. An approach similar to step 2 is taken for step 3 (with a difference in the computation which takes place on the subsets of the rows as well) and step 4 (computation of mean squared residue is considered for both rows and the inverse of the rows).

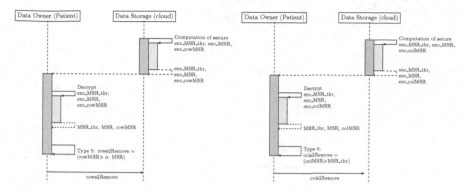

Fig. 2. Rows and Columns to Remove in Multiple Node Deletion Step (SeCCA steps 5 and 6)

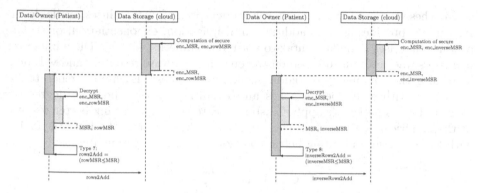

Fig. 3. Rows and Inverted of the Rows to Add in Node Addition Step (SeCCA steps 7 and 8)

5 Experiments

In this study, we have used the yeast cell cycle expression data that was used for testing the original implementation of the algorithm [2]. The data consists of 2884 genes and 17 conditions; a matrix of integers in the range between 0 and 600 that were selected according to Tavazoie et al. [18]. Missing data are also replaced with generated random numbers that form a uniform distribution between 0 and 800. Furthermore, these random values are the candidates to get removed in the node deletion phase as they would not form recognisable patterns [2]. Additionally, we have executed our experiment on synthetic data sets based on the bicluster model (i.e., constant) according to a procedure developed by [16]. Thus, for further testing in this paper, we focus on making a constant data set consisting of 300 rows, 50 columns with 5 biclusters as a sample data set. We measured the performance of encryption and decryption processes inside SeCCA steps 1 to 4. We then carried out the comparison of the secured version of the algorithm with the original one to examine the accuracy of our proposed

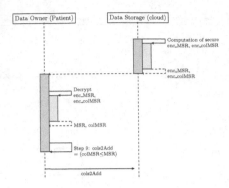

Fig. 4. Columns to Add in Node Addition Step (SeCCA step 9)

approaches. We used the homomorphic encryption functionalities available in Pyfhel [12] provides such as addition, multiplication, exponentiation, or scalar product that uses a similar syntax to normal arithmetic (+, -, *). The number of biclusters was determined based on the current hardware resources and without increasing the complexity of the implementation phase. Each step generates 5 biclusters, with a number of genes and conditions with a possible degree of overlap. In this paper, we apply Clustering Error (CE), achieving better results in the empirical analysis [16]. The CE measure ranges over the interval [0, 1], with higher values indicating better solutions. The CE is formulated as:

$$CE(A, \hat{A}) := \frac{d_{max}}{|U|}$$

where d_{max} is a measure of intersection of biclusterings and $|U|$ the total space covered by the biclusterings considering overlaps [3]. We perform a comparison of the four encrypted versions, steps 1 to 4 of the Cheng and Church algorithm to the non-encrypted version (as the ground truth) by CE over the input data set. By comparing step 1 of SeCCA with the non-encrypted Cheng and Church algorithm (CCA), the corresponding evaluation measure CE shows an outstanding result with a score of 0.97662. Similarly, step 3 of SeCCA represents a considerably high similarity score close to 1 with 0.99611. Despite the high similarity of steps 1 and 3 to CCA, our experiment produces striking dissimilarity among step 2 and the non-encrypted version of CCA with a score of 0.10659. We tried to improve this result by adjusting different HE parameters (like $p = 65537$, $m = 4096$, $base = 2$, $intDigits = 16$, $fracDigits = 64$) as parameter setting 2 in Fig. 5 and 6, resulting in a slight improvement reaching a score of 0.18207 (further information about HE parameters in Sect. 3.2). In Fig. 5 (a), results of accuracy between two different HE parameter settings over yeast cell cycle data set are shown. An improvement can be seen in the performance of step 4 with a score of 0.32225. Consequently, the combination of the four aforementioned steps is affected by what we achieved so far in steps 2 and 4, thus showing a notable difference between SeCCA and CCA with 0.10458. Actually, the context of Pyfhel in our project is set according to available hardware resources to make the project run on a large amount of data. The settings include adapting the parameter fracDigits which specifies the number of bits that are used to encode the fractional part; thus, all the fractional parts, in case of an insufficient amount of this parameter, will be coerced into invalid result. We observed that the noise budget can reach zero soon after each squaring residue operation leading to an incorrect decrypted result. To solve these issues, we set the encryption parameters to have a high noise budget and enough fraction digits at the beginning. Still, there is room for improving accuracy in working with floating points by changing to the appropriate schemes. To compare the resulting biclusters with another data set, we choose synthetic data based on the constant bicluster model. Figure 5 (b) depicts the CE scores on yeast gene expression data and synthetic data for individually implemented steps (1 to 4) and their combinations.

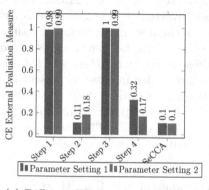

(a) Different HE Parameter Settings

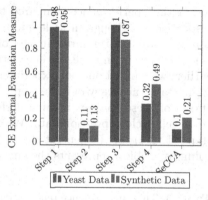

(b) Different Data sets

Fig. 5. Comparison of SeCCA with CCA by CE

Computational Performances. We conduct the experiment on a single server with Intel(R) Xeon(R) Silver 4314 CPU @ 2.40GHz and 131182528 kB RAM with Rocky Linux 8.6 (Green Obsidian). The Python version used in the project is 3.8 on the PyCharm environment. Table 3 demonstrates the time performance of encryption and decryption for four implemented steps of SeCCA (steps 1 to 4) and 5 biclusters for yeast gene expression data and Table 3 for time performance of these steps on synthetic data. Hence other parts of the code in each step that run without homomorphic encryption can be found by subtracting the total execution time from the summation of encryption and decryption time. Large-scale gene expression data sets such as our two-dimensional input matrices need Pyfhel's vector operations; thus, it leads to dramatically increased execution time in performing computationally inten- sive tasks, including multiplication, compared to the non-encrypted Cheng and Church algorithm. As shown in Table 3, there is relatively no delay in doing encryption on maximum mean squared residue accepted homomorphically (step 1) with 0.0372 s in encrypting and 0.00254 for decryption of required parame- ters. Although, it takes a considerable amount of time for the remaining three steps to complete their tasks (encryption, decryption), where the computation of mean squared residue for node deletion/addition relies on a number of loops and different homomorphic encryption operations. Step 2 of SeCCA is one of the most time-consuming tasks by far, with 26513.85849 s executing encryption tasks (which also takes 132034560 in Bytes memory after creating an instance of Pyfhel) due to its applications in node deletion phase and recomputation of mean squared residue score after each update in node addition step. As steps 3 and 4 are exclusively designed for encrypting score in node addition, they show better time performance compared to step 2 by 2081.72169 and 21393.38351 s, respectively, although in node addition phase, inverted of the rows extends the computation to form mirror images of the rest of the rows in the bicluster results (see Sect. 4.2) in an increased encryption/decryption time for step 4. As discussed earlier, we carried out our experiment on different HE parameters which leads to increased accuracy of some steps. Figure 6 is provided in order to present the effects of these changes in time performance (encryption and decryption) over yeast cell cycle expression data. We also tested the execution time of individual steps (1 to 4) for the generated synthetic data that consists of 300 rows and 50 columns; Table 3 represents the encryption as well as decryption time.

Table 3. Time performance (encryption and decryption) of steps 1 to 4 of SeCCA for Yeast Gene Expression Data (left) and Synthetic Data (right)

Step	Encr. Time (Sec.)	Decr. Time (Sec.)	Step	Encr. Time (Sec.)	Decr. Time (Sec.)
1	0.0372	0.00254	1	0.03656	0.00247
2	26513.85849	104.25779	2	6918.90463	33.05609
3	2081.72169	0.73747	3	522.23543	0.85587
4	21393.38351	173.88712	4	1629.95298	12.71682

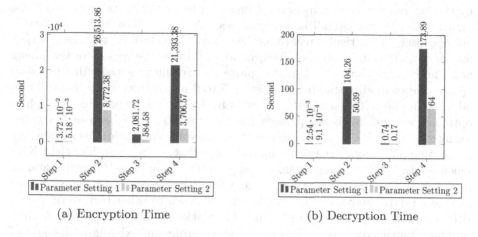

(a) Encryption Time

(b) Decryption Time

Fig. 6. Time Performance According to Different HE Parameter Settings on Yeast Cell Cycle Data

6   Conclusion and Future Work

In this paper, we proposed the Secured Cheng and Church Algorithm (SeCCA) to find a given number of biclusters with predefined parameters and showed the applicability of homomorphic encryption over biclustering algorithms – particularly Cheng and Church algorithm – with a number of steps encrypted with homomorphic operations. To the best of our knowledge, the Secured version of the Cheng and Church algorithm (SeCCA) is the first application of homomorphic encryption in biclustering algorithms that enhances the overall genomic privacy of data owners. Based on what we have achieved so far, homomorphic encryption operations are capable of calculating the maximum mean squared residue accepted and mean squared residues score in both phases (node deletion and addition) for an input data matrix with predefined parameters. Our experiment throughout steps 1 to 4 reveals a meaningful analysis of the sample yeast gene expression data and synthetic data based on a constant bicluster model with 5 biclusters and subsets of rows and columns (genes and conditions, respectively). Each step provides partial security for the entire procedure. SeCCA follows the original algorithm, but the number of biclusters is reduced to run the project in a reasonable amount of time. Moreover, nine SeCCA steps were determined to represent the overall required computations that are part of the Cheng and Church algorithm, and the storage system (public cloud service) is responsible for their execution. Among them, only four steps have specific computations that were feasible with the applied homomorphic encryption library; for the rest of the SeCCA steps, we have to rewrite the expressions in future work. Computational performance is greatly affected by the algorithm's complexity, which consists of heavy-duty computations (e.g., multiplication), leaving room for future improvements. We also compare SeCCA with the original algorithm by the external evaluation measure, Clustering Error (CE). As future work, we plan to improve the overall accuracy of SeCCA and increase the scalability of our approach (in particular regarding the number of biclusters) for which performance optimisation is required. To generate a fully secure version of the Cheng and Church algorithm, it is of great importance to come up with further practical approaches to modify statements in steps 5 to 9 straightforwardly. We will also address the computational performance in future work. One possible solution to optimise performance is the packing mechanism. SIMD has been implemented for integers in Pyfhel==2.3.1; however, homomorphic encryption operations rely on floating-point numbers in our application so that, we will consider the CKKS scheme with SIMD packing for improved performance in terms of computational overhead and accuracy. Moreover, we aim to generalise privacy-preserving gene expression data analysis by extending our approach to other biclustering algorithms and developing a secure biclustering platform with the aim to achieve a profound impact on personalised medicine, regardless of existing limitations of current homomorphic encryption libraries.

References

1. Jose-Garcia, A., Jacques, J., Sobanski, V., Dhaenens, C.: Biclustering Algorithms Based on Metaheuristics: A Review. arXiv preprint arXiv:2203.16241 (2022)
2. Cheng, Y., Church, G.M.: Biclustering of expression data. In: ISMB, vol. 8, pp. 93–103 (2000)
3. Nicholls, K., Wallace, C.: Comparison of sparse biclustering algorithms for gene expression datasets. Briefings Bioinform. **22**(6), bbab140 (2021)
4. Naveed, M., et al.: Privacy in the genomic era. ACM Comput. Surv. (CSUR) **48**(1), 1–44 (2015)
5. Tu, W., Subedi, S.: A family of mixture models for biclustering. Stat. Anal. Data Mining ASA Data Sci. J. **15**(2), 206–224 (2022)
6. Maâtouk, O., Ayadi, W., Bouziri, H., Duval, B.: Evolutionary biclustering algorithms: an experimental study on microarray data. Soft. Comput. **23**(17), 7671–7697 (2019)
7. Ngo, M.N., Pluta, D.S., Ngo, A.N., Shahbaba, B.: Conjoined Dirichlet Process. arXiv preprint arXiv:2002.03223 (2020)
8. Byun, J., Lee, J., Park, S.: Privacy-preserving evaluation for support vector clustering. Electron. Lett. **57**(2), 61–64 (2021)
9. Lee, J.-W., et al.: Privacy-preserving machine learning with fully homomorphic encryption for deep neural network. IEEE Access **10**, 30039–30054 (2022)
10. Tu, Z., Wang, X.A., Su, Y., Li, Y., Liu, J.: Toward secure K-means clustering based on homomorphic encryption in cloud. In: International Conference on Emerging Internetworking, Data & Web Technologies, pp. 52–62 (2022)
11. Zhang, C., Li, S., Xia, J., Wang, W., Yan, F., Liu, Y.: BatchCrypt: efficient homomorphic encryption for cross-silo federated learning. In: 2020 USENIX Annual Technical Conference (USENIX ATC 2020), pp. 493–506 (2020)
12. Ibarrondo, A., Viand, A.: Pyfhel: python for homomorphic encryption libraries. In: Proceedings of the 9th on Workshop on Encrypted Computing & Applied Homomorphic Cryptography, pp. 11–16 (2021)

13. Brakerski, Z., Gentry, C., Vaikuntanathan, V.: (Leveled) fully homomorphic encryption without bootstrapping. ACM Trans. Comput. Theory (TOCT) **6**(3), 1–36 (2014)
14. Paverd, A., Martin, A., Brown, I.: Modelling and automatically analysing privacy properties for honest-but-curious adversaries. Technical report (2014)
15. Demirci, H., Lenzini, G.: Privacy-preserving Copy Number Variation Analysis with Homomorphic Encryption (2022)
16. Padilha, V.A., Campello, R.J.G.B.: A systematic comparative evaluation of biclustering techniques. BMC Bioinform. **18**(1), 1–25 (2017)
17. Chialva, D., Dooms, A.: Conditionals in homomorphic encryption and machine learning applications. arXiv preprint arXiv:1810.12380 (2018)
18. Tavazoie, S., Hughes, J.D., Campbell, M.J., Cho, R.J., Church, G.M.: Systematic determination of genetic network architecture. Nat. Genet. **22**(3), 281–285 (1999)
19. Bozdemir, B., Canard, S., Ermis, O., Möllering, H., Önen, M., Schneider, Th.: Privacy-preserving density-based clustering. In: Proceedings of the 2021 ACM Asia Conference on Computer and Communications Security, pp. 658–671 (2021)
20. Mohassel, P., Rosulek, M., Trieu, N.: Practical privacy-preserving k-means clustering. Cryptology ePrint Archive (2019)
21. Jäschke, A., Armknecht, F.: Unsupervised machine learning on encrypted data. In: International Conference on Selected Areas in Cryptography, pp. 453–478 (2018)
22. Perscheid, C., Uflacker, M.: Integrating biological context into the analysis of gene expression data. In: International Symposium on Distributed Computing and Artificial Intelligence, pp. 339–343 (2018)

Author Index

© IFIP International Federation for Information Processing 2023
Published by Springer Nature Switzerland AG 2023
F. Bieker et al. (Eds.): Privacy and Identity 2022, IFIP AICT 671, p. 215, 2023.
https://doi.org/10.1007/978-3-031-31971-6

Printed in the United States
by Baker & Taylor Publisher Services

Printed in the United States
by Baker & Taylor Publisher Services